WIXSE3 MEMI ... ME IP ARY

D1194762

PRESS

why aren't they there?

the political representation of women, ethnic
groups and issue positions in legislatures

Didier Ruedin

aspos
WISSER MEMORIAL LIBRARY

JF 1051
·R843
2013
C·1

© Didier Ruedin 2013

First published by the ECPR Press in 2013

The ECPR Press is the publishing imprint of the European Consortium for Political Research (ECPR), a scholarly association, which supports and encourages the training, research and cross-national cooperation of political scientists in institutions throughout Europe and beyond.

ECPR Press
University of Essex
Wivenhoe Park
Colchester
CO4 3SQ
UK

All rights reserved. No part of this book may be reprinted or reproduced or utilised in any form or by any electronic, mechanical, or other means, now known or hereafter invented, including photocopying and recording, or in any information storage or retrieval system, without permission in writing from the publishers.

Typeset by ECPR Press.

Printed and bound by Lightning Source.

British Library Cataloguing in Publication Data.

A catalogue record for this book is available from the British Library.

Paperback ISBN: 978-0-955820-39-7
eBook PDF Format ISBN: 978-1-907301-62-9

Further resources from the author can be found here: http://figshare.com/articles/Political_Representation_of_Women_Ethnic_Groups_and_Issue_Positions/675917

www.ecpr.eu/ecprpress

ECPR – Monographs

Series Editors:

Dario Castiglione (University of Exeter)
Peter Kennealy (European University Institute)
Alexandra Segerberg (Stockholm University)
Peter Triantafillou (Roskilde University)

Please visit www.ecpr.eu/ecprpress for information about new publications.

This page is intentionally blank

contents

This page is intentionally blank

| list of figures and tables

Figures

Tables

Further resources from the author can be found here: http://figshare.com/articles/
Political_Representation_of_Women_Ethnic_Groups_and_Issue_Positions/675917

| list of abbreviations

CSES	Comparative Study of Electoral Systems
GDP	Gross domestic product
HDI	Human Development Index
IDEA	Institute for Democracy and Electoral Assistance
IPU	Inter-Parliamentary Union
M	District magnitude
Mj	Majoritarian
MMD	Multi-member district
MMM	Mixed-member majoritarian
MMP	Mixed-member proportional
OECD	Organisation for Economic Cooperation and Development
PR	Proportional representation
Q	Representation score, the main dependent variable, see Appendix
SMD	Single-member district
UK	United Kingdom
UN	United Nations
US	United States
WVS	World Values Survey

This page is intentionally blank

acknowledgements

I would like to thank Steve Fisher, Sara Hobolt, Alistair McMillan, James Tilley and Matthew Bond for their support during different stages of the research leading to this publication. I would also like to thank Marc Carinci, David Rueda, John Fox, David Firth, Bernard Grofman, Anthony Heath, Edmund Chattoe-Brown, Gianni D'Amato and Gallya Lahav for support and encouragement. My grateful thanks are also extended to Neli Demireva, Lily Qianhan Lin, Alexey Bessudnov, Silke Schneider, Charles Laurie, Laurence Lessard-Phillips, Pär Gustafsson, Siana Glouharova, Krishna Omkar, Elina Kilpi-Jakonen, Thees Spreckelsen, Thomas Grund, Christina Fuhr, Rolando Ochoa Hernandez, Maria Grasso, Shreya Sarawgi, Irum Shehreen Ali, Alex Sutherland, Soomin Chung, Samina Luthfa, Sumeet Mhaskar, AJ Adrienne Rivlin, Ken Okamoto-Kaminski, Sum Yin Kwong, Maria Sobolewska, Robert Ford, Jeehun Kim, Raya Muttarak, Ping Lin, Flora Pui-Yan Lau, Declan Hill, Moonju Seong, Jing Yang, Chinnawut Techanuvat, Eline De Rooij, Carmel Hannan, Sieglinde Rosenberger, Jae-Hyeong Choi, Mona Lena Krook, Natalja Mortensen, Daniel Bochsler, Georg Lutz, Ed Fieldhouse, the anonymous reviewers, Alexandra Segerberg and staff at ECPR press, and everyone who should have been mentioned here but inadvertently has been left out. Finally, I would like to thank members of parliamentary services across the world who responded to my requests for data.

Didier Ruedin
March 2013

This page is intentionally blank

introduction

In the primaries of the 2008 US presidential election, the battle between Barack Obama and Hillary Clinton for nomination by the Democratic Party grabbed headlines. Both candidates were different from the stereotypical white men who tend to dominate governments and legislatures across the western world. Voters were not only presented with the possibility of an alternative to the stereotypical white man, but they also had the opportunity or obligation to choose between one of them. In this sense, the 2008 US presidential election highlighted the importance of gender and ethnicity in political representation, and the tensions that may exist at their interface. Indirectly, the voters faced the question of whether a black man or a white woman should lead the country.

Perhaps less visible internationally was the renewed debate on gender quotas in Germany in 2011 and early 2012 – exemplified by the website Pro Quote in support of quotas. In contrast to the 2008 US election, debates on gender quotas address questions of political representation more directly. Although there is an unmistaken claim that there should be more women in legislatures, debates on gender quotas revolve mostly around the means to achieve this aim, not the aim itself. They draw directly on the radical expansion of citizenship in the twentieth century, namely the understanding that all humans are essentially equal. This argument of justice emphasises principles of fairness and mutual respect. In politics, this is well reflected in the mantra of one person, one vote: the principle that the voice of every citizen counts the same. The inclusiveness that underlies citizenship is a fundamental criterion for democracy (Dahl 1985). Debates on gender quotas and the attention both Hillary Clinton and Barack Obama received highlight that despite remarkable advances, ideals of equality are far from realised. In some places, women and ethnic minority groups remain systematically marginalised, and in almost all countries they are significantly under-represented in national legislatures. For example, the average legislature in 2013 comprises just 20 per cent women. Such political under-representation is problematic because the proportion of women and minority groups in national legislatures is indicative of their status in society.

This book seeks to understand why the proportion of women and ethnic minority groups in national legislatures varies across countries, and why legislatures are reflecting the issue positions of citizens to a different degree. There are various reasons to insist on representation in national parliaments and legislatures. For instance, it is often argued that women and ethnic minorities have interests that are distinct from those of the broader population. In order to accommodate these interests, it is vital to include women and minority groups in legislatures. Examples of such distinct interests include birth control for women or issues of land resources that may affect certain ethnic groups. The argument put forward is that certain issues are only representable by those directly affected because it is impossible to appreciate the importance of such issues without direct experience. The contention that certain interests are unrepresentable is certainly controversial, but representation is thought to ensure that particularised and uncrystallised interests can be defended in the legislature. Such 'descriptive representation' of group members is necessary because sometimes women and ethnic minority groups do not trust men or members of the ethnic majority to represent their substantive interests (Mansbridge 1999). For a fuller understanding of political representation, this book also examines the representation of policy preferences and issue positions separately. These are considerations of what is commonly referred to as 'substantive representation'.

In most cases, the argument for including various groups and views in legislatures is based on concerns about the legitimacy and accountability of representative institutions. Where certain views, ideas or groups are excluded from the processes of decision-making, the political legitimacy of those institutions can be called into question. Accordingly, an institution consisting only of men, or one where only left-wing ideas are present, for instance, is seen as deviating from the ideal of inclusiveness to such an extent that some may question its legitimacy. This view is rooted in the ideals of direct democracy, where representation in the legislature is understood as entrusting someone else with one's right to participate in decision making processes. Where there are no legitimate representatives or some groups are significantly under-represented, social cohesion can be affected negatively.

Both approaches – whether based on legitimacy or the representation of interests – insist that national legislatures should be representative of the population. In this book, the level of political representation is considered high where the legislature resembles the population and low where the legislature differs significantly. Legislative representation is employed as a case of political representation, and consequently the two terms are largely used synonymously. Some studies concerned with policy-making focus on governments rather than legislatures, arguing that in advanced democracies governments are the drivers of public policy. In practice, there is little difference between the two foci (Powell 2000; Furedi 2005), possibly because government formation is intrinsically linked to the composition of the legislature (Gamson 1961; Manin *et al.* 1999; but see O'Brien 2012).

Not all legislatures are representative to the same degree. This book first examines the vastly different levels of representation in national legislatures, the representation of women and ethnic groups, as well as issue positions. As is common in the literature, I refer to the representation of women and ethnic groups as 'descriptive representation' and use the term 'substantive representation' for the representation of policy preferences and issue positions in different domains. I use the terms 'gender representation' and 'ethnic group representation' interchangeably with the representation of women and ethnic groups respectively, and use a group perspective commonly referred to as 'collective representation'. Similarly, I use policy representation as a synonym for the representation of issue positions and policy preferences.

In order to establish which factors are associated with higher levels of representation, it is first necessary to outline different conceptions of representation. This brief discussion clarifies the existence of different understandings of political representation and helps to approach the representation in national legislatures in a systematic manner. Based on a clear understanding of what political representation means, it is possible to establish the levels of representation in different countries. The first research question of this book is: How can we explain differences in the levels of political representation? In other words, applied to the specific forms of representation examined in this book: What factors are associated with levels of gender representation, ethnic group representation and policy representation in different domains?

In order to address this question, this book uses a cross-national comparison to tease out significant patterns. Throughout the book, institutional, cultural, and other factors are considered as variables that are associated with the different levels of representation observed. Very broadly, institutional factors refer to aspects of the electoral system and cultural variables capture the prevalent attitudes towards women and ethnic minority groups in different societies. The systematic inclusion of institutional and cultural factors in the empirical chapters (see Chapters Two – Five) leads to a better understanding of how these variables influence levels of representation. Existing studies on the representation of women may be most complete in this regard, but cultural variables are often an afterthought, despite the recognition that attitudes of the population and the elite may be substantial in shaping levels of representation.

Regarding the representation of women, almost all studies find a strong association between the presence of proportional electoral systems and higher levels of representation. In a similar vein, the presence of gender quotas is generally found to be associated with higher levels of representation. Party ideology is often highlighted, but it no longer appears that stronger left-wing parties result in higher levels of representation. More consistent are findings based on the supply of qualified women, although it is not entirely clear how the stipulated variables affect levels of representation. The variables might capture how established a democracy is or acknowledge economic modernisation; both aspects are thought to affect the prevalent attitudes in society. Studies that include cultural variables consistently find very strong associations with the representation of women. In the empirical chapter (see Chapter Two), both institutional and cultural variables are included in a systematic manner, leading to a better understanding of how these variables work when considered simultaneously.

As far as the representation of ethnic groups is concerned, lack of data prevented the multivariate comparative studies common for the representation of women. Instead, it is often assumed that findings from the representation of women apply equally to the representation of different kinds of ethnic groups, including immigrants in Western societies. This assumption seems to be supported by single-country studies. In particular, the role of proportional electoral systems is highlighted. Supply factors are sometimes discussed, but interlocking statuses make it more difficult to examine their influence than is the case for women. Cultural factors are also invoked, such as when certain groups are considered unsuited for office or when discrimination is discussed. In Chapter Five, the assumption that different forms of descriptive representation are shaped by the same factors is also addressed by comparing levels of gender representation with levels of ethnic group representation. This way, assumptions and speculations based on studies covering gender or ethnicity separately can be tested directly. Specialist papers frequently make claims about the relationship between the representation of gender and ethnicity, such as trade-offs, for example where levels of gender representation are directly traded off against ethnic group representation. This book tests such claims directly, drawing on a theoretical framework that allows cross-fertilisation.

Studies on the representation of issue positions and policy preferences, by contrast, tend to focus on institutional variables. In particular, they explore the influence of various aspects of the electoral system, highlighting the proportionality between votes cast and seats gained. Some recent contributions, however, question the importance of proportionality. In the literature, influences on vote choice are not generally treated as part of the representative relationship between citizens and the legislature. Studies that consider such influences separately tend to highlight the same variables that are found to influence the vote choice leading to descriptive representation. Such variables include party identification and the role of the political environment – aspects of culture and their salience, i.e. the importance conferred to them. The salience of divisions, in the case of gender and ethnic group representation, refers to the awareness and politicisation of under-representation.

Chapter Four examines multiple issue domains rather than concentrating on the representation of left and right as is commonly done. The chapter, however, does not examine the substantive representation of specific groups. Rather than taking a specific group in society as the starting point (e.g. Thomas 1991; Berkman and O'Connor 1993; Chen 2009), it remains focused on policy preferences to cover a different aspect of political representation. By looking at different forms of representation, this book aims to achieve a better understanding of political representation more generally.

Part of the book explores the influence of – and possible interdependence between – cultural and institutional factors for representation. The perception is that the effects of institutional factors may be limited if they are not accompanied by analogous cultural attitudes. In Chapter One, I present a theoretical framework to further develop the anticipated role of institutional, cultural and other variables. By systematically considering both institutional and cultural factors, this book is also able to examine whether current approaches to improving levels or descriptive representation – principally by means of quotas – are effective in achieving this goal. This framework is a synthesis of influences that have been suggested or established in the existing literature. The presentation makes it clear that similar influences are recognised for different forms of representation. In this sense, it becomes possible to refer to political representation in more general terms. The result of such a perspective is a fuller understanding of variables that influence levels of representation, as theoretical contributions from different fields are combined.

When talking about political representation in general, it is explicitly acknowledged that political representation is multifaceted and multi-dimensional. To reflect this, different forms of political representation are examined: the representation of women and ethnic groups, as well as the representation of issue positions in different domains. At the same time, the relationship between different forms of representation is of key interest. The book examines whether there are factors that are associated with higher levels of representation in all cases, or whether there is a trade-off between different forms of representation. With an eye on electoral engineering, it is particularly interesting to determine whether improving one form of representation necessarily comes at the cost of another or whether different forms of representation can be reconciled, or can even be mutually supportive. The guiding research question is: How are levels of representation in different forms linked? In other words, and as applied to the specific forms of representation examined in this book: What is the relationship between levels of gender representation, ethnic group representation and policy representation in different domains?

This research question highlights the fact that issues of inter-sectionality are of concern when it comes to the political representation of women and ethnic minority groups (Walby 2009; Smooth 2011). Multiple forms of inequality can affect levels of representation. For example, women from ethnic minorities may be particularly under-represented in national legislatures or there may be no women representatives from the working class, leaving a particular group without a voice in legislative decision making. While these concerns are important, they cannot be addressed explicitly in this book for reasons of data availability. Data on the representation of women, ethnic groups and policy domains are collected independently to retain a large sample of countries. The systematic study of different forms of representation in itself is a substantive expansion of the scope of studies on political representation.

In contrast with most previous studies, this book focuses on both descriptive and substantive representation. Descriptive representation is associated with group rights, an aspect of citizenship more commonly recognised and emphasised in recent years. In free societies where all citizens are considered equal, everyone has the same right to representation in positions of decision making. Consequently, the under-representation of certain groups is an issue concerning the legitimacy of the legislature in question. At the same time, most voters arguably care about substantive representation: the representation of issue positions and policy preferences (Darcy *et al.* 1994). In this case, the focus is on the role of the legislature in policy making: either actively in creating policies or passively as watchdogs of the government. The intuition is that voters care about their interests and are concerned with how well representatives in the legislature defend their policy preferences.

The presence of like-minded representatives, however, does not guarantee their active involvement in the policy-making process to further particular interests. For example, a politician elected on a ticket critical of privatisation may later vote in favour of privatisation. Considerations of what representatives do once elected are beyond the scope of this book for a number of reasons. The biggest challenge is the lack of adequate data for many countries (the voting patterns of representatives are commonly used, but such data are unavailable for many legislatures). Data availability notwithstanding, voting patterns in the legislature might not be the best indication, since a representative may have an impact on a particular bill through discussions and arguments put forward in select committees, even in places where party discipline encourages him or her to vote differently. Minta (2011) highlights oversight hearings as a potential site where minority groups can shape policy. Moreover, there are also factors outside the legislature that affect policy, such as the influence of big business, civil society, the media or government committees. The result is that a proper examination of the impact of a representative on policies is highly complex and difficult to capture empirically.

Other arguments for political representation are not affected by such potential limitations. The representation of women and ethnic minorities in legislatures can be defended as a sign of justice and equality of citizens. Following this argument, presence in the legislature is regarded as intrinsically valuable. Other contributions focus on the symbolic value of inclusion and women and ethnic minorities as role models for future generations. The assumption is that the presence of women or minority candidates encourages children and young adults to seek similar positions in decision making or the public sphere in general. Particularly in the context of immigrant groups, political representation can be considered conducive to integration in society. The most important case for political representation, however, remains the representation of interests. The experience of living in a particular society means that women and ethnic minorities can be considered as groups with specific interests, whether such interests are explicit or uncrystallised. Throughout the book, political representation is rooted in concerns of justice: it emphasises the equality of citizens and that the legislature should mirror the citizenry as closely as possible, representing the interests of everyone – a microcosm of society.

Following this argument on justice, the book focuses on countries that are free and partly free. In unfree countries, the fundamental assumption of justice and democracy is often violated, such as in repressive regimes (de Rezende Martins 2004; Rehfeld 2006; Matland 2006; Baldez 2006). In such countries, the dynamics related to political representation may differ significantly (Yoon 2004; Hassim 2009; Krook and O'Brien 2012) and it would be inappropriate to equate representation with legitimacy. Members from different groups may be present in the legislature of such countries, but if the legislature has no real power, representation in the name of justice seems pointless. Without meaningful and competitive elections, it is unlikely that presence in the legislature is linked to decision making power, so the interests of groups and individuals may not be represented adequately. Moreover, in some unfree countries, members from certain minority groups may be reluctant to disclose their ethnic identity publicly, making it difficult to quantify political representation. In this book, I circumvent these issues by excluding unfree countries in the empirical analyses. The analysis in this book is based on 131 countries classified as free or partly free by Freedom House (2006). The Freedom House classifications reflect the inherent difficulty of classifying regimes into free and unfree since many regimes are in fact hybrid cases (Diamond 2002).

To some extent, the insistence in this book on countries that are free and partly free reflects Walby's (2009) reflections on the depth of democracy. The starting point is largely what she calls a suffrage democracy, with free, fair, and competitive elections. Walby outlines additional indicators to develop the concepts of presence democracy and broad democracy. Whilst her ninth indicator of 'proportionate presence of women and minorities' (p.180) resonates with this book, she seems to confound different indicators. Insisting on the presence of quotas or proportional representation systems, as Walby does, removes the focus on the representational outcome. It is unclear why Walby insists on particular means for achieving what she calls a presence democracy. For this reason, Walby's indicators of the depth of democracy unfortunately do not help directly in informing this book on a theoretical level. Nonetheless, as Walby outlines, the inclusion of different forms of representation is necessary for a better understanding of the inequalities that shape modern societies.

The remainder of the book is structured as follows. In Chapter One, I examine the concept of political representation in detail. This review of different conceptualisations builds up to a theoretical framework of political representation. Using this framework it is possible to coherently integrate findings from previous studies and political theory to present the different factors that are thought to influence levels of representation. It is not intended that the framework provides a unifying theory, but it is a tool to bring together the different, separate facets of political representation. It helps to identify the institutional and cultural factors associated with different levels of representation, and is useful in recognising potential links between different forms of representation.

The first two empirical chapters are dedicated to levels of descriptive representation. Chapter Two examines the representation of women. The strong effects of the electoral system and voluntary gender quotas are reduced once cultural factors are taken into consideration. Contrary to the strong expectations in the literature, there is no clear evidence that the institutional setting has a significant impact on levels of gender representation. With regard to the representation of ethnic groups, Chapter Three is dedicated to a different form of descriptive representation. As in the preceding chapter, cultural rather than institutional factors appear to be dominant. This contradicts strong expectations in the theoretical literature, but I suggest that the incentives of the political elite may offer an explanation. Perhaps surprisingly, quota regulations appear to be unsuccessful, but this might be because of poor implementation in many cases.

Chapter Four focuses on the representation of policy preferences and issue positions: substantive representation. As in the chapters on descriptive representation, the electoral system appears to be of little significance, despite very strong expectations in the literature. This might reflect recent changes in substantive representation in countries with majoritarian systems. The final empirical chapter examines the relationship between different forms of representation. The argument examined in Chapter Five is that the same institutional and cultural factors are associated with high levels of representation in any form and, therefore, levels of representation in different forms are positively correlated. The chapter finds no evidence for this and, instead, highlights the salience of issue domains and descriptive divisions. Levels of representation tend to be higher in the forms that are thought to be more salient. By comparing levels of representation, the chapter helps to consolidate different forms of political representation. It encourages future investigation in an area that, to date, has been neglected, despite the direct implications for electoral engineering. The final discussion in Chapter Six brings together the different empirical chapters to present a more complete picture of political representation. In this context, limits to electoral engineering are discussed taking into account institutional and cultural influences on levels of representation.

chapter one | political representation: a framework

The concept of political representation is often used in the literature, but its exact meaning is rarely examined in detail (Birch 1971; Eulau and Wahlke 1978; Blondel *et al.* 1997; Brennan and Hamlin 1999; Miller *et al.* 1999).[1] When looking at the concept in detail, it becomes clear that there is no single understanding (Pitkin 1967; Brennan and Hamlin 1999). It is therefore helpful to reflect on the different notions of representation. It is the central concept of this book and this chapter unpacks its complexity, bringing together the varied approaches into a comprehensive understanding of political representation.

The chapter begins by looking at the different components of the concept of representation, which helps to define the scope of this book. The role of representatives is investigated, as well as which characteristics should be represented. This discussion builds towards the theoretical framework by selecting the forms of representation most relevant to the empirical analysis. The framework itself is a new synthesis of previous contributions and forms the basis for the chapters that follow. Whilst the framework integrates different facets of representation, it does not attempt to provide a comprehensive theory. It is a tool to inform the hypotheses presented at the end of the chapter.

What is representation?

Whilst political representation is frequently studied, surprisingly few contributions work towards a better understanding of its meaning. In this book, representation in legislatures refers to a case of political representation. At its most general, representation is defined as '[being] present on behalf of someone else who is absent' (*Britannica* 2006a). In the context of politics, this describes 'the idea that people, while not in person present at the seat of government are to be considered present by proxy' (Ford 1925: 3). In order for representation to take place, two conditions are required: a person or group of persons that should be present, and a person or group of persons to take their place instead. This process implies a specific purpose that representation serves (Fairlie 1940a, 1940b). For political representation, this specific purpose is involvement in decision-making, and it requires a specific means of selecting representatives.

Implicit in this classic view of representation is the contention that the citizens deserve a voice: they are sovereign citizens. The fundamental moral principle is

---

1. This has changed recently with new theoretical developments that examine the concept of representation in detail. See, for example, Rehfeld 2006, 2009, 2011; Mansbridge 2003, 2008, 2011; Saward 2006, 2010; and Severs 2010.

that the preferences of the citizens should prevail. For practical or other reasons, the sovereign citizens cannot be present at a place, and they elect representatives to look out for their substantive interests. The basis of the notion of sovereign citizens is the concept of equality. If the citizens are of equal worth, this means that all citizens should be eligible to vote, as well as to stand for election (Rehfeld 2006). Whilst most classical contributions emphasise the representation of policy preferences, the general argument equally applies to the representation of women and ethnic groups.

There are two sets of principles of social justice that can be applied to political representation. First, there are principles of distributive justice, as championed by Dahl (1985) or Rawls (1999). Secondly, there is Young (1990) arguing for a justice of difference. Rawls' approach regards justice as fairness, and it is based on a thought experiment involving rational actors behind the veil of ignorance. For Rawls, justice means that people are not discriminated against because of criteria such as skin colour or age. The principle of equality is based on individual rights. Young's argument contradicts both the logic and consequences of Rawls' approach. Young focuses on domination and oppression as the basis of injustice. Groups are regarded as oppressed if they are marginalised and powerless, amongst others, because they cannot take part in decision making. Justice can only be achieved where all voices can be heard, no matter how dominant one group may be. Her argument is based on the rights of groups. Whereas Rawls pays attention to the outcome of policy making, Young's approach includes an unmistakable claim that all minority groups should be present in the legislature to defend their interests.

Almost all accounts of political representation agree that the representatives should *act for* the citizens. The interests of individuals, however, can rarely be said to be singular. Together with different social roles and group membership – reflected in different and multiple identities – come different needs and interests (Squires 1996; Walby 2009; Smooth 2011). For example, a person's interests as a car driver may differ from those of the same person as an employee or as a parent. As a car driver, I might be interested in quick roads for short journey times. As a parent, I might be concerned with my children's safety when walking to school along busy roads. For all different roles, there are separate political interests that may not agree. When faced with the task of choosing a representative, these differing interests may complicate matters, since voters are normally only allowed a single vote. Most contributions to political representation ignore such cross-pressures or assume the primacy of certain political domains, such as concerns for the economy. The approach in this book allows for such influences and is open about which issue domain matters most to citizens.

Saward (2006, 2010) takes quite a different approach to the active aspects of political representation. Rather than simply insisting that representatives should act for citizens, he presents political representation as a question of claims-making, thus an active and creative process. Modern democracies are regarded as representative because they claim to be. Whilst this perspective expands the scope to non-electoral representative relationships, it can distract from the special role of electoral representation. Elections provide a systematic claim to legitimacy that is widely accepted – other representative claims may speak to a more limited audience. Because of its institutional nature, electoral representation may also increase the chances that uncrystallised interests will be represented should the need arise. The claims-making perspective regards such interests as not represented until someone claims to do so. Moreover, because it is possible to remove representatives, elections can ensure formal accountability.

Questions of accountability are made more difficult because different forms of representation can be differentiated (Mansbridge 2003, 2011; Rehfeld 2011). For example, the relationship between citizens and representatives can be shaped in terms of electoral promises made during campaigns, but it is also possible that representatives focus on the interests of citizens outside their constituency. Seen this way, issues of responsiveness – acting for citizens – appear in a new light. Despite highlighting various possible relationships, recent theoretical developments contribute a clear insistence on the relational nature of political representation. While the comparative approach of this book is unable to capture all the different relationships possible, the theoretical framework used in the empirical chapters agrees with these theoretical developments and regards representation as a relationship between citizens and representatives. By looking at the representation of women, ethnic groups and different policy preferences, this book works towards a wider understanding of political representation, particularly in terms of representative outcomes. The exact relationship these entail will remain unexplored. The focus on electoral representation limits the scope of this book to forms where accountability and legitimacy are clearer than in many other representative relationships that can and do exist.

Linked with accountability is, to a certain extent, the question of whether citizens are the best judges of their own interests. On the one hand, citizens are regarded as independent and able individuals, capable of judging their own needs and desires better than anyone else can (Williams 1995; Thompson 2001). In this case, the possibility to remove unwanted representatives is an important part of political representation. On the other hand, the view that citizens are not very capable of knowing or expressing their priorities is also common (Ross 1943; Schumpeter 1996/1976; Eichenberg 2007). In this context, the concept of guardianship is often cited, emphasising the common good thought to be beyond the grasp of the ordinary person. Whilst there might be a case for disregarding some declared wishes, the concept of guardianship is in danger of legitimising undemocratic governments that no longer act for its citizens.

The claim that representatives should mirror the population may appeal even to those insisting on guardianship, provided it does not contradict the selection of individuals qualified for work as representatives (Dunn 1999; Mansbridge 2005). Most of the literature is silent on how the legislature should mirror the population, although the next section will explore different possibilities.

In order to ensure a legitimate and responsive government, this book insists on democracy, as do most accounts of political representation. Representative democracy is by far the most common means for selecting representatives, although other approaches are possible, such as direct appointment (Pennock 1968; Rehfeld

2006). Democracy is the preferred means of selection because of accountability (Cheibub and Przeworski 1999; Dunn 1999). Since the representatives are elected to act for the citizens in the first place, they should be held accountable for their actions. The fact that free elections are held every few years is often considered a sufficient criterion for accountability (Plotke 1997; Manin *et al.* 1999). In elections, a particular representative may be replaced; this implicit threat is thought to work as an incentive for representatives to act in the interests of the citizens. Consequently, given the possibility to remove representatives, the result of any free election is regarded as legitimate.[2] Paxton (2008) makes a strong argument that we can only speak of democracies where women have the right to vote (see also Walby 2009).

Forms of representation

The two most commonly considered forms of political representation are descriptive and substantive. Descriptive representation is concerned with matching the demographic characteristics of the population, whilst substantive representation deals with issue positions and how well the representatives match the ideological views and policy preferences of the citizens.

Descriptive representation is the extent to which demographic characteristics, such as ethnicity, gender or class, are reflected in the legislature (Pitkin 1967; Birch 2000; Paxton *et al.* 2007). Descriptive representation exists between two

---

2. Legitimacy means that a group of representatives is considered the rightful group to represent the citizens. Although the literature is ambivalent on who is to judge the rightfulness of a representative relationship, the best approach is probably to combine Weberian approaches with Rehfeld (2006). Weber argues that a representative relationship can only be legitimate if those giving up the power accept it as such (Grafstein 1981; Matheson 1987). A representative is the legitimate one, if he or she acts with the consent of those whom he or she represents. This means that any representative elected fairly is a legitimate representative. This view is not entirely satisfactory, because it is unclear how those unable to authorise a representative can be represented – such as children, foreign citizens or future generations. Rehfeld underlines the fact that a representative needs to be recognised as such by the specific audience to whom he or she represents the citizens (see also Saward 2006, 2010). He substantiates this argument with the example of ambassadors from undemocratic regimes, where the citizens have no possibility to voice their agreement or lack thereof with the chosen representative. This argument is unsatisfactory on its own, as it implies that the most dominant power in a society is generally also the legitimate authority. The lack of agreement by the audience renders representation futile, but at least passive consent on behalf of the citizens is necessary to implement laws for example. Representation arguably only takes place where there is legitimacy. By focusing on free and partly-free countries, this book focuses on cases where legitimate political representation can be assumed to a certain degree. Hayward (2009) takes a slightly different position, arguing that legitimacy does not stem from the democratic means in themselves, but from the inclusiveness free democratic countries tend to come with.

members of the same group, one in the citizens and one in the representatives. A male citizen is therefore represented by any male representative, a person from Scotland by a Scot. Throughout the book, I use the term 'descriptive *dimension*' to refer to the different groups within which representation can occur, such as gender or religious groups.

Interest in descriptive representation is rooted in the normative argument that the legislature should mirror the population. It is significant for several reasons related to the representation of interests. The absence of certain groups from legislatures – or their presence in only a reduced number – is sometimes taken as a sign that certain views and voices are suppressed (Phillips 1993). The underlying assumption is that whoever is not present in the legislature – be it in person or by proxy – has no means to express his or her views (Ganghof 2010). The absence or under-representation of certain groups is a concern to those who believe that the groups identified by demographic criteria have distinct interests (Wittman 1990; Fearon 1999). The argument is that there are certain (relevant) views or experiences that cannot be represented by anyone who is not directly affected (Schwartz 1988; Phillips 1995). For example, it can be argued, that the experience of racial discrimination cannot be understood unless experienced from the receiving end. Without an understanding of the issue, it follows that there is no appreciation for the importance of certain policy changes, for example (Arscott 1995; Allwood and Wadia 2004). The politics of presence theory introduced by Phillips contends that descriptive representation increases the chances of the substantive representation of such group interests. What is more, the presence of the groups affected ensures that policies are well informed in the sense that all legislators made their policy decisions based on knowing the potential impact on different groups. The presence of different groups thus ensures that policy debates are better informed – and because legislators are aware of different policy options, the conditions for transforming group interests into policy are optimised.

It is certainly controversial to argue that demographically-defined groups have intrinsic interests (Mansbridge 1999; Schwindt-Bayer and Mishler 2005), but the focus on experience makes it a more compelling case. A woman's interests are justified not because she was born with two X-chromosomes, but because of her experience of being a woman in a particular society. For example, Campbell *et al.* (2010) show that men and women have different attitudes with regard to gender equality (see also Shapiro and Mahajan 1986; Tremblay 1995; Minta 2011). Although difficult to ascertain (Chen 2009; Gray 2003), it is sometimes argued that the increasing number of women in the Norwegian legislature is associated with substantial shifts in policy such as on birth control (Bystydzienski 1995). It is thought that this is achieved through the representation of uncrystallised interests (Mansbridge 1999; Campbell *et al.* 2010). However, Osborn (2012) makes a convincing case that while women do represent women's interests, they do so primarily as partisans. Put another way, parties remain dominant over gender differences. Mansbridge argues that descriptive representation is also necessary where women and members of ethnic minority groups do not trust others to represent their substantive interests, even though such substantive representation would be possible by non-members. In certain contexts, descriptive representation is necessary for substantive representation, but this is not universally the case.

There are also instrumental reasons to insist on descriptive representation. These include incorporating a wider pool of talents (Duverger 1955; Henig and Henig 2001; EHRC 2008), women and ethnic minorities as positive role models, considerations of efficient decision making and less alienation of minorities. Some writers highlight the lack of women as positive role models in public life in general, and in legislatures in particular (Phillips 1995; Wolbrecht and Campbell 2005; Girlguiding 2009). Their argument is that the little subtleties of everyday life help socialise men and women into distinct roles that recreate the gender divide and perpetuate associated injustice (Sharpe 1976; Okin 1994). The potential impact on future generations adds some urgency to this argument. There are also practical considerations of efficiency in decision making resulting from the composition of groups. Gratton et al. (2007) studied the impact of the gender composition of groups on the efficiency of decision making. They found that where the proportion of men and women is equal, decision making is associated with greater efficiency and innovation. When applying their argument to representation in legislatures, a call for select committees to be gender equal follows, something more likely to happen where the proportion of women in the legislature is high. The application to ethnicity and substantive representation is unclear.

As a symbol of equal treatment, higher levels of representation can work to reduce political alienation and increase trust (Saideman et al. 2002; Bochsler 2006; Schwindt-Bayer 2012) or indeed increase political participation (Uhlaner 2002; Banducci et al. 2004; Bühlmann and Schädel 2012). The idea that higher levels of descriptive representation can reduce societal conflict is commonly presented as a reason for the representation of ethnic groups. It is argued that without representatives in the legislature, members of minority groups are less likely to accept the outcome of elections as legitimate and will be more prone to conflict. This means that higher levels of descriptive representation are generally associated with political stability (Van Cott 2005; Cederman et al. 2010; Wucherpfennig et al. 2012), although the way minority groups are integrated may be as crucial as their presence in the legislature (Sisk and Reynolds 1998; Reynolds 2006). Traditional ethnic groups and immigrant groups may differ significantly in the extent that under-representation and conflict are linked. This can be explained by differences in group consciousness and political organisation, and also the exclusion of immigrant groups through citizenship. As such, claims to representation may differ, but the right to inclusion should not be reduced to conflict and a potential threat to social cohesion.

For empirical analysis, it is necessary to quantify the levels of representation. Based on the normative argument that legislatures should mirror the population, measuring descriptive representation is straightforward. The proportion of the population with a particular attribute is compared to the proportion of the representatives with the same attribute. This measurement is introduced formally in the chapters on the representation of women (see Chapter Two) and ethnic groups (see Chapter Three). The more difficult aspect of measurement is choosing the attributes that are compared, since there is no established normative claim that one descriptive dimension is more valuable than another. Whilst the representation of class was studied extensively in the past (e.g. Ross 1943; Birch 1971), recent contributions focus on gender and to a much lesser extent, ethnicity and age (Birch 2000; Childs 2000). Interest in ethnic group representation has increased in recent years (Rothman 2004; IPU 2010; Bird *et al.* 2010). I use the salience and degree of politicisation of social divisions as guidance to select descriptive dimensions. Of interest is the degree to which groups in society are aware of their identity and concerned by their level of representation in the legislature. The availability of comparable cross-national data also influences the choice of descriptive dimensions, as do considerations of inequality (Walby 2009). For many of the potential categories, including class and age, there are simply no data available for the representatives, or the data available are insufficient. In this book, I consider descriptive representation in terms of gender, ethnic groups and, to a much lesser extent, religious and language groups. Similarly, Egan (2012) highlights that group identification without mobilisation is possible, leading to a situation where claims to representation are unlikely.

For ethnic group representation, it is necessary to classify ethnic divisions in a country. The approach taken in this book does not attempt to compare across groups; in other words, ethnic groups are compared only with other ethnic groups, not with purely religious or geographical groups. The advantage of this approach is that countries with multiple salient divisions can be covered adequately. This differs from Norris (2004), who considers a wide variety of groups, depending on the country: language groups, religious groups, national groups or inhabitants of peripheral areas. It is unclear whether such different groups really can be compared.

In many Western societies, immigrant groups may be perceived as ethnic groups. Kymlicka (1995) argues that immigrant groups and indigenous ethnic groups should be treated separately, because they have different claims to representation. Whilst claims to representation and the politicisation of such claims are indeed often different, arguments of justice do not make a difference between minority groups based on *how* a group has become a minority or how long a group has been present in society (see also Jung 2009). Indeed, the distinction between different types of minority groups is often less clear than implied by Kymlicka (Packer 2005; Brock 2005). By using salience to identify relevant ethnic groups in the 131 countries that are free and partly free, immigrant groups are picked up in some countries. Often, however, immigrant groups are too small to be salient on their own. In contrast, looking at immigrants – as opposed to non-immigrants – does usually not fulfil the criteria of being a group in the sociological sense, because members of different immigrant groups often do not identify with such a label. For those countries for which I have information on immigration groups specifically, the resulting level of representation tends to be similar irrespective of whether immigrant groups are considered exclusively ($p<0.001$, but see also the Appendix). The visibility of minority groups is sometimes used as a criterion to identify immigrant groups (Bird *et al.* 2010), but on its own, visibility need not lead to salience or group consciousness.

Whichever social division they focus on, most studies concerned with descriptive representation find a significant discrepancy between the proportions of the groups in the population and the elected representatives (Norris 1993; Paxton *et al.* 2007). For example, in none of the legislatures in free and partly-free countries are there as many women as there are men (IPU 2009). At the same time, writers concerned with women's rights or social justice in general often celebrate the fact that in many places there are now more women in legislatures than in the past (Norris and Lovenduski 1993; IDEA 1998). Women in the Nordic countries now occupy a significant number of seats in government. In other Western European countries, the number of female representatives has increased at a slower rate (IPU 2009). There are also places where the number of women in the legislature seems to stagnate. The end of Soviet influence in much of Central and Eastern Europe and Asia meant a significant drop in the number of women in legislatures in the affected regions (UN 1992; Dahlerup 2006). These changes, however, are generally interpreted in a positive light. It is the freer elections and the increased power of the legislature vis-à-vis the executive that are thought to outweigh the fact that the legislature is now less of a demographic mirror. Moreover, for many observers the representation of demographic groups seems to be secondary to the representation of policy positions, since people appear primarily to vote on the basis of policies and opinions (Vallance 1979; Darcy *et al.* 1994; Osborn 2012).

Substantive representation is based exactly on this premise: it refers to the representation of the issue positions and policy preferences of citizens (Pitkin 1967; Powell 2004). As was the case with descriptive representation, the normative claim is that legislatures should mirror the population as closely as possible, this time in terms of political views and issue preferences. Of interest is how accurately the legislature matches the preferences of the citizens. Most commonly, issue positions are measured on the political left–right spectrum, even though it is not always clear what *left* and *right* mean (Laponce 1981; Knutsen 1995). Nonetheless, the concepts are relatively stable within a country (Fuchs and Klingemann 1989; Herrera 1999). In addition to left and right, other policy domains are also of interest (Miller and Stokes 1963; Thomassen and Schmitt 1997). Throughout the book, I use the term 'issue' or 'policy *domain*' to refer to the different issues for which representation can occur. The term '*policy representation*' describes the representation of policy preferences and issue positions.

Studies of substantive representation normally assume voting behaviour is best approximated with a spatial approach to voting. For example, issue positions can be expressed as left wing and right wing, or being for or against liberalising the economy. The assumption of spatial voting means that it is not only possible to state that person A is further to the left than person B, but also by how much. In addition, it is often assumed that voters act in a way that minimises the distance between their own position and that of the representative they voted for (Downs 1957; Pierce 1999).

This book does not examine how well representatives of particular parties represent their voters, partly because of the complexity other influences have on voter choice. Substantive representation is approached in a way that addresses the political representation of all citizens.

Substantive representation is paramount because of its direct relationship to policy. It is argued that citizens primarily vote based on issue positions and policy preferences (Mueller 1988; Darcy *et al.* 1994). The fact that most citizens vote in terms of issue positions, however, does not therefore imply moral desirability. Some writers argue that policy preferences are all that matter, since other distinctions, such as gender or age, are considered irrelevant. The primacy of policies is emphasised by the fact that most parties define themselves in terms of policy and ideology – often political left, centre, or right (Dalton 1985; Wittman 1990).

The quality of substantive representation is measured in terms of how well the representatives reflect the issue positions and policy preferences of the population. The congruence between the population and their representatives is thought to make the elite sensitive to the interests of the population. In practice, there are many ways to measure the congruence between the views of citizens and their representatives. All these measurements suffer from the difficulty of comparing distributions (Leik 1966; Holmberg 1999), but in fact, they tend to correlate highly with one another (Converse and Pierce 1986; Herrera *et al.* 1992). In this book, a simple comparison of means is used, possibly the most common measurement in the literature (see, for example, Weissberg 1978; Marsh and Wessels 1997; Schmitt and Thomassen 1999; Powell 2000; Golder and Stramski 2010). In order to calculate representation scores, data on the issue positions of the citizens and the representatives are required – something not available in most countries. The weighted averages of party positions are a reasonable approximation of the positions of representatives, particularly when considered as a part of the legislature as a whole. By so doing, it is possible to maintain a large and diverse sample with multiple policy domains.

Regardless of the measurement used, studies on policy representation tend to identify a certain discrepancy between the issue positions of citizens and representatives (Eulau and Wahlke 1978; Powell 2000). Some studies find relatively high levels of representation in certain domains, such as the economic domain or the less specific political left–right spectrum. This can be interpreted as good representation in the areas people care about (Birch 2000; Lutz 2003). However, Thomassen (2012) outlines situations where representation fails in the sense of significant differences on policy positions that citizens care about.

On the side of the representatives, it is unclear to what extent such concerns are reflected. A person elected to the legislature may not necessarily act in the way voters expect (Childs 2002; Curtin 2008). Being a woman does not necessarily mean that a female representative will vote in favour of what are widely considered women's issues;[3] a representative from a particular ethnic group may not

---

3. Women's interests are often assumed to align with the feminist agenda, but feminists do not necessarily speak for women in general (Squires 1996; Waylen 2008). Indeed, Smooth (2011) demonstrates that black women consider political issues important that are not traditionally part of the feminist agenda, such as crime or children's issues. She highlights that women are not a group with singular interests.

represent the interests that group is thought to have; and a left-wing representative might vote to privatise key industries (van Heelsum 2002). Studies on the topic commonly compare policy preferences with the voting pattern of representatives or the spending decisions in legislatures. Such an approach is unable to capture the multiplicity of interests often involved or the fact that the actions of individual representatives may not always translate into policy outcomes. For example, this is often the case when members of a minority group are outvoted on legislation that directly affects them. In the free and partly-free countries covered in this book, it can be assumed that levels of descriptive and substantive representation are largely linked to the extent to which representatives act for citizens (Saggar 2000; Chaney 2006; Dodson 2006; Farrell and Scully 2007). Whilst not every woman would represent what are widely considered women's interests, in places where there are more women in the legislature, it is more likely that women's issues will be discussed in the legislature (Thomas 1991; Mateo Diaz 2005). Focusing on ethnicity, Saalfeld (2009) shows similarly that parliamentarians from ethnic minorities in the United Kingdom are more likely to ask about ethnic minority groups in parliamentary questions.

This section has outlined different forms of representation and I have argued that both descriptive and substantive representation is relevant. These forms of representation are largely complementary – separate facets of political representation. The different forms of representation are discussed further in separate empirical chapters. In addition to examining descriptive and substantive representation, this book is also interested in the relationship between different forms of representation. Contrary to most studies on the relationship between different forms of representation, this book is focused on the representative outcome, not specific groups. It follows that the substantive representation of specific groups is not dealt with. However, at the same time – and unlike studies that focus on just one form of political representation – the theoretical framework outlined below integrates different forms of representation. A more complete understanding of political representation can be achieved by studying its many forms.

Representative relationships

Representation can take different forms, depending on particular types of representative relationships: who represents whom? This is a question of the proper role of the representatives, for which there are many different possibilities (Mansbridge 2003, 2011; Rehfeld 2009, 2011). Recent developments have highlighted the many forms of representative relationships, paying attention to new forms of responsiveness. A central distinction remains between *delegation* and *trusteeship*, commonly attributed to a speech by Edmund Burke (2004/1774). Burke argued that the proper role of a representative is not to be a mouthpiece for the wishes of his constituents, but to use his intelligence and experience to decide what is best for the constituency and the country. Today these two roles – commonly referred to as delegates and trustees respectively – are better understood as ideal types. Overall, it appears that citizens prefer delegates, which implies that any deviation from the microcosm ideal is of great concern. In contrast to the claim of Mansbridge (2008), survey evidence suggests that representatives prefer to regard themselves as trustees, which gives them more leeway to deviate from the citizens' ideal (Esaiasson and Holmberg 1996).

This book approaches representation by means of a collective relationship, which is different from a dyadic relationship (Miller and Stokes 1963; Dalton 1985; Herrera *et al.* 1992; Bartels 2005). When a dyadic relationship exists between a representative and the citizens of his or her district, the representative is expected to follow the opinion of the district or work in the interests of the district's citizens by securing resources for them (Copeland and Patterson 1998; see also Colomer 2011). The implicit assumption that only the legislator of a district can represent the citizens' views ignores the fact that in most cases interests and opinions will overlap district boundaries (Weissberg 1978). Mansbridge (2003) uses the term 'surrogate representation' to describe such representation without a direct electoral link. Focusing on the outcome rather than the representatives, a collective relationship concentrates on representation at the national level. The focus is entirely on the outcome and little attention is usually paid to how a particular result comes about, that is which party or district contributes to the outcome. The citizens as a whole are regarded as being represented by the elite. This aspect of representation – *as a whole* – is the key aspect of collective representation, rather than the distribution of preferences. Political parties may play an important role in the relationship between the masses and the elite. By choosing a particular party, citizens are assumed to be voting for the issue positions they prefer. However, even if that party fails to win a seat in the citizen's district, or the representative of that district does not reflect the voter's issue positions, other representatives from the same party might represent the citizen's views (McLean 1991; Wessels 1999a).

Examining a collective relationship is important because citizens care more that their views are represented in the legislature; they are less concerned about who does the representing (Weissberg 1978). Similarly, citizens from minority groups may be more concerned with their group being represented in the legislature than which district the corresponding representative comes from. Indeed, with a focus on districts, the dyadic relationship is unable to address descriptive representation adequately and is, therefore, unsuited for the analysis presented in this book. Only a collective perspective can serve both descriptive and substantive forms of representation. Nonetheless, there remains tension between representation for a specific district and representation at the national level (Colomer 2011). For issues limited to a specific geographical area, the collective perspective used in this book might fail to appreciate significant details. However, it can be argued that there are few such cases since most issues are not restricted to the bounds of a single district.

It is also possible to look at the presence of a single group member. An individual – or a group of citizens possessing a particular characteristic – can be considered represented if there is at least one representative sharing their particular characteristic. For example, if I am black and at least one representative is black, I could be regarded as represented in the legislature. This binary view of representation is not concerned with proportions. Groups can be defined by demographic features or certain policy preferences. In multiparty elections, it can be assumed that legislatures represents all major issue positions, considering one domain at a time, and this relationship does not merit further investigation. The case is different for women and ethnic minority groups that may be absent from the legislature. Insisting on having at least one group member in the legislature reflects Young's (1990) conception of group justice to a certain extent: all voices should be heard and included in legislative discussions; here, diversity is positively valued (Walby 2009). However, it is frequently argued that a certain threshold needs to be reached before numerical presence translates into changes in legislatures. This argument usually draws on a case study by Kanter (1977), who demonstrated that the composition of groups affects the behaviour of group members. Whilst the presence of a single woman technically fulfils the requirement of women's voices being present, Kanter's study demonstrated that in groups dominated by one kind, the minority group often simply adopts the views and values of the dominant group. In rare cases, the visible prominence of minorities leads to over-achievers. Differences are likely to be emphasised and stereotyped. With a more balanced group composition, Kanter observed different kinds of behaviour. However, it is unclear to what extent these findings can be applied to national legislatures (Mackay 2004; Childs 2006; Childs and Krook 2006, 2008).

This book implicitly supports the idea that collective representation means that membership of the legislature should reflect the different groups and issue positions in society. Based on the view that all citizens are equal and should have their views represented in the legislature, the book goes further: higher levels of descriptive representation can be regarded as an indication of the status of the respective groups in society. The key argument is that the number of women in legislatures, for example, is a reflection of women's real position in the public sphere (Thomas 1994; Kimmel 2004). Indeed, in countries where the number of female representatives is high, the number of women in public positions of responsibility also tends to be high (Vallance 1979; Ruedin 2009). In this sense, it can be argued that high levels of descriptive representation are indicative of a society with harmonious gender and race relations. Identifying the factors shaping levels of representation may also help understanding and ultimately improve the status of women and minority groups.

A framework of political representation

So far, this chapter has focused on disentangling the different aspects of legislative representation. This has helped to delimit the research focus to a collective relationship between citizens and their representatives in national legislatures. This relationship covers both group membership – descriptive representation – and issue positions and policy preferences – substantive representation. In both cases, there is a normative assumption that legislatures should reflect the groups and preferences of the population. However, examining the nature of representation in isolation does not help to explain the different levels of representation observed in national legislatures. Thus, I will introduce a theoretical framework in this section that draws on previous studies in the field, case studies from single countries as well as theory on political representation. It identifies factors that are thought to influence levels of representation and helps to bring the different facets of representation together in a new synthesis. With that, the framework provides the theoretical grounding to address the first research question (*How can we explain differences in the levels of political representation?*).

Given that the theory on the representation of women is more developed than the representation of ethnic groups, this literature is drawn on more frequently. Although significant differences are recognised in some instances (Bird 2003; Htun 2004; Walby 2009), there are many reasons to expect similar influences (Taagepera 1994; Lijphart 1999; Heath *et al.* 2005), perhaps with a different focus in each form of representation. Following this argument, the framework draws on research about different forms of political representation and applies these different contributions to other forms of representation as far as possible. Throughout the chapter, it becomes apparent that in most cases the same institutional and cultural variables are suggested as influences on the levels of representation. For that reason, a single theoretical framework for different forms of representation seems appropriate, even in the light of questions of intersectionality – the argument that multiple inequalities may lead to different outcomes (Weldon 2006; Walby 2009; Krook and O'Brien 2010; Hughes 2011). However, as well as presenting an integrated framework, I also highlight some differences. Whilst the theoretical framework aims to be integrated and coherent, it does not claim to provide an exhaustive or unifying model of political representation. In other words, if one of the factors identified is in reality unrelated to levels of representation or not significant in a particular form of representation, the remainder of the framework is unaffected. The framework also helps to recognise how different forms of representation might be linked, which is valuable to address the second research question (*How are levels of representation in different forms linked?*).

The framework presented in this section covers both descriptive and substantive representation and assumes a collective relationship between citizens and representatives. It is introduced gradually in order to discuss relevant views without losing sight of the overall idea. Ultimately, the theoretical framework allows testable hypotheses to be generated, which form the basis for the subsequent empirical chapters. The framework outlines the variables in question, and where appropriate, discusses details of how the variables are thought to affect levels of representation. Details of the operationalisation of the variables can be found in the Appendix.

Throughout this book, political representation refers to the relationship between citizens and the legislature. This describes a collective representative relationship: citizens are represented by the legislature as a whole. This relationship applies to both descriptive and substantive representation. In order to understand political representation, it is necessary to consider the nature of this relationship. How is representation created? As outlined in Figure 1.1, the chain begins on the left with citizens. Each citizen considers the options available and makes a vote choice. Here the options are not only to cast a vote, but also to not vote at all. The votes are counted and aggregated into seats in the legislature, completing the chain. In short, representation is created through elections. The basic setup is the same for both substantive and descriptive representation. The literature often implies that the first step in Figure 1.1 is negligible for representation in the legislature, focusing entirely on the relationship between votes cast and the representational outcome. This approach is particularly common for substantive representation, but as outlined below, such an approach is likely to lead to a partial treatment of political representation (Mutz 2007).

Figure 1.1: Basis of political representation

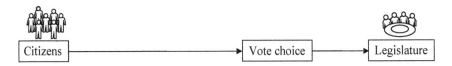

Based on the fundamental relationship between citizens and the legislature it is now possible to consider influencing factors. As outlined in Figure 1.2, different variables may shape the overall representative relationship at different stages. At their broadest, these variables can be understood as instances of the political context and key institutions affecting levels of representation in various ways. In the paragraphs that follow, I will add variables to the basic setup outlined in Figure 1.1, and discuss them in turn. The different variables can affect levels of representation via the voters by influencing voting behaviour, via the elite by influencing the selection of candidates, and directly by influencing the aggregation of the votes cast.

Starting on the right side of the diagram, the electoral system and other key institutions have a significant influence on the relationship between vote choice and the resulting composition of the legislature (Benjamin 1998; Lijphart 1999; Farrell 2001). Of these, only the electoral system has a direct influence. It determines the proportionality of the system: how the number of votes translates into seats in the legislature. This factor affects both substantive representation and descriptive representation (Grofman 1983; Taylor 2005; Johnston *et al.* 2006). Assuming that citizens vote sincerely, disproportionality between votes and seats means that those who vote for certain parties are numerically under-represented in the legislature. More specifically, majoritarian systems augment the votes of the largest parties, giving them and their policies greater weight in the legislature. Descriptive representation may be affected by the proportionality of the system if different groups are not equally present in all parties, such as when left-wing parties have more female candidates. The proportionality between votes and seats itself is largely influenced by the district magnitude, the electoral formula, the ballot structure and the number of parties.

Figure 1.2: Variables influencing political representation

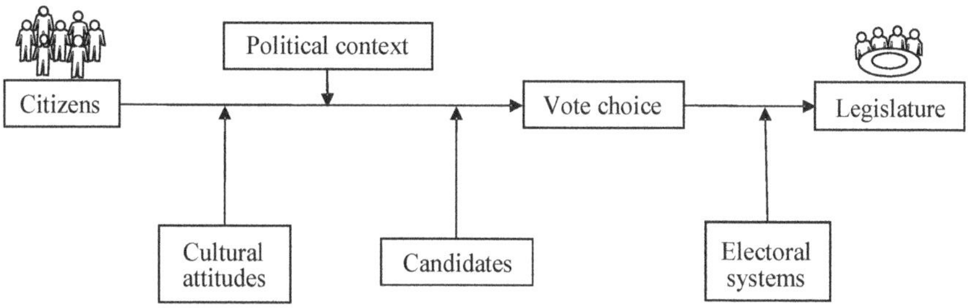

The electoral system is not the only factor thought to shape political representation. The candidates available to the voters directly influence the processes leading to vote choice, and some writers bemoan the lack of choice available to the voters (Ross 1943; Pulzer 1975). For example, a voter with communist tendencies might have no choice of a like-minded candidate or party. The candidates standing for election effectively limit the options available to the voters. Suitable candidates may not come forward and stand for election, a fact that might be more of an issue for descriptive representation, as outlined below. For example, not enough women or persons from ethnic minorities may come forward as candidates. The citizens' votes are constrained by the electoral system and the political context because some candidates are unlikely to win a seat, given the particular electoral rules and party system in place. Voters may discount candidates who would otherwise appeal to them when they are nominated by a party with little hope of winning a particular seat. For example, a candidate from a minority group may not gain many votes from voters from that minority group if the party in question is unlikely to win a seat at all. More generally, the political context influences how candidates are evaluated, and thus affects the likelihood that certain candidates are elected to the legislature.

On the far left of the diagram, the vote choice is influenced by cultural attitudes. This assumes that an individual's vote is the product of endogenous views, such as party identification, and influences from the social environment (Fiorina 1976; Inglehart and Norris 2003; Galligan 2005). For substantive representation, party identification is thought to be particularly important, but influences from the political and social environment are also important in determining individual vote choice. The influence of the social environment can be described in terms of cultural attitudes. It is worth examining the predominant attitudes in society towards women as political leaders, or towards marginalised groups. In the case of descriptive representation, such views and attitudes may directly affect the probability of an individual voting for a woman or a member of an ethnic minority group. The influence of cultural attitudes on levels of ethnic group representation is often implied, especially when discussing historical under-representation and discrimination (Geisser 1997; Darity and Mason 1998; Saggar and Geddes 2000; Moser

2004). Johnson (1998), for example, examines the role of black Brazilians in the *National Congress*, where non-whites are still considered by many to be less suited for public office. The experience of discrimination, often perhaps unintentional, may inhibit women and members of ethnic minority groups from entering politics (Johnson 1998; Saggar and Geddes 2000). In the case of substantive representation, such views and societal attitudes may affect the salience of different domains. In other words, attitudes affect the issues that are widely considered important.

I have outlined four different areas where the representative relationship between citizens and legislatures is influenced by outside factors. Next, I will examine underlying factors. To this extent, Figure 1.3 adds further details to Figure 1.2. The lack of influencing variables in Figure 1.3 illustrates that the electoral system and its key institutions are regarded as fixed. Whilst such a view is not tenable in the long term (Lijphart and Grofman 1984; Reynolds *et al.* 1997; Bogaards 2004), for the purpose of this book where a cross-sectional perspective is used, such a position can be defended. By insisting on the short-term stability of the electoral system, the possibility of change in the long term is explicitly acknowledged (Zimmerman and Rule 1998; Colomer 2004), although in established democracies such changes are relatively rare (Shugart and Wattenberg 2003; Colomer 2004; Cox 2006). Changes from outside the time period covered in the empirical analyses will be addressed in the discussion of the results.

The nature of the electoral system is often identified as a key factor in explaining the varying proportions of women in legislatures. With the exception of a few (Oakes and Almquist 1993; Moore and Shackman 1996), almost all studies find the electoral formula to be a useful predictor. Proportional representation (PR) systems, in particular, are associated with higher levels of representation than majoritarian ones (for example Darcy *et al.* 1994; Paxton 1997; Ballington 1998; Galligan and Tremblay 2005). Many even find that the electoral formula is the single most important factor in explaining differences in gender representation (Rule 1987; Norris 1987; Lovenduski and Norris 1993; Kenworthy and Malami 1999). The reason the electoral system is thought to be a significant factor for the representation of women in legislatures is the larger districts found in PR systems (Lijphart 1994; Rule and Zimmerman 1994; Katz 1997). Although it is rarely noted, women in large districts have a higher probability of being elected; the assumption is that there are only a few female contenders. In larger districts more candidates are selected, so there is an increased likelihood that one of the female candidates will be elected.[4]

---

4. Matland (1993) attempted to better understand how the electoral system influences the representation of women. He introduced a new concept of party magnitude and argued that it is causally closer to levels of gender representation than the underlying district magnitude. Party magnitude is calculated by dividing the district magnitude by the number of parties in the district. This concept adds a further dimension to that of district magnitude. The implicit assumption is that men are more likely to take the top spot of party lists than women. Where there are fewer parties

The electoral system and its key institutions are also mentioned in studies on ethnic group representation (Engstrom and McDonald 1982; Spirova 2004; Bochsler 2006). Togeby (2005) highlights the role of preferential voting combined with a proportional representation system, although no adequate comparison to other cases is included. The supposition is that proportional systems with preferential voting allow voters to select ethnic minority candidates without compromising on their preferred party. It assumes that, all things being equal, voters would prefer a higher number of ethnic minority representatives and that all parties nominate some candidates from ethnic minority groups. Reynolds (2006) takes a different approach and suggests the electoral system is a factor that can foster cooperation between members of different ethnic groups.

In studies of substantive representation, the focus is often on the multifaceted electoral system as a key explanatory variable (Farrell and Scully 2007). The electoral formula is of particular interest, as is the district magnitude, or electoral thresholds. Many studies find better congruence between the policy preferences of citizens and representatives in countries with PR systems rather than in places with majoritarian systems (for example Huber and Powell 1994; Lijphart 1999; Powell 2006; Budge and McDonald 2007). This is because majoritarian systems tend to significantly augment the majority position. In other words, the proportionality between votes and seats is the underlying factor behind differences between electoral formulas (Nordlinger 1968; Katz 1997). Powell (2000) elaborated on this approach, arguing that more attention should be paid to the role of the opposition. Where the opposition is stronger, levels of representation tend to be higher; and in PR systems, the opposition is predisposed to be strong.

Not all studies, however, support the finding that countries with PR tend to have higher levels of policy representation than those with majoritarian systems. There is some indication that, when considering subsequent elections under majoritarian systems, the average level of representation increases when opposing parties alternate in power (McDonald *et al.* 2004; Budge *et al.* 2012). In a similar vein, Blais and Bodet (2006) report that PR systems tend to lead to a larger number of political parties, but also to parties that are less centrist than found under majoritarian systems. Whilst PR systems thus offer more choice to voters, the positions of the main parties means that, overall, there is no noticeable difference

---

competing in a district, the likelihood that a woman will be elected increases by reaching further down the party list. The concept of the party magnitude combines the two effects and it becomes apparent why, as Matland acknowledges, the effects of party magnitude are temporarily limited. The association between party magnitude and levels of gender representation is weak where levels of gender representation are low. In this case, the likelihood that a woman is elected will always be low. The association increases as levels of representation increase: more women are elected where the districts are larger and where the number of parties is smaller. When women are just as likely to be candidates as men, and they are equally likely to appear at the top of party lists, the association decreases again. The likelihood that a woman will be elected in this case approaches 50 per cent.

between countries with PR and majoritarian systems. Powell (2007) suggests the time frame accounts for the difference: the differences between PR and systems with single-member districts (SMD) are actually declining in real terms. Powell elaborates that in some SMD elections in the past decade, convergence towards the median position could be observed. Since the number of countries with SMD is relatively small, these changes mean that the advantage of PR systems previously noted has largely disappeared.

In Figure 1.3, quotas and related interventions are considered as part of the electoral system and its key institutions.[5] As is common in the literature, this book considers three kinds of quotas: voluntary party quotas, statutory or legal quotas, and reserved seats. Quotas for women are generally implemented within parties and realised on a voluntary basis, with no further consequences if the target is not achieved (Htun 2004; Dahlerup and Freidenvall 2005). This means that a political party decides to include at least a certain proportion of women candidates, often a value between 20 and 30 per cent. Of the parties, it is often parties on the left that are first to introduce quotas, possibly a reflection of their focus on inclusiveness (Matland 2006; McLeay 2006; Paxton et al. 2006). The term 'gender quota' is common, and sometimes quota rules are formulated in a way that includes both women and men. For example, in some cases both genders are entitled to be at least 30 per cent of candidates. In addition to voluntary quotas, there are also statutory quotas: a law is passed that requires all parties to nominate a certain percentage of women or ethnic minorities. The degree to which statutory and voluntary quotas are enforced varies, but often there are no serious consequences for failing to reach a quota. Most studies on quotas for women find that such interventions result in a higher proportion of women in legislatures (for example McAllister and Studlar 2002; Yoon 2004; Tripp and Kang 2007; Chen 2009; Krook 2010; Hughes 2011).

---

5. There are two different arguments for the introduction of quotas. The *fast-track* approach deems current progress towards higher levels of representation too slow. Quotas are introduced to achieve higher levels of representation without having to wait for what is often projected to take decades or longer (Dahlerup and Freidenvall 2005; Lovenduski 2005; Norris 2009; Chen 2009). The *blockage* argument suggests is that some factor prevents levels of descriptive representation from increasing, and quotas or affirmative action are needed to break through these barriers. Both approaches to quotas assume that the best way to achieve higher levels of descriptive representation is by asserting and politicising difference by means of special rights specific to the group (compare Lijphart 1977; Horowitz 1985). Claims to self-control do not rule out moderation of conflict in the long term, but there is a danger that group differences are accentuated by the accommodation of difference in the short term. Asserting difference may be necessary, since a focus on assimilation and moderation from the outset could involve ignoring the root of any difference. This is a case of domination through universalisation (Young 1990; Phillips 1993; Williams 1995).

Figure 1.3: Underlying factors for representation

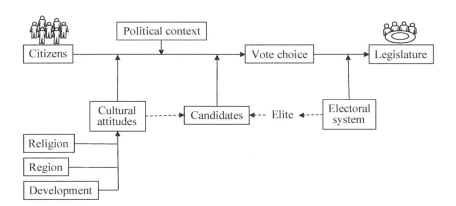

Notes: The predominant religion, the region and the level of development influence cultural attitudes. These cultural attitudes affect candidate selection (dashed line). The electoral system – through the political elite – also influences candidate selection (dashed lines).

The influence of quotas on levels of representation is two-fold. First, quotas and related measures may directly affect the relationship between votes cast and seats gained. Indeed, they are implemented exactly for increasing the level of representation for specific groups without necessarily affecting the proportionality for parties. In India, for example, there are reserved seats for Dalits.[6] This direct influence is included in Figure 1.3 as a straight line originating from the electoral system. Secondly, quotas and related measures may affect the selection of candidates. This is particularly obvious with voluntary party quotas. In Sweden, for instance, the *Liberal Party* reserves at least 40 per cent of all candidate places to either men or women (IDEA 2006). The influence works via the elite, as indicated in Figure 1.3 using a dashed line. For the purposes of this book, quotas are regarded as instigated by the elite (Simms 1993; Childs 2000; Sawer *et al.* 2006). There are other views, however, like the propensity of implementing quotas is directly linked to positive attitudes in the population towards women and ethnic minorities in power (Inglehart and Norris 2003; Norris and Inglehart 2004; Norris 2009), the presence of quotas in neighbouring countries (Aroújo and García 2006) or more established democracies (Schwindt-Bayer and Palmer 2007). I was unable to support these views with the data used.

The political context may shape political representation in two ways: through political rights and the age of democracy, although these are not listed separately

---

6. Dalits are often called *untouchables* – people in India who fall outside the four castes, considered to be below them. In the Indian constitution, the term '*scheduled caste*' is used.

in Figure 1.3. Both factors influence levels of representation or moderate other variables in the theoretical framework. In freer and more established democracies, the elite and the citizens are more able to learn and improve their expectations. Such political freedom can be measured with reference to the political rights in a country. Political rights are associated with the formulation of attitudes towards women as political leaders and marginalised groups in society (cultural attitudes), the supply of candidates, the formulation of vote choice – through the information on the candidates available – and the actions of the elite. At each stage, the role of political rights may be small, but it is always theoretically important (Rule and Zimmerman 1994; Paxton 1997; Matland 1998; Reynolds 1999; Diamond 2002; Paxton *et al.* 2007; Viterna *et al.* 2008; Viterna and Fallon 2008). Political rights may ultimately play the biggest role in affecting political representation by enabling political communication and making sure citizens and members of the elite are able to express their views openly. Like other institutional factors, political rights affect the incentive structure that shapes electoral behaviour. This is more apparent in the absence of political rights and freedom, which is associated with the oppression of such groups as ethnic minorities, opposition party supporters or others with dissenting views. In all cases, political representation will be affected.

A political system can be considered more or less established by measuring the number of years democracy has been in place. The political elite may become more experienced over time and therefore better able to judge the electoral system's influence on the expected success of candidates (Crigler 1996; Herrera 1999). For instance, a longer tradition of democratic rule infers that the elite had more time to incorporate demands for the representation of ethnic minority groups. The literature on the influence of political rights, or the age of democracy, on levels of policy representation is relatively sparse (Birch 2000; Olson and Crowther 2002; Banducci *et al.* 2004; Luna and Zechmeister 2005). Over time, electoral systems are likely to become more solidified. As a result, the importance of certain domains is highlighted in more established systems, which influences the level of representation achieved in different domains.

The candidates who are available at an election exert a significant influence on levels of representation. Two underlying factors are commonly suggested: the role of the elite in selecting and nominating candidates, and the so-called supply of candidates who stand for election. The political elite is thought to have a considerable impact by nominating candidates and, more generally, by controlling internal party structures. The political elite essentially acts as gatekeeper. This may negatively affect candidates from minority groups or, in the case of substantive representation, candidates with certain views (Lovenduski and Norris 1993; Bylesjö and Seda 2006). The political ideology of parties may be important, particularly regarding the representation of women. In the past, it was observed that left-wing parties were more likely to include women on their party lists and place them higher up on the lists. Consequently, where left-wing parties were stronger, the proportion of women in the legislature tended to be higher. In recent years, it seems that the strength of left-wing parties no longer makes a significant difference to levels of gender representation (Skjeie 1991; Matland and Studlar 1996; Leyenaar 2004;

Kunovich 2012; Krook and O'Brien 2012). A similar influence can be expected for the representation of ethnic minority groups. The elite may be influenced by the political context and, more particularly, the electoral system when determining strategies for candidate recruitment. The probability of a candidate succeeding in an election also depends on the nature of the political system, and the elite takes those factors into account. This includes the presence of quotas, but also other considerations. For example, it is often argued that women are not nominated as candidates in national elections because the party leadership consider them an electoral risk. Given a particular political system, the elite will often calculate that a male candidate is more likely to be elected than a female (Norris and Lovenduski 1995; Norris 2000). In the case of policy representation, the link from attitudes to candidates describes a political climate and attitudes in society that may limit or prevent the formation of certain parties, e.g. communist or openly racist parties. In the case of descriptive representation, this link is more about individual candidates coming forward, such as women and members of ethnic minorities. Suitably qualified members will come forward in significant numbers only in a society where their role in public life is widely supported.

The number of suitably qualified candidates willing to stand for election is commonly referred to as 'the supply of candidates' (Randall 1987; Norris and Lovenduski 1995; Norris and Franklin 1997; Childs 2000). Rather than focusing on the elite's role in selecting candidates, the focus is on the individual coming forward as a potential representative. The social background of the individual influences the likelihood that hopefuls come forward because this factor reflects the resources and motivations available. Such motivations are probably shaped by primary and secondary socialisation and the internalisation of social roles (Froman 1961; Mueller 1988; Wolbrecht and Campbell 2005; Lawless and Fox 2005; Moore 2006; Jennings 2007). Potential candidates are likely to consider the hurdles that will impede their chances of success. Necessary investments will be compared against the demand for women or ethnic minority candidates by voters and the elite (Leyenaar 2004; Bird *et al.* 2010). Saggar (2000) outlines the complex interplay of class and ethnicity, and Banda and Chinkin (2004) highlight how different minority statuses often interlock. For example, a member of an ethnic minority may be doubly disadvantaged by both her ethnicity and her religion. Walby (2009) uses the expression of complex inequalities to describe such issues of 'intersectionality'. Gershon (2012), for example, provides evidence that media coverage for women and ethnic minority candidates is not particularly negative, but coverage for ethnic minority women is notably more negative. Differences in motivation can influence both descriptive and substantive representation, such as when women or members of the working class stay out of elections because they consider themselves unsuited for political office.

Socioeconomic issues are often cited in the literature as factors affecting the number of women who consider becoming a candidate. These variables probably account for the supply of candidates, although this is rarely acknowledged. Factors like the proportion of women in higher education can be considered approximations of the actual number of qualified women in the wider population. Many studies find that the size of women's share of the labour force is associated with the proportion of women in the legislature (Rule 1981; Norris 1985, 1987; Oakes and Almquist 1993; Mateo Diaz 2005). A particularly relevant factor is the proportion of women in professional jobs. Where this proportion is higher, there tends to be more women in national legislatures (Rule 1987; Moore and Shackman 1996; Kenworthy and Malami 1999; Paxton and Kunovich 2003). Socio-economic constraints are also cited for ethnic minority groups (Geisser 1997; Chaney and Fevre 2002). Some studies focus on educational variables rather than labour force participation. Of these, the proportion of girls in secondary education is the most common factor studied (Rule 1981, 1987; Norris 1987; Oakes and Almquist 1993; Matland 1998). Intuition suggests that where the proportion of girls in secondary education is higher, the supply of suitably qualified women candidates should also be higher, although the evidence for such educational variables is mixed. Educational variables may be too generic, and do not incorporate women's participation in public life in general. The proportion of women in professional jobs, by contrast, covers all aspects of supply, including qualifications, and the willingness of women to accept public roles of responsibility. The argument is that in countries where women are free to participate in the labour force, there are fewer constraints on women to participate in the public sphere in general. Measures of supply may therefore also incorporate cultural factors that affect the likelihood of candidates running for election.

Cultural variables are included on the left in Figure 1.3. The level of development, religion, and historical regional differences are all potential influences for cultural attitudes. Such attitudes include prescriptive gender roles or attitudes towards marginalised groups in society. Perhaps surprisingly, cultural factors are far less frequently studied than institutional and socioeconomic factors. For example, popular attitudes towards women or ethnic minorities occupying public positions can be a significant factor. Many studies recognise this factor without testing it directly (for example Paxton 1997; Arcenaux 2001; Galligan and Tremblay 2005; Abou-Zeid 2006). Both the supply and demand side are thought to be affected by relevant attitudes. Where attitudes are more positive, more women and ethnic minorities are expected to enrol as candidates – and there is a greater chance of them being chosen. There are, however, different approaches to capture the influence of cultural attitudes on levels of descriptive representation. On the one hand, the focus can be on any of the underlying factors shaping cultural attitudes, while on the other hand, it may be attempting to capture cultural attitudes directly.

One such underlying variable is the level of 'development'. A useful concept is the *Human Development Index* (HDI), a measure of development that goes beyond purely economic considerations. The assumption is that with increasing development, concerns for equality in general and women and ethnic minorities in particular increase. There are no convincing arguments to explain this, but it could be linked to people having more time and resources to focus on issues beyond basic needs (Norris and Inglehart 2010). Consequently, development is not commonly treated as a covariate in its own right (Matland 1998). Instead, many have emphasised the difference between industrial and post-industrial countries, paralleling the trend towards post-material values in more highly-developed societies (Peterson 1990; Inglehart 1997; Matland 1998; Welzel 2007; Inglehart and Welzel 2010). The understanding of development remains wide, highlighting trends of modernisation going beyond economic aspects. The shift towards post-materialist values leads to heightened concerns for the rights of ethnic minority groups and women, as well as social issues or the environment (Schmitt 1990; Norris and Lovenduski 1995; Moser 2004). As societies become more stable and stronger economically, attitudes tend to shift beyond the primary impulses of security and self-preservation. The attitudes in question evoke the concept of sociological liberalism: support for peaceful cooperation and coexistence of different groups in society, rooted in ideals of equality and social justice (Crouch 1999).

A different influence on relevant attitudes is the predominant religion of a country, a variable sometimes used to account for cultural aspects. Relatively large categories are used to tease out relevant differences, recognising predominantly Protestant, Catholic, and Muslim countries. All other countries are combined into the category 'other'. The predominant religion of a country is thought to reflect generally held views, particularly views on the appropriate role and behaviour of different groups in society (Chafetz 1984; Bystydzienski 1995; Henig and Henig 2001; Rabb and Suleiman 2003; Inglehart and Norris 2003; Mateo Diaz 2005; Norris 2009). In studies on the representation of women, predominantly Catholic countries are sometimes highlighted (Rule 1987; Paxton 1997; Leyenaar 2004). Catholicism is singled out for its prescriptive views on the role of women in public life whereby, to a certain extent, individuals have internalised gender roles that culturally restrict women's access to the public sphere. Equivalent limits can be expected in predominantly Muslim countries. Similarly, religious influences may affect the ability of ethnic minorities to reach public office, such as when religion condones particular social divisions and hierarchies (Mateo Diaz 2005). In this sense, one can speculate that some domains of substantive representation are also affected by the predominant religion of a country. Working through internalisation and socialisation, both the public and the political elite may be influenced by religion. This may result in certain issue domains becoming politicised and could make it more difficult for women and ethnic minorities to enter politics (Kunovich and Paxton 2005).

A rather different approach to cultural differences is the use of regional variables, an approach frequently employed with regard to the representation of women (Moore and Shackman 1996; Kenworthy and Malami 1999). Regional variables may explain cultural differences resulting from different historical experiences. For example, access to trade routes, relative isolation or involvement in seafaring can be thought to influence attitudes in a wider sense. The intuition here is that regular contact with other cultures fostered a certain degree of open-mindedness, reflected in present-day attitudes towards different groups in society (Bystydzienski 1995; Forbes 1997; Emerson *et al.* 2002; Rabb and Suleiman 2003; Pettigrew and Tropp 2006). This argument can be applied to changes in attitudes both at the individual and group level. Whilst regional variables incorporate historical cultural differences, they also encompass institutional and economic factors. Despite

NEW YORK INSTITUTE
OF TECHNOLOGY

this, however, regional differences are a suitable measure of cultural differences. Regional variables are highly correlated with other factors such as the predominant religion or attitudinal variables (p<0.001), as further outlined in the Appendix. The frequent use of regional variables as a measure of the cultural attitudes relevant to the representation of women and ethnic minorities is normally justified on a theoretical basis (Paxton 1997; Inglehart 1997; Contreras 2002; Paxton and Kunovich 2003; Nanivadekar 2006; Tripp and Kang 2007).

Instead of focusing on underlying factors, it is also possible to examine directly the position of women and ethnic minorities in society and related attitudes (Norris and Inglehart 2001, 2004; Paxton and Kunovich 2003). As outlined in Figure 1.3, it would seem that relevant attitudes are influenced by a multitude of factors. Besides the aforementioned differences in development, region and religion, there may be other influences, but it seems difficult to capture them empirically. Considering a single underlying variable, therefore, necessarily means that some aspects of cultural attitudes are missed. Instead, if possible, capturing relevant attitudes in an immediate sense should be more successful in explaining differences in political representation. This is not to say that the underlying factors are of no importance. Rather, we should recognise that they may be too confounded to be included separately in the empirical analysis because the respective variables are highly correlated. With a direct measure of cultural attitudes, however, the link to political representation is clearer. Women and ethnic minorities are more likely to come forward as candidates in a more supportive environment. The elite is more likely to support these candidates, and the electorate is more likely to vote for women and ethnic minorities in elections.

Having outlined the underlying factors, Figure 1.4 adds further influences for levels of political representation. These include the role of salience, influences from other places and the composition of society. When considering salience, it becomes apparent that attitudes and culture can also affect substantive representation. Salience in the context of political representation refers to the awareness of and importance given to different policy domains and descriptive dimensions. The importance assigned to certain issue domains or the awareness and politicisation of certain social cleavages may differ from country to country, or even from citizen to citizen. The salience may be affected by the level of development, the composition of society, religion, regional differences, as well as levels of representation in other places. The composition of society is included because in nearly homogeneous societies, little notice may be paid to this homogeneity. For example, in a country where nearly everyone speaks the same language, language as a political factor may not be very salient or politicised. Similarly, the level of development and religious differences can be considered factors shaping salience, paralleling the argument outlined for cultural attitudes. Religions with prescriptive world views tend to consider particular public roles undesirable for women and ethnic minorities, and tend to emphasise particular issue domains, such as social issues. By comparing levels of representation in different forms, the significance of the salience of different domains and dimensions can be appreciated. Although they are not treated directly in the empirical chapters, civil society organisations

Figure 1.4: Framework of political representation

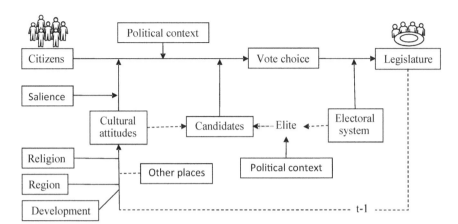

Notes: Political representation links citizens (top left) and the legislature (top right) via vote choice. This relationship is influenced by the political context, the electoral system, the candidates standing for election and predominant cultural attitudes. These variables, in turn, are affected by differences in the predominant religion, region, or the level of development. The salience of social divisions (left) and the level of representation achieved in other places or dimensions (bottom) as well as in the previous legislature (t-1) influence how the other variables shape the basic relationship between citizens and the legislature.

may play an important role in influencing and shaping the salience of different domains (Jacobs and Townsley 2011).

Furthermore, as noted in Figure 1.4, levels of representation achieved in other dimensions and other places may affect cultural attitudes to some extent. The argument is that higher levels of representation in one area may influence attitudes towards other dimensions of representation. For example, in a country where ethnic minorities are successfully integrated in the legislature, women may start demanding better representation, and the wider population is more likely to support them (Phillips 1993; Allwood and Wadia 2004; Tereskina 2005). The equivalent argument – essentially an argument of imitation – can be made for policy representation. Election results in one country may affect elections in other countries by influencing the salience of certain issue domains. Indeed, events in one country may shape attitudes towards women or ethnic minorities as political leaders in other countries. The argument is that once one country successfully integrates more women into the legislature, for example, attitudes in neighbouring countries are equally affected (Matland and Studlar 1996; Baldez 2006; Aroújo and García 2006). Similar influences can be expected from cultural links, international organisations or global summits (Dahlerup and Freidenvall 2005; Viterna and Fallon 2008). In Figure 1.4, these effects are summarised into a single label ('other places'). However, both the influence of neighbouring countries and levels of representation in other dimensions describe a temporal effect. For reasons of data availability, this book uses a cross-sectional design. This makes it impossible to include influences from other countries systematically in the empirical analyses.

For the representation of ethnic groups, the composition of society may be a relevant factor. Focusing on Britain, Anwar (1994) highlights the geographical concentration of many ethnic minority groups. In certain districts, ethnic minorities have become a significant electoral constituency, sometimes even forming a numerical majority locally. In such cases, political parties often actively woo ethnic minority voters. Nonetheless, ethnic minorities remain grossly under-represented in national legislatures (Anwar 1994; Bogaards 2004). Togeby (2005) outlines a similar story for local councils in Denmark, but concludes that ethnic minorities are comparatively well represented at the local level. The difference may result from the political parties in place, as argued in Bird's (2005) account of visible minorities in France, Denmark, and Canada. The argument is that historically minority groups, including ethnic minorities, tend to be under-represented in almost all countries. Bird outlines how parties actively recruit ethnic minority candidates in some areas for strategic reasons to present an alternative to the 'traditional' white candidates. Messina (1989), again focusing on Britain, argues that racial difference is still largely absent from mainstream political discourse, despite increasing demands for inclusion. This is echoed by Saggar and Geddes (2000). In other words, the geographical concentration of ethnic groups may result in increased salience and politicisation, but it is not inevitable.

The theoretical framework summarised in Figure 1.4 outlines variables that are thought to influence levels of representation. Where possible, the accompanying text discusses how the variables are expected to affect levels of representation. However, the empirical analysis examines associations and is thus unable to test whether the outlined variables work as suggested. Having introduced the different variables, however, it is also necessary to examine the causality of cultural factors. Consistent with all literature considering political culture, the theoretical framework cannot completely resolve issues of causality (Fuchs 2007). For levels of descriptive representation in particular, the argument is not only that attitudes towards women and marginalised groups as political leaders affect levels of representation (Norris and Inglehart 2001; Paxton and Kunovich 2003; Leyenaar 2004), but it is also that such attitudes may be influenced by the actual number of women or ethnic minorities present in the legislature. Figure 1.4 reflects this by a dashed line from the legislature to cultural attitudes. A similar argument is made for substantive representation, where representatives may significantly shape the views and opinions of citizens (Jacobs and Shapiro 2000; Shapiro et al. 2009; but see Somin 2000), although such assertions are difficult to test.

The argument that attitudes influence levels of representation is well rehearsed. Cultural attitudes in society are thought to influence both demand (by the voters and within parties) and supply (as in candidates coming forward) (Chafetz 1984; Norris 1993; Leyenaar 2004; Galligan and Tremblay 2005). At the same time, particularly in the case of gender representation, some argue that societal attitudes towards women as political leaders are partly shaped by the levels of representation in national legislatures. In this case, women in legislatures are regarded as role models (Thomas 1994; Arcenaux 2001; Tinker 2004; Wolbrecht and Campbell 2005; McAllister 2006; Dovi 2007). However, there are many other influences on cultural attitudes, including the dominant religion of a country, the level of development, historical regional differences and prominent role models from outside politics (Sharpe 1976; Goffman 1976; Fuchs 2007). For this reason, it can be assumed that the legislature has a limited influence on issue positions and policy preferences. Unfortunately, in most cases, I am unable to address the issue of reverse causality with the data available. In the chapter on gender representation (see Chapter Two), I include a limited analysis of representation over time. This analysis suggests that attitudes towards women as political leaders are closely associated with levels of gender representation. It also casts doubt on the argument that levels of representation in the past have a significant influence on current attitudes towards women as political leaders, at least for the time period examined.

Evidence that social changes occur prior to the corresponding political changes also comes from Togeby (1994). Togeby uses longitudinal data from Denmark to support the view that attitudinal changes are indeed causally prior to changes in the levels of descriptive representation. With a time span of thirty years, Togeby's study should cater for the argument that the effects of presence in the legislature may take time to be picked up (Phillips 1995; Stimson 2007). Togeby argues that, initially, changes in education and the employment status of women lead to changes in their attitudes. Next, women start to change their behaviour within the family and their immediate environment. However, sooner or later, the individuals with changed attitudes will face inequalities they cannot change as individuals. These encounters lead to political activism and ultimately to changes in mainstream attitudes. The underlying argument is that cultural attitudes shift to fit changes in the social structure (Chafetz 1984; Togeby 1994; Fernández et al. 2004; Häusermann and Schwander 2010). This is not to deny that the presence of women and ethnic minorities in the legislature can lead to an adjustment of societal attitudes. Rather, it highlights that the main effect is that societal attitudes can shape levels of political representation.

In this section, I have developed a theoretical framework of political representation. Starting with the relationship between voters and representatives, I outlined the underlying causes, and discussed how the variables are understood to affect levels of representation. In so doing, it should be possible to better understand and explain the differences in the levels of descriptive and substantive representation observed around the world. The framework was designed with both descriptive and substantive representation in mind, but different areas may be emphasised in each case. This means that different forms of political representation are regarded as separate facets of political representation. Nonetheless, the basic procedure for both forms of representation is assumed to be the same. Indeed, the same underlying variables are shown to influence levels of political representation. For this reason, some similarities between levels of descriptive and substantive representation can be expected. Consequently, the framework is also useful for addressing the relationship between different forms of representation.

Hypotheses

It is possible to derive a number of hypotheses from the theoretical framework outlined above. I begin with hypotheses of a general nature, followed by specific hypotheses for the different forms of political representation – the representation of women, the representation of ethnic groups, and the representation of issue positions. A final section on methods and models completes this chapter.

Assuming that most voters cast a sincere vote expressing their true preferences, the proportionality between votes cast and seats gained may lead to misrepresentation in legislatures. In other words, *systems that are more proportional lead to higher levels of representation*. Consistent with the literature and the theoretical framework, we can expect the proportion of women in national legislatures to be associated with the proportionality of the electoral system. Proportional representation (PR) systems should be associated with a higher proportion of women in the legislature. The same argument can be applied to the representation of ethnic groups. Higher levels of ethnic group representation are expected in countries with more proportional systems. The influence of the electoral system on the level of substantive representation is also highlighted in the existing literature. Because they are designed to reproduce a microcosm of the population, systems that are more proportional can be expected to lead to higher levels of policy representation. This argument should apply to all policy domains.

Other institutional aspects are also thought to be associated with higher levels of substantive and descriptive representation, such as low electoral thresholds or larger districts; but institutionalised practices can also affect the probability of women and minority candidates winning seats in the legislature. More generally, higher levels of descriptive representation can be expected in places where the institutional setting encourages the inclusion of women and ethnic minorities. The proportionality of a system itself is probably also affected by factors other than the electoral formula, such as electoral thresholds or the district magnitude (Kolinsky 1993; Blais and Massicotte 2002). It can be summarised using measures of proportionality, such as the *Gallagher Index* (or least squares index) (Gallagher 1991). The electoral formula largely accounts for the effect of district magnitude and proportionality, since PR systems tend to come with larger districts than their majoritarian counterparts. As outlined further in the Appendix, the electoral formula is the best available measurement of institutional influences for the large number of countries included in this book.

The experience of working within certain parameters also has links to institutional factors. The more established democracies have better political communication and systemic efficiency, meaning that *levels of representation should be higher in more established democracies*. Regarding the representation of women, a longer tradition of democratic rule means that there was more time to incorporate demands for women's inclusion in the legislature. It is thought that, over time, the actors involved learn to effectively deal with demands for inclusion. Consequently, a positive correlation can be expected between levels of gender representation and the age of democracy. The equivalent argument applies to the representation of ethnic groups. For the representation of women, the time elapsed since women's suffrage was granted is probably another suitable approximation of the relevant political context. For reasons of consistency across chapters, the age of democracy (measured in years since democratic rule last introduced) is used, although in the empirical chapter the same substantive results are achieved with the variable of women's suffrage. For levels of substantive representation, the intuition is that the experience of working within certain parameters can increase levels of representation. All the involved actors, from voters to the elite, need some time to understand the effects of the electoral system and its key institutions. What follows is that the efficiency of political communication, and thus the system itself, improves in the more established democracies. Thus, levels of policy representation are expected to be higher in more established democracies.

The political context is likely to affect all the stages of political representation outlined in the framework, particularly the vote choice of the citizens and the actions of the elite. In particular, political rights can affect political communication and the level of representation. The perception is that in places where individuals enjoy greater political rights, the citizens and the elite are better able to communicate their preferences. The expectation that follows is that *there is a positive correlation between the level of political rights and the level of political representation.* This argument applies to the representation of women and ethnic groups, as well as issue positions. In addition to the age of democracy, it is possible to understand the level of political rights as an indicator of how well a democracy is established. In practice, the two factors are relatively independent, suggesting that there are different aspects of established political systems relevant for political representation.

It is possible to implement quotas for all kinds of groups, but in practice quotas and similar measures are introduced to address the under-representation of women and ethnic minority groups. Quotas play a central role as a form of political engineering to increase levels of descriptive representation. As such, quotas are treated as a separate factor in this book. Quotas and related measures work in parallel to the electoral system and key institutions. Their main intention is to improve the representation of certain groups, so it can be expected that *the presence of quotas or similar measures is associated with higher levels of representation for specific groups.* In the case of gender representation, measures to include women are generally implemented as voluntary party quotas. Although the enforcement of such targets could be an issue, it can be assumed that the presence of quotas increases the number of female candidates to some extent. In other words, in places where parties implement gender quotas, the number of women in the legislature can be expected to be higher. Also counted are reserved seats and statutory quotas. These measures are more common for specific ethnic groups, with the aim of increasing the level of ethnic group representation. In practice, voluntary party quotas are rare for ethnic groups, and reserved seats or statutory solutions are the norm. The expected impact of these interventions, however, is unchanged: where quotas for ethnic groups are present, the level of ethnic group representation can be expected to be higher.

Factors that relate to candidates operate on a different basis and they are considered in Chapter Two. Unfortunately, the lack of reliable data for ethnic groups means that the effects exerted by candidates can only be tested for the representation of women. Where not enough candidates come forward, it is impossible to achieve high levels of representation, even if the elite and voters would support more women in the legislature. *Where there are more suitably qualified candidates, levels of descriptive representation can be expected to be higher*. The potential supply of qualified candidates can be approximated by measuring women's involvement in the labour force. A positive correlation can be expected between the proportion of women in the labour force and the level of gender representation in the legislature.

The demand for candidates – the vote intention – can be analysed with cultural variables. The concept of demand includes the willingness to support women or ethnic minority candidates. Where popular attitudes are favourable towards ethnic minority groups and women in public roles of authority, women and members of ethnic minority groups are more likely to occupy positions of power. Attitudes are thought to influence a citizen's inclination to vote for a female or ethnic minority candidate. However, these attitudes also affect the processes of candidate selection within political parties. *In a society where attitudes are more positive towards women or ethnic minorities in public office, levels of representation tend to be higher*.

The influence of cultural factors on vote choice, however, is not limited to descriptive representation. It can be expected that cultural factors affect levels of substantive representation, approximated by variables of religion or development. This is because, as outlined in the theoretical framework above, the perceived importance of policy domains might be affected by cultural variables. Differences in the salience of policy domains will then affect voting behaviour. On one level, the prevalence of post-material views potentially affects all kinds of domains, especially social and environmental issues. On a different level, religious parties may play a significant role because of the prescriptive world views of some religions. The definition of religious parties should be comprehensive, including parties that traditionally draw from a specific religious community. The influence on levels of policy representation stems from the fact that religious parties tend to be conservative on social issues. In predominantly Catholic or Muslim countries, a significant number of citizens may vote for religious parties for reasons of social identity and party identification, despite disagreeing with the social positions of the parties. As a result, levels of substantive representation can be expected to be lower in predominantly Catholic and Muslim countries. The influence of cultural variables on levels of substantive representation is a new area of research – and the hypothesis is also included to encourage future research in this area.

As outlined in the theoretical framework above, there are different underlying variables shaping cultural attitudes and the importance of each may vary from country to country. For this reason, an immediate measure of attitudes towards women as political leaders and marginalised groups in society can be thought to lead to a better appreciation of the effects. A direct measure should also be reflected in a better model fit. In the case of ethnic groups, I use attitudes towards marginalised groups in society as a variable, as outlined in more detail in the Appendix. This variable is highly correlated with attitudes towards ethnic minorities, but is chosen for reasons of data availability. In the relevant surveys, questions on attitudes towards ethnic minorities are covered in fewer countries. Although direct measures are preferred, it can be expected that each of the underlying variables – the predominant religion, regional differences, the level of development, and post-materialism – is associated with the level of representation. The argument that cultural factors shape levels of representation is a generic one and, therefore, applies to all of these variables. The theoretical framework also recognises the importance of the level of descriptive representation achieved in other places and in other dimensions. Unfortunately, such influences are intangible in a cross-sectional design, and no reliable data appear to be available for changes over time.

The same variables that shape attitudes towards women as political leaders and towards marginalised groups in society play a role in shaping the salience of demographic divisions and policy domains. The salience of divisions, in the case of gender and ethnic group representation, refers to the awareness and politicisation of under-representation. In the case of policy representation, it refers to the importance assigned to different domains. Salience may influence the decisions of individual voters. For example, a voter can face pressures to use their single vote for several purposes, like holding the legislature to account and choosing candidates in terms of descriptive and substantive representation. These cross-pressures are likely to lead voters to compromise between different considerations. In this case, the salience of divisions may be a common heuristic to resolve such pressures. It can be expected that levels of representation are higher in the forms of representation that are considered more important by the voters and the political elite – the forms of representation that are more salient.

The measurement of ethnic group representation used in this book does not control for the heterogeneity of society because all ethnic groups have a right to be included in legislatures, irrespective of the makeup of society. In a more heterogeneous society, where ethnic minorities form a significant proportion of the population, the possibility to exclude ethnic minorities from the legislature in a significant number is greater. With the measurement used, it follows that *in more homogeneous societies the level of ethnic group representation is expected to be higher*. This is an important factor, not because it contributes to higher levels of representation, but because it is a necessary control given the characteristics of the measurement used.

Another factor related to the composition of society is the geographical concentration of ethnic minorities. This factor is unrelated to the measurement of ethnic representation used. Where ethnic groups are concentrated, members of an ethnic minority may constitute a local majority and are more likely to be elected (Anwar 1994; Ruiz 2002; Bogaards 2004; Norris 2004; Bird 2005; Togeby 2005). A local concentration of ethnic minorities results in the same effect as there being an overall more homogeneous society. This effect is caused by the nature of the electoral system (Taylor 2005; Latner and McGann 2005; Bochsler 2006). *Where minorities are geographically concentrated, levels of ethnic group representation can be expected to be higher.* The effect of geographical concentration on levels of ethnic group representation is expected to be more significant in majoritarian systems.

In the chapter on the relationship between different forms of representation, the argument of shared covariates applies to all forms of representation. The theoretical framework includes the same explanatory factors for all forms of political representation. The same variables are expected to influence levels of representation in each form, and they are thought to do so largely in the same manner. The argument is that some factors are positively correlated with higher levels of representation in general. Shared covariates, of course, need not necessarily lead to positive correlations. In addition, positive correlations can be the result of other – unidentified – underlying causes. The argument, however, is made on a theoretical basis. For instance, it is expected that levels of descriptive representation in different dimensions are linked because of the shared variables and mechanisms involved. In fact, Taagepera (1994) and Lijphart (1999) argue that because of shared mechanisms, the measurement of gender representation can be a reasonable approximation of levels of ethnic group representation, if no data are available. They emphasise the proportionality between votes and seats. Heath *et al.* (2005) make the case that both women and ethnic minorities are relative newcomers to national legislatures and can thus be expected to face very similar challenges. Rule and Zimmerman (1994) claim that the combination of cultural factors and the electoral system form a barrier to the inclusion of women and ethnic minority groups in legislatures. A similar argument can be made based on a concurrent awareness of the under-representation of women and ethnic minority groups (Baldez 2006; Aroújo and García 2006; Kostadinova 2007). In each case, the resulting expectation is that *levels of gender representation are positively correlated with levels of ethnic group representation.*

The argument that the same explanatory factors influence levels of representation also applies to different policy domains. The perception is that there are institutional aspects associated with higher levels of representation, like the level of vote–seat proportionality. Similarly, some political systems create an environment that facilitates high levels of substantive representation. The age of democracy may reflect such an environment. If such facilitating factors exist, the levels of representation in different policy domains can be expected to correlate positively. Moreover, the theoretical framework suggests the same underlying variables and mechanisms – the electoral system, the age of democracy, and the level of development – for both substantive and descriptive forms of representation. Institutional and cultural factors can be considered as underlying covariates. In practice, however, particular institutional settings are often thought to be associated with higher levels of representation in general, such as the vote–seat proportionality (Horowitz 1985; Lijphart 1999). In a similar vein, certain political environments may encourage higher levels of representation more universally. Because of these shared factors, it is expected that levels of substantive and descriptive representation are positively correlated.

Methods and models

In the empirical chapters that follow, I draw on reputable sources such as the *World Values Survey* (a global research project that explores people's values and beliefs) and recently-collected data for the representatives to address levels of political representation in different forms. The dependent variable is a coefficient of political representation, describing the extent to which the legislature reflects the population. As outlined in the Appendix, the same logic to measuring political representation is applied to descriptive and substantive representation. The explanatory variables capture the main influences outlined in the theoretical framework: the electoral formula, the presence of quotas, political rights, the age of democracy and cultural attitudes. In each case, but particularly in the case of cultural attitudes, different operationalisations are considered in order to ascertain the robustness of the results. The Appendix outlines the data in more detail and elaborates on the measurement of political representation. Regression analyses (OLS) are applied to the hypotheses outlined here. The study is comparative at the country level in order to clarify significant patterns. Most of the analyses are cross-sectional because of data availability, although the chapter on the representation of women includes a limited analysis over time.

With regard to institutional factors, special measures for women and ethnic minorities are treated separately – voluntary quotas or statutory provisions are indeed factors independent of the electoral formula. All variables addressing cultural aspects are closely associated. Political rights and age of democracy (measured in years since democratic rule last introduced) are also included as variables, since they may be modifying variables affecting many of the other variables. Regional differences are used in order to maximise the number of cases, consistent with Paxton (1997), Moore and Shackman (1996) and Kenworthy and Malami (1999). However, there is a strong theoretical reason to directly capture attitudes towards women as political leaders and marginalised groups in society, namely that there are significant differences within regions (Norris 2009). Unfortunately, this reduces the sample size significantly. Consequently, the multivariate analysis in Chapters Two and Three are carried out twice: first to cover all cases and approximate attitudes through regional differences; second to cover fewer cases and use a variable that measures relevant cultural attitudes. Both empirically and theoretically, all the identified key dimensions are reasonably independent.

This page is intentionally blank

chapter two | the representation of women

Women in most countries remain greatly under-represented in positions of power and decision making despite constituting half the population. What is more, there are significant differences between countries and world regions. For example, in 2006, there were 33 per cent women in Iceland's *Alþingi*, whereas only 7 per cent women were present in the *National Assembly* of Madagascar. In this first empirical chapter, I examine how the absence and numerical under-representation of women in national legislatures can be explained. To do so, I look at the influence of institutional, cultural, and other factors on levels of gender representation. I use the term 'gender representation' to emphasise that both men and women should be present in legislatures, although women tend to be under-represented.

I commence with a very brief summary of existing research and discuss aspects of methodology and modelling specific to this chapter. Next, in those countries called free and partly free, I present the levels of gender representation achieved, i.e. the extent to which women are included in national legislatures. The main part of the chapter is dedicated to examining the contributing factors that shape the differences between countries. By considering both institutional and cultural aspects, it will be possible to appreciate the effectiveness of gender quotas whilst also catering for directly measured cultural attitudes.

There have been many attempts to explain the varying proportions of women in national legislatures. Numerous previous studies have concentrated on highly-developed countries, often focusing entirely on institutional variables, of which the electoral system is consistently identified as relevant. Countries with proportional representation (PR) systems tend to have a higher proportion of women in the legislature than countries with majoritarian systems. Some studies highlight a low proportion of women as related to candidate selection and the lack of candidates standing for election. The participation of women in the labour force, particularly in professional jobs, also appears to be a good indicator. In the past, left-wing parties had more women candidates, but in recent years this difference seems to have waned. Cultural and ideological variables are not always perceived as such and are sometimes merely discussed rather than included in the models. Consistent results can be found pertaining to the predominant religion of a country. Catholicism, in particular, is highlighted for its tendency to produce a lower proportion of women in the legislature. Similarly, geographical and/or regional differences are associated with differences in the levels of representation. Nordic countries, for example, are generally noted for their relatively high levels of gender representation. The few studies that included a direct measure of attitudes towards women in politics found very strong associations, with more positive views linked to higher levels of representation. In view of this influence, a direct measure of attitudes towards women in politics is in many ways preferable to measures that capture underlying factors. In this chapter, I use a direct measure of attitudes towards women in politics where possible, but also pay attention to different measures that might approximate cultural attitudes. In so doing, conclusions can be drawn for all free and partly free countries.

The multivariate models in this chapter closely follow the theoretical framework outlined in Chapter One. Starting with institutional factors, the electoral formula is used to capture the proportionality of electoral systems. A distinction is made between PR and mixed systems with proportional tendencies on the one hand, and majoritarian systems and mixed systems with majoritarian tendencies on the other. The use of more elaborate classifications of the electoral formula leads to the same substantive result as presented in this chapter. Quotas for women include voluntary party quotas and statutory quotas that apply to all parties. Reserved seats are rare for women and these are considered separately below. The age of a democracy counts the number of years since democratic rule was (last) introduced in a country. It is a measure of how well the political system in a country is established. In a similar vein, political rights are captured with a variable from *Freedom House*. Cultural aspects are captured with regional differences and, where possible, with a direct measure from the *World Value Survey*, using a question on women as political leaders. The text also explores the addition of other variables and alternative operationalisations. A particularly relevant variable may be the number of women in professional jobs as a measure of women candidates standing for election. In order to maintain comparability with subsequent chapters where no equivalent data are available, the factor of labour force participation is not included in the main models and therefore does not appear in the tables.

The data used to examine the representation of women are based on established reference works and further outlined in the Appendix. Most studies on the representation of women take the proportion of women in the legislature as the dependent variable. I use an approach formulated in more gender-neutral language, equally concerned with the representation of men and women. To do so, the representation scores used in this chapter consider the proportion of women in the population. This is an important technicality to prepare the measurement in Chapter Three, where multiple ethnic groups are considered. However, when interpreting the results for the countries included in this chapter, the representation scores used can be interpreted in the same manner as the proportion of female representatives. There are only negligible substantial differences between measures controlling for the proportion of women in the population and those that do not. The values correlate at a rate of 0.99 (p<0.001).

Formally, the representation score Q_G is calculated as the difference between the proportion of women in the population ($\Pi_{Z,f}$) and the equivalent in the legislature ($\Pi_{R,f}$). The representation score is thus: $Q_G = 1 - |\Pi_{Z,f} - \Pi_{R,f}|$. Q_G denotes the quality of gender representation, and the subtraction from 1 is used so that higher values of Q_G stand for higher levels of representation. The representation scores theoretically range from 0 to 1. In a country where the percentage of women in the population is exactly matched by the percentage of women in the legislature, a representation score of 1 would be achieved. By contrast, in a country where there are no female representatives in the legislature, the value for Q_G is around 0.5. This is because all men in the population are reasonably represented by the men in the legislature. For example, in 2006, the proportion of women in the population of Spain was 51 per cent, whilst the proportion of women in the *Congress of Deputies* was 36 per cent. The difference between the two values is 0.15. This value is subtracted from 1 to give a representation score $Q_{G,Spain} = 0.85$.

Findings

The extent to which women are represented in national legislatures varies noticeably between countries. Figure 2.1 presents the distribution of representation scores in the 131 free and partly free countries studied in this book. The representation scores of all countries are presented in the Appendix. This chapter focuses on the situation in single and lower chambers, but there is no apparent difference between the levels of gender representation in lower and upper chambers in countries with bicameral systems. As shown in Figure 2.1, it is uncommon for women to be represented in proportion to their share of the population. In this case, the representation score would be around 1. Sweden achieves the highest value, with a representation score of 0.95 – not far off the aim of including men and women in equal measure. The proportion of women in national legislatures is highest in Nordic countries, where, in 2006, 40 per cent of representatives were women. Excluding Nordic countries, the average share of women in European legislatures is 19 per cent. A similar percentage is found in the Americas. The lowest proportion of women in legislatures can be found in the Arab states, where, in 2006, just 8 per cent of representatives were women.

Figure 2.1: Levels of gender representation

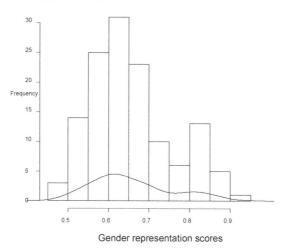

Gender representation scores

Notes: the distribution (frequency and density) of gender representation scores in lower and single chambers in free and partly free countries. N=131.

Across the globe, it is rare to find legislatures completely devoid of women. In almost all free and partly-free countries, there is at least one woman in the legislature. In 2006, the exceptions were Kyrgyzstan, Micronesia, Nauru, Palau, Saint Kitts and Nevis, the Solomon Islands, and Tuvalu. In Kyrgyzstan, two women lost their court case and the *Supreme Council* was temporarily without women (IDEA 2006). *Freedom House* apparently took the Tulip Revolution of 2005 as significant enough to upgrade the classification of Kyrgyzstan from *unfree* to *partly free*. In a similar vein, the Solomon Islands were still recovering from a coup. Whilst a number of women stood for parliament in the most recent elections, none of them was elected. A single-member system is sometimes blamed for the absence of women in parliament. The other countries with no women in the legislature are all micro-states. Although they are free countries as classified by *Freedom House*, they all have very small legislatures. A single seat in such small chambers may constitute as much as 7 per cent of all the seats available.

The proportion of women in the legislature is sometimes regarded as a general indication of women's status in society (for example Walby 1997; Novosel 2005; *Social Watch* 2008). Indeed, there are strong correlations between the level of gender representation and commonly-used measures of women's status in society. These include the participation of girls in secondary education, the WEF *Gender Scale* (Lopez-Carlos and Zahidi 2005; $r=0.61$, $p<0.001$), and the UN *Gender Empowerment Index* (UNDP 2005; $r=0.72$, $p<0.001$). These latter two sophisticated scales combine measures of economic participation, economic opportunity, political empowerment, educational attainment, control over economic resources, and the health and wellbeing of women (Ruedin 2009).

By looking at bivariate associations, it is possible to see if the variables identified in the model are associated with higher levels of gender representation in the sample of free and partly-free countries used in this chapter. This constitutes initial hypothesis testing and can highlight areas that need attention in the subsequent multivariate analysis. The electoral formula and its proportionality are often highlighted and, indeed, the level of gender representation in countries with proportional representation (PR) is higher than in majoritarian systems ($p<0.001$). The mean representation score for countries with PR is 0.70, as opposed to 0.61 for majoritarian systems. Whilst PR is no guarantee of high levels of representation, majoritarian systems never do very well in terms of the representation of women and the highest scores are exclusive to countries with PR.

Gender quotas are often held up as a means to improve the representation of women in legislatures. The evidence suggests that in countries where one or more parties have gender quotas, the representation score is higher by 0.06 ($p<0.01$). This is equivalent to about 6 per cent more women in the legislature. Statutory gender quotas seem to improve gender representation to the same magnitude as voluntary party quotas ($p<0.05$). In sum, the presence of either kind of quotas is associated with a higher proportion of women in the legislature. Similarly, the argument that political rights are constitutive to higher levels of representation is supported in the bivariate analysis. More rights are associated with higher levels of representation ($r=0.27$, $p<0.01$). The other aspect of having an established political system considered in this chapter is age of democracy. The older a democracy is, the higher the proportion of women in the legislature tends to be ($r=0.32$, $p<0.001$).

Institutional factors apart, the supply of suitable candidates may be an issue, because without a sufficient number of women coming forward as candidates, high levels of representation are impossible. The measure most frequently referred to in the literature is the proportion of girls enrolled in secondary education, for which there is a weak association ($r=0.23$, $p<0.05$). In line with Kenworthy and Malami (1999), I find women's share in professional jobs ($r=0.24$, $p<0.05$) to be a stronger correlate for women's representation in the legislature than women's share in paid work more generally ($r=0.07$, $p>0.1$). Put differently, where the pool of suitable female candidates is larger, the level of representation tends to be higher.

One reason that more women come forward as candidates may be a cultural setting that encourages inclusion. Regional variables are a common way to approximate relevant cultural differences. Nordic countries are often singled out, but the argument applies worldwide. Compared to the base category (Western Europe, United States, Canada, Australia and New Zealand), all the regional variables are significantly different ($p<0.01$). Levels of gender representation are higher in Nordic countries, whilst levels of representation are lower in other regions. It is also possible to view religious differences as a proxy for cultural attitudes. Compared to predominantly Protestant countries, only predominantly Muslim countries have significantly lower levels of gender representation ($\Delta Q_G = 0.08$, $p<0.05$). This result contradicts the importance of Catholicism reported by some previous studies (Rule 1987; Paxton 1997; Leyenaar 2004), whilst maintaining the significance of religion as an overall factor. In the same way, post-industrial countries are associated with higher levels of gender representation than industrial countries ($\Delta Q_G = 0.10$, $p<0.001$). Capturing cultural attitudes more directly seems to confirm that positive attitudes towards women in society are linked to higher levels of representation ($r=0.71$, $p<0.01$). This supports the findings of other studies that include a direct measure of attitudes towards women (Norris and Inglehart 2001, 2004; Paxton and Kunovich 2003).

In the bivariate analysis, the variables outlined in the literature and the theoretical framework are supported as significant covariates. In accordance with expectations, both the electoral system and cultural variables are associated with levels of gender representation. In order to see how these factors fare when considered simultaneously, the levels of gender representation are now examined using multivariate regression analysis. As noted at the end of Chapter One, the analysis is carried out twice: first with all free and partly free countries, and secondly with the – arguably better – variable of cultural attitudes. Unfortunately, this second analysis reduces the number of countries for consideration. Initially, the modelling is designed to maximise the number of cases in the analysis.

Table 2.1 outlines the results of three multivariate models. Starting with the electoral formula, additional variables are introduced to increase the model fit. Model 1 includes both the electoral formula and variables capturing the presence of gender quotas. Both voluntary party quotas and their statutory counterparts are included. The percentage of women in legislatures is about 8 per cent higher in countries with PR systems than in countries with majoritarian systems. The effects of voluntary party quotas are equivalent to about 3 per cent more women in legislatures (p<0.1), whilst the association of statutory quotas is statistically not significant (p>0.1). In all the models, the results are the same when all kinds of statutory quotas are considered and when only enforced quotas are included.

Following the theoretical framework, Model 2 adds considerations of political rights and age of democracy. The intuition is to increase the model fit by adding variables capturing the political context. In Table 2.1, age of democracy is given in hundreds of years, because the size of the effect is so small. Considering the other variables in the model, the effects of political rights seem negligible (p>0.1). The age of democracy, by contrast, appears to be a significant, although very small factor. The results of Model 2 suggest that it takes just over a decade for the number of women in legislatures to increase by about 1 per cent. Given the low number of female representatives in many countries, this seems a very small effect. It is conceivable that the effects of the electoral system are dependent on the age of democracy. This can be tested with an interaction term in the model, but the interaction between the age of democracy and the electoral formula is not significant (p>0.1), and does not add to the model fit. I have also tested various other interaction effects, with no significant results. In particular, no significant interaction could be observed between institutional and cultural factors.

The predicted effects of gender quotas are reduced once the age of democracy is added, but they remain significant covariates (p<0.1). Trying to cater for the supply of candidates, adding variables on education or labour-force participation does not increase the model fit and the additional variables are statistically insignificant (p>0.1). The same is true for subsequent models. The supply of suitably qualified candidates appears to be a negligible factor, contradicting some previous studies that did not include the age of democracy. Given the small number of seats in legislatures compared to the number of women in the population, this finding is not entirely surprising.

Norris and Inglehart (2001) used the *Human Development Index* (HDI) instead of the age of democracy. Although the HDI is significantly associated with levels of gender representation, this is not the case in the multivariate analysis. Substituting the age of democracy with the HDI leads to a slightly lower model fit ($R^2=0.35$), but the other variables in the model are not notably affected by this substitution. Neither the variables of political rights nor the HDI are significant, but after including the interaction between the two factors, both the interaction and the HDI become significant (p<0.05). This suggests that political rights may be necessary for the effects of development to work. With reference to modernisation theory, it could be argued that the *Human Development Index* captures cultural attitudes to some extent. Empirically, this is reflected by high correlations with other variables that account for attitudes towards women as political leaders. A more common approach, however, is to focus on regional differences. Here, the perception is that regional differences capture relevant differences in attitudes. Moreover, the variable is easy to measure, and thus the entire sample of free and partly-free countries can be retained.

Table 2.1: Multivariate models of gender representation 1

	Model 1			Model 2			Model 3		
	B	SE	p-value	B	SE	p-value	B	SE	p-value
Constant	0.60	0.01	0.000*	0.58	0.02	0.000*	0.65	0.03	0.000*
Electoral formula									
Mj/MMM (Base)									
PR/MMP	0.08	0.02	0.000*	0.07	0.02	0.000*	0.04	0.02	0.007*
Quotas									
No quotas (Base)									
Party quotas	0.03	0.02	0.08+	0.01	0.00	0.023*	0.01	0.00	0.137
Statutory quotas	0.05	0.03	0.117	0.03	0.02	0.066+	0.04	0.02	0.021*
Political rights				0.00	0.01	0.502	0.00	0.01	0.560
Age of democracy				0.08	0.02	0.001*	0.02	0.03	0.391
Regions									
Western (Base)†									
Nordic							0.14	0.04	0.000*
Eastern European							-0.05	0.03	0.091+
Asia and Pacific							-0.09	0.03	0.003*
Middle East‡							-0.10	0.04	0.011*
Sub-Saharan Africa							-0.02	0.03	0.468
Latin America							-0.03	0.03	0.268
R²	0.26			0.39			0.54		

Notes: Three multivariate models (OLS) with gender representation scores as the dependent variable. *Significant at p<0.05, + significant at p<0.1. The age of democracy is given in 100s of years. †The base category includes Western Europe, the US, Canada, Australia, and New Zealand. ‡ "The category Middle East also includes North African countries". N=131. Model 3 includes a variable for regional differences.

The predicted effect of having PR rather than a majoritarian system is reduced, but it remains statistically significant (p<0.01). When the regional variable is added, party quotas no longer seem to make a significant difference (p>0.1), whilst the stricter statutory variant appears to perform (p<0.05). Using variables that consider the size of the quotas – the proportion reserved for women – does not change this finding.

The age of democracy is the factor probably most affected by the introduction of regional variables. Rather than being a large positive factor, Model 3 suggests that the age of democracy has little significant impact after considering regions. Instead, regional differences matter most. Nordic countries have higher levels of gender representation than elsewhere. All other regions have lower levels of gender representation compared to the base category of Western Europe, the United States, Canada, Australia and New Zealand. Some of these differences are marked and most of them are statistically significant. The same substantive results can be found when using the predominant religion of a country as a variable of cultural difference.

The use of regional difference is somewhat unsatisfactory because it can only capture attitudes by proxy. The results so far suggest that the role of cultural attitudes should be pursued in more detail. This is done by capturing the relevant attitudes directly, using a question from the *World Values Survey*. However, this survey does not cover every country, and not every country taking part in the survey asks all the questions. This means that the use of measured attitudes – as opposed to proxies – reduces the number of countries in the sample. In spite of this, a significant number of countries from various regions of the world is retained for the analysis that follows. I consider the impact of the smaller sample on the results presented in this chapter. Therefore, Table 2.2 includes Model 3 with only the countries where data are available on measured attitudes towards women in politics. A key difference to Model 3 with the full sample is that, in the reduced sample, the variable on the electoral system is no longer a significant factor. However, the size of the estimated effect remains the same. This difference is because of the sample, since the electoral system is also not a significant variable in Model 2 when restricted to the reduced sample. Another difference is that the estimated effect of statutory quotas is reduced in the model in Table 2.2 (p>0.1). This might indicate potential issues of enforcement in some of the countries in the reduced sample. For all the other variables, the results are substantively the same, with any differences being negligibly small. The coefficients for the different regions remain almost unchanged, even though in some cases the number of cases is small. This means that the results from the smaller sample are likely to apply to all free and partly-free countries.

Having considered the impact of the smaller sample, the next variable included is measured attitudes. Based on the theoretical framework and the bivariate associations, a strong association is expected. The difference between Model 4 and Model 3 is that in Model 4, cultural attitudes are measured directly. It directly measures the attitudes towards women as political leaders. As such, the link to political representation is closer than with underlying cultural variables, like the regional differences included in Model 3. The introduction of this variable not only increases the model fit significantly, it also overrides all the other variables.

Table 2.2: Multivariate models of gender representation II

	Model 3 (reduced sample)			Model 4			Model 5		
	B	SE	p-value	B	SE	p-value	B	SE	p-value
Constant	0.67	0.05	0.000*	0.73	0.05	0.000*	0.69	0.02	0.000
Electoral formula									
Mj/MMM (Base)									
PR/MMP	0.04	0.03	0.142	0.02	0.03	0.367	0.05	0.02	0.002*
Quotas									
No quotas (Base)									
Party quotas	0.01	0.00	0.160	0.01	0.01	0.297	0.00	0.00	0.689
Statutory quotas	0.02	0.02	0.326	0.02	0.03	0.511	0.01	0.02	0.510
Political rights	0.00	0.01	0.723	−0.01	0.01	0.266	0.00	0.01	0.479
Age of democracy	0.01	0.03	0.722	−0.03	0.04	0.483	−0.02	0.02	0.474
Cultural attitudes: region									
Western (Base)									
Nordic	0.14	0.04	0.001*						
Eastern European	−0.06	0.03	0.080+						
Asia and Pacific	−0.09	0.05	0.066+						
Middle East	−0.15	0.06	0.024*						
Sub-Saharan Africa	0.11	0.06	0.080+						
Latin America	−0.04	0.03	0.210						
Attitudes: women leaders				0.19	0.04	0.000*	0.21	0.03	0.000*
R²	0.53			0.58			0.60		

Notes: Three additional multivariate models (OLS) with gender representation scores as the dependent variable. *Significant at p<0.05, + significant at p<0.1. Model 3 is identical to the one used in Table 2.1, but only includes the cases also used in Model 4. N=48. Model 5 includes all 131 cases, relying on predicted attitudes where no data are available.

The estimated effects of the electoral system become smaller when attitudes are considered. The overriding nature of the cultural variable reflects findings by Paxton and Kunovich (2003). However, at this point I also consider quotas as an institutional factor, which seem to make no difference when directly controlling for attitudes towards women in political roles ($p>0.1$).[1] It is not possible to include regional variables and the variable on women as political leaders because they both deal with the same concept and lead to serious collinearity issues.

The variable on attitudes towards women in politics is measured using a four-point scale, averaged for each country. The scale is centred to ease the interpretation of the other coefficients in the model. The range across all countries is about two points on this scale. In a country where the national mean differs from another by one point, the number of women in the legislature is affected by about 19 per cent. In other words, a country where the average position towards women is most liberal is estimated to include about a fifth more female representatives than an average country. A country with the least liberal attitudes will have a fifth fewer women in the legislature than an average country.

In a similar analysis, Norris (2004) relied on an indirect measure of cultural attitudes: the predominant religion of a country. She suggests that political factors are more significant than cultural factors, as indicated by the standardised values. Based on Model 3, using regional or religious variables, and Model 4, using a direct measure of attitudes towards women in politics, it appears that the conclusion needs to be reversed (see also Paxton and Kunovich 2003). With the data used in this book, I am unable to replicate Norris's findings.

Norris added 'the time since women's suffrage was granted' to the final model. Adding suffrage to Model 4, however, does not increase the model fit, and the variable is not significant ($p>0.1$). None of the coefficients in any of the models is significantly affected by this additional variable. In a similar analysis, Paxton and Kunovich (2003) found that Nordic countries remain significantly different, even when considering attitudes towards women. I am unable to replicate this finding with the data used in this chapter. Adding regional or religious variables to Model

---

1. Propensity score matching is a statistical method to test whether the lack of association is due to possible sampling bias concerning the presence of quotas (Rosenbaum and Rubin 1983). To this extent, the propensity of having quotas in the first place is predicted, before examining their effectiveness in regression analysis. Inglehart and Norris (2003) and Norris and Inglehart (2004) argue that the propensity of implementing quotas should be directly linked to positive attitudes towards women in power, but no such association can be determined ($p>0.1$). Empirically, the best prediction of the presence of quotas was achieved using the *Human Development Index* (HDI), political rights, as well as the time since suffrage was gained ($R^2=0.26$). Using propensity score matching, the sample could be improved, but the presence of quotas remained insignificant. This suggests that quotas may not be the driving force behind increasing numbers of women in legislatures, but possibly an extra step to reflect advances elsewhere in society (Freidenvall *et al.* 2006).

4 – ignoring collinearity issues – does not notably change the coefficients already in the model, and none of the additional variables is significant.

Another approach is to look at the difference between industrial and post-industrial countries to replace the age of democracy variable. Doing so in Model 4 has no substantial effect on the reported coefficients. This suggests that the variable on the age of democracy may capture, to some extent, the effects of modernisation outlined by Inglehart and Norris (2003). Because of collinearity issues, it is impossible to include both variables at the same time. Some studies suggest that the presence of preferential voting is a significant covariate (Sainsbury 1993; Reynolds *et al.* 1997), but I am unable to find a direct association. There is no significant interaction between the presence of preferential voting and attitudes towards women in politics ($p > 0.1$), nor do such considerations significantly increase the model fit. This suggests that voters may not actively seek women candidates, even where they are given the chance on the ballot paper.

Although the reduced sample does not appear to be problematic, I used predicted values of attitudes towards women as political leaders in Model 5. Based on the theoretical framework, it is possible to predict the predominant attitudes in countries not covered in the *World Values Survey*. As a result, the whole sample of free and partly-free countries can be used, and most of the results are unchanged. The variable on the electoral system is affected most, with PR systems now associated with higher levels of representation. The magnitude of the other variables does not change. In a different analysis, I tried to address the nature of the reduced sample using a sub-sample of the highly industrialised OECD countries. As with Model 5, the presence of PR systems remains a significant factor in the full model ($p < 0.05$). However, when excluding Nordic countries from the OECD sub-sample, the variable on the electoral formula no longer remains significant. This suggests that, apart from the Nordic countries, there appears to be no substantive difference between OECD countries and free and partly-free countries. The results for the electoral formula remain unclear because in Models 3 and 4 the variable was not significant, even though the sample was reasonably large.

So far, this chapter has not addressed the impact of reserved seats for women on levels of representation. In contrast to voluntary party quotas and statutory interventions, reserved seats for women are rare in the free and partly-free countries included in this book. Because of serious collinearity issues, it was impossible to include reserved seats in the main analysis: all the countries with reserved seats for women in this book also use majoritarian systems. By limiting the focus to these countries, it is possible to substitute the variable of statutory quotas with one that accounts for the presence of reserved seats. In contrast to other quotas, reserved seats affect the number of elected representatives, not just those standing for election. By their very nature, reserved seats are essentially enforced quotas. Substituting statutory quotas and reserved seats in Model 4 suggests that reserved seats are indeed a significant factor ($p < 0.05$), even after controlling for attitudes towards women in politics.

Changes over time

There is tension between the theory on the representation of women that highlights changes over time and the cross-sectional analysis possible with the available data. This section seeks to address the problem by presenting a limited analysis over time. The analysis is limited because of data availability, but it helps understand which factors are associated with changes in the proportion of women in national legislatures. Moreover, an analysis of changes over time is also valuable as a test of robustness. It can indicate whether variables are likely to be causally linked. Taking account of the different samples used in the main analysis of this chapter, these tests of robustness are important. The results are considered robust if changes in the key variables are associated with changes in the levels of gender representation. Questions capturing attitudes towards women in public life were added recently to the *World Values Survey*. Thus, I compare values for 2006 with 1995 for reasons of data availability.

Paxton (1997) also compares changes in gender representation over time. In contrast to her analysis, this section does not rely on proxies. Instead, it directly measures attitudes towards women in politics. Additionally, I consider the implementation of gender quotas, which are probably the most commonly commended intervention for increasing the number of women in legislatures. Paxton finds no effect for supply factors, but suggests that proportional representation (PR) systems and ideology are significant. Paxton *et al.* (2010) compare levels of gender representation over time, but focus on the effect of legislative quotas and the electoral formula. This section also considers party quotas and cultural variables, and covers more recent developments.

Over the time period covered in this section, there were no major changes in electoral formulas. Evidence from outside this period casts doubt on the suggestion that the electoral formula is associated with sustained increases in the number of women in the legislature. Although the 1996 switch to PR in New Zealand is associated with a significant increase in the number of women in parliament (Grey and Sawer 2005; IPU 2009), that large initial increase could not be sustained in subsequent elections. Based on a linear trend that started in the 1970s, the proportion of women in 2005 and 2008 was foreseeable, irrespective of the change in electoral formula. It is, therefore, difficult to speak with any confidence of an electoral system effect.[2] In France, there was a short trial of PR in 1986, but it did not result in above average gains for women in parliament. Whilst the electoral system may be a significant factor for levels of gender representation, it does not seem useful for explaining changes over time.

During the period of the study, there was a general trend towards higher levels of gender representation. This trend is consistent with modernisation theories that predict higher levels of representation as countries develop economically.

---

2. The proportion of women after the 2011 election is somewhat below the linear trend, further questioning the purported effect of the electoral system.

Countries that saw an increase in political rights over the time period studied are associated with noticeably higher levels of gender representation. The difference compared to other countries, however, is not statistically significant (ΔQ_G =0.06, p>0.1). Only a few political parties introduced quotas for women during the period considered. In most countries there were no changes; in fourteen countries, one or more parties introduced voluntary gender quotas between 1995 and 2006. Of these, thirteen countries have increased their level of gender representation. The exception is Botswana, where two parties introduced quotas, but both failed to reach their target (IDEA 2006). However, the estimated effect of party quotas is small and there is no significant difference compared with countries that did not introduce party gender quotas (p>0.1). The small substantive impact of quotas reflects findings by Paxton *et al.* (2010) focusing on legislative gender quotas. Iceland is different: here the number of parties with quotas decreased, whilst the number of women in the *Alþingi* increased. Taken together, it only appears at first sight that the introduction of quotas is associated with a higher proportion of women in legislatures. Because there is a general trend towards more women in legislatures, the observed increase is indistinguishable from countries where no quotas were introduced. The higher proportion of women in legislatures cannot be attributed to the introduction of quotas.

In contrast, there is a strong correlation between changes in attitudes and changes in the level of gender representation (r=0.46, p<0.1). Counter to this trend, Bangladesh increased the number of women in parliament only after implementing reserved seats for women (IDEA 2006). With the data available, it is impossible to say whether in this case diminishing popular support for women politicians is linked to the establishment of reserved seats. In the cross-national analysis, quotas and reserved seats are not significantly associated with attitudes. Similarly, in the Philippines, an all-women's party was elected during the period considered, and it accounted for almost all the changes. No changes in attitudes were recorded. In India, the failure to increase the number of women in parliament can be attributed to partisan political factors or a possible backlash in attitudes. In sum, in only a few countries there appear to be explanations for higher levels of representation other than changes in attitudes.

It is possible that the earlier presence of women in the legislature affects current levels of representation, mediated by attitudes. This explanation merits further consideration. Unsurprisingly, the proportion of women in legislatures in 1995 is strongly associated with the proportion of women in legislatures in 2006 (r=0.88, p<0.001). The proportion of women in legislatures in 1995 is also associated with positive attitudes towards women in politics in 2006 (r=0.73, p<0.001). This association, however, does not hold when controlling for underlying factors: the prevalent religion, region, or the level of development. In regression analyses, the predominant religion of a country, regional differences, and the level of development are all good predictors for attitudes towards women as political leaders in 2006 (p<0.05). In contrast, the age of democracy, the level of political rights, the electoral system and the proportion of women in legislatures in 1995 are not significantly associated with attitudes towards women as political leaders in 2006 (p>0.1). This casts doubt on the argument that the proportion of women in legislatures in the past has a significant impact on present attitudes towards women in politics, at least for the period considered.

Although the evidence is limited, the analysis over time suggests that the findings reported in this chapter are robust and apply to changes over time: where attitudes towards women as political leaders become more liberal, levels of gender representation tend to increase. This finding is in line with Paxton (1997), who used religion and other proxies as measures of ideology. What is more, the analysis here fails to find a clear indication that the introduction of quotas is associated with higher levels of gender representation. Up to this point, I have interpreted this lack of association as a sign that quotas may not work. Following the blockage argument, the lack of association in the cross-sectional analysis might mean that quotas have indeed worked, and that without quotas it would not have been possible to break through gender barriers. However, if such blockages exist, over time the introduction of quotas should be associated with an increase in the level of gender representation. The results here indicate that in countries where quotas were introduced, the level of gender representation did not increase significantly more than in countries where no quotas were introduced. This casts doubt on the argument.

Quotas and cultural attitudes

This chapter has looked at the factors associated with levels of gender representation. The variables suggested in the literature and the theoretical framework initially seemed to be associated with the proportion of women in legislatures. Bivariate analyses seem to confirm that the electoral system is a factor that affects the representation of women. Gender quotas appear to be successful. The proportion of women in the legislature is larger in countries with quotas compared to those countries without quotas. Similarly, variables thought to approximate cultural attitudes are associated with differences in levels of gender representation. Causally, attitudes towards women in politics are more closely linked to gender representation than other cultural variables, and they are highly correlated with levels of representation.

In the multivariate regression analysis, the inclusion of cultural variables led to a surprising result. Whilst the relationship between attitudes and gender representation might be as expected, the size of the effect is surprising. The effectiveness of gender quotas becomes questionable after considering cultural factors: the presence of quotas is no longer associated with higher levels of representation. The size of the quotas – for example whether 20 per cent or 40 per cent of seats are reserved for women – does not change this finding. Sanctions for failing to reach the quota's target appear to make no difference. Furthermore, the lack of association between the presence of quotas and levels of gender representation was also apparent from the analysis over time. The introduction of quotas is not associated with increases in the levels of gender representation greater than in countries where no quotas were introduced. This weakens the blockage argument that quotas may have worked and are therefore no longer significant in the cross-sectional analysis. The lack of association between quotas and the level of gender representation should be a serious consideration for policymakers seeking to increase the number of female representatives.

The results do not necessarily mean that quotas are ineffective. Rather, they indicate that the effect of quotas on levels of political representation may be more cosmetic. Unenforced voluntary gender quotas may merely reflect a society that wants more women in politics. The quotas act as an extra assurance rather than jump-starting a process. Alternatively, quotas might indicate that a liberal elite is more supportive of women in politics than the general public. In this case, quotas might help to avoid lower levels of representation. This argument would explain why there is no association between public attitudes and the presence of quotas in the cross-sectional analysis, contrary to the predictions of Inglehart and Norris (2003). Unfortunately, I have no data on the attitudes of the elite to test this. Unless the presence of women in legislatures affects attitudes towards women in politics, the increase in female representatives will probably be limited to the time it is enforced by reserved seats or mandatory quotas. This point is illustrated by the drastic drop in the number of female representatives in former communist countries after the transition to democracy (Tinker 2004; Dahlerup 2006).

The introduction of reserved seats, as in Bangladesh, or other forms of enforced electoral engineering may have an immediate impact on the number of women in legislatures (Jacquette 1997; Kostadinova 2002; Norris 2004; O'Flynn and Russel 2005). In order to assess the impact on representation, however, the context in which quotas are adopted must be considered (Hassim 2009). It has to be assumed that those advocating this type of affirmative action are concerned with the lasting effects rather than merely the number of women in the legislature. Based on the analysis in this chapter, it appears that trying to change attitudes towards women in politics may be an effective way to change levels of gender representation, mainly because this influences both the supply and demand sides. More women will come forward as candidates, and women will be chosen more often by political parties and voters. Further research is needed to understand which factors influence the changing attitudes towards women in politics over time, such as changes in the level of development, advocacy work, or other variables. Norris (2009) suggests religion is a key variable, but it is unclear how the predominant religion of a country can explain changes over time.

Whilst enforced quotas can be used to increase the number of women in legislatures, they come with the risk of popular backlash (Wilentz 2003; Mansbridge 2005). The Rawlsian theory of justice rejects preferential treatment for women, but quotas are largely compatible with Young's approach (Young 1990; Bacchi 2006). Some argue that the liberal tendency to disregard differences is a failure because it ignores rather than addresses these differences (Williams 1995). Quotas are therefore justified as a necessary means to address differences. The effectiveness of unenforced gender quotas, however, became doubtful in the analyses in this chapter. Once controlling for regional differences or attitudes towards women in politics, gender quotas do not appear to be associated with higher levels of representation. Contrary to many previous studies, the electoral formula was not a significant variable in all the models presented. This can be explained by sampling issues, although it seems difficult to suggest a systematic effect for the electoral formula. It is possible that in previous studies some cultural aspects were erroneously associated with the electoral formula. For instance, it may be that part of the cultural heritage of the Nordic countries becomes associated with the electoral formula, namely PR systems.

The mixed findings on the importance of quotas and the electoral formula, however, do not affect the overall message of this chapter. Cultural attitudes appear to be the key drivers for levels of gender representation. What follows is that studies focusing entirely on institutional factors probably overestimate the effects of the electoral system, and especially the effectiveness of voluntary party quotas. As indicated in the theoretical framework, the effects of positive attitudes towards women in politics may also extend to the supply of suitable candidates. In the cross-national analysis, variables on the supply of candidates remained insignificant. It is possible, however, that such a supply – as captured in levels of education or engagement in professional work – is secondary to actually coming forward as a candidate. Additionally, given the relatively small number of seats in a legislature, the respective variables may be too generic. By contrast, a supportive environment – defined in terms of attitudinal variables – appears to be the dominant factor for supply. Unfortunately, with the data available it is impossible to untangle separate effects of supply.

The variable on attitudes towards women as political leaders works best on statistical grounds. The exact measure of cultural attitudes does not seem to matter. Since the underlying argument is linked to attitudes similar to sociological liberalism, the same substantive results can be obtained using more general attitudes towards marginalised groups in society. Likewise, causally prior measures of cultural attitudes – such as regional or religious differences – lead to similar results, with the exception that the electoral formula is a significant covariate in the full model. This is important because, for the direct measure of cultural attitudes, the causal direction may not necessarily be clear. Although it is a contested idea, increased numbers of women in legislatures may lead to positive attitudes towards women in public life. In this sense, it could be argued that positive attitudes towards women in politics are partly the result of higher levels of gender representation in previous legislatures.

There are many reasons to believe that the more significant influence is from attitudes to levels of representation, rather than the other way round. The examination of changes over time highlighted cases where levels of representation increased without corresponding changes in attitudes. This was most notable in Bangladesh with the implementation of reserved seats. In this case, the resulting higher levels of gender representation are in fact associated with slightly less positive attitudes. At least in the short term, higher levels of representation did not seem to lead to more positive attitudes. Conversely, in other countries and regions, changes towards more positive attitudes are associated with higher levels of representation. In these places, however, there are no other obvious causes for the increased levels of representation, such as reserved seats, or an all-women's party. Moreover, the theoretical framework underpinning this book suggests that representation is primarily caused by relevant attitudes, not the other way round. I have successfully outlined underlying factors for cultural attitudes, from religion to the level of development, and have demonstrated their statistical association. This adds further weight to the claim that the main influence is as indicated. Empirically, this view is reinforced by the fact that these underlying variables are significant predictors in their own right (although, as expected, in a somewhat weaker form). It therefore seems reasonable to assume that the main direction of influence is as outlined.

The view that institutional factors only work in conjunction with the right cultural environment is unsupported statistically, where relevant interactions remain insignificant variables. The exclusion of 'unfree' countries from analysis in this book can be regarded as an admission that on theoretical grounds, the institutional setting is expected to have a large impact. However, it appears that in most free and partly-free countries the political elite is able to adjust to the institutional setting, which is reflected in the lack of association between levels of gender representation and the electoral system.

The dominance of cultural factors can also be found at the more fundamental level of counting at least one woman in legislatures. In almost all the free and partly-free countries included in this chapter, there is at least one women present in the national legislature. For the few countries where women are completely absent, cultural and, particularly, religious factors appear to be the key inhibitors. It is possible to speculate that political rights are another significant factor, albeit not in the sample of free and partly-free countries covered in this book.

chapter three | the representation of ethnic groups

In Trinidad and Tobago, about 38 per cent of the population are African and they are present in the House of Representatives in more or less this proportion. At the same time, individuals of mixed descent are numerically under-represented. Indeed, in many countries, ethnic minority groups are under-represented or even absent, such as in Chile. In this chapter, I examine ethnic group representation to examine why in many places ethnic minority groups are marginalised and under-represented in national legislatures. Although theories of justice emphasise both the under-representation of ethnic minorities and the under-representation of women, the political representation of ethnic groups is studied far less frequently. Studying ethnic groups is no less important than studying women, since ethnicity is the source of much segregation and discrimination. I define ethnic groups as groups of people who are related through kinship and have an awareness of a shared culture and ancestry. This means that ethnicity refers to self-declared group membership (Jenkins 1997). Despite some elements of choice, since ethnicity is what one identifies with, ethnic identities are rather stable (Green 2005; Hoddie 2006). For this reason, a systematic analysis of ethnic groups is possible. I examine the covariates of high levels of ethnic group representation, complementing the previous chapter with a different dimension of descriptive representation.

As a comparative analysis, this chapter breaks with the established literature where single-country studies are the norm (Messina 1989; Anwar 1994; Geisser 1997; Ramet 1997; Geddes 1998; Saggar 2000; Delemotte 2001; Pantoja and Segura 2003; Togeby 2008). Bird (2005) compares three developed countries, but stays clear of a numerical assessment; Banducci *et al.* (2004) compare the situation in the United States and New Zealand. Reynolds (2006) only addresses individual groups, focusing entirely on the role of the electoral system, whilst Bird (2003) examines the situation of individual visible minorities in fourteen countries, but avoids multivariate comparisons. Despite covering multiple countries, Bird *et al.* (2010) do not include comparative statistical analyses. Norris (2004) approaches the representation of ethnic groups with a survey question on whether members of different groups feel represented. Whilst her approach allows a numerical comparison, Norris cannot say anything about actual levels of representation. The systematic comparative consideration of ethnic group representation in this chapter leads to a better understanding of why levels of representation vary across countries.

Initially, I assess previous research, followed by a brief discussion of methodological aspects specific to this chapter. I then present the levels of ethnic group representation in free and partly-free countries: the extent to which different ethnic groups are present in national legislatures. The level of representation of some individual ethnic groups is discussed to highlight the diversity across ethnic groups and countries. The main part of the chapter is dedicated to examining the contributing factors that shape the differences between countries in a multivariate cross-national manner.

Research on ethnic group representation is notably sparser than research on gender representation. Most of the literature concerned with ethnic group representation regards representation at the local level and does not cover representation in national legislatures (Engstrom and McDonald 1982; Welch 1990; Saggar and Geddes 2000; Garbaye 2000; Bousetta 2001; van Heelsum 2002; Togeby 2005, 2008). In single-country studies, the focus is often on a specific minority group, ethnic minorities as opposed to the majority population, or in Western Europe immigrant groups. It is also often argued that ethnic minorities are traditionally under-represented (Rothman 2004; Bird 2005).

When it comes to the different levels of ethnic group representation, party political explanations are probably most common. Sometimes candidates do not come forward for election in sufficient numbers, although this factor is difficult to capture. No systematic data exist to deal with 'candidate effects' in an adequate manner in this chapter. Where collected, such data – measuring participation in education or the labour force – tend to use nationality rather than ethnicity as the basis (OECD 2006; ILO 2007). The resulting indicators allow no reasonable conclusions about the supply of candidates. Following the theoretical framework in Chapter One, however, it is likely that models that account for differences in cultural attitudes to some extent cover issues of supply. Nonetheless, the absence of data should not be interpreted as a lack of association. Institutional factors are also mentioned in some studies, especially the presence of proportional electoral systems. Proportional systems are thought to benefit all kinds of minorities and their political representation. Discrimination on behalf of the party elite or voters is also mentioned, but this tends to be argumentative rather than based on clear evidence. It seems that many members of ethnic minorities think that their interests can only be appropriately represented by another group member (Ross 1943; Schwartz 1988; Phillips 1993; Williams 1995). In other words, they demand descriptive representation to achieve substantive representation.

There are also utilitarian arguments for increased levels of ethnic group representation, since levels of representation are associated with better integration: where levels of representation are higher, fewer members of ethnic minorities feel alienated by the political system (Pantoja and Segura 2003; Norris 2004; Banducci et al. 2004). Saggar (2000) is more cautious, suggesting that in Britain higher levels of representation at the local level did not lead to reduced alienation from the system overall. Reynolds (2006) follows a similar line of thought, arguing that only where minority communities are properly included can ethnic conflict be avoided. Minorities in many places are systematically excluded from significant decisions, such as electoral reform, government, or the drafting of a new constitution. It is argued that where certain ethnic groups are excluded, such as the Roma in many European countries, there is potential for future conflict (Ramet 1997; Rothman 2004; Cederman et al. 2010; Wucherpfennig et al. 2012).

What unites almost all studies on ethnic group representation is that they find a significant under-representation of ethnic minorities in positions of power. The popular view that ethnic minorities are completely excluded from positions of power, however, is often an exaggeration (Alba and Moore 1982; Geddes 1998). Geisser (1997) highlights that, despite much talk of what he calls an ethnification of the world, the integration of ethnic minority groups is incomplete. In France, this is reflected in the low level of Algerians and Muslims in local councils. Saggar (2000) equally focuses on representation at the local level, and argues that local representation stands for a certain degree of local autonomy, assuming a geographical concentration of ethnic groups.

It is sometimes argued that both women and ethnic groups are under-represented in positions of power for similar reasons. Consequently – as reflected in the theoretical framework – the same hypotheses can be applied to gender representation and ethnic group representation (Taagepera 1994; Lijphart 1999; Heath *et al.* 2005; but see Walby 2009). In broad terms, this means that both the electoral system and cultural aspects can be expected to contribute to levels of ethnic group representation. More specifically, the presence of PR systems and liberal cultural attitudes is thought to be conducive to higher levels of ethnic group representation. Where there are quotas for specific ethnic groups, the expectation would be that levels of representation are higher. Similarly, more developed political rights and more established systems are thought to be associated with higher levels of representation. These general expectations reflect the findings of single-country studies (Welch 1990; Geisser 1997; Saggar 2000; Saggar and Geddes 2000; Spirova 2004; Moser 2004; Bochsler 2006).

Newly collected data and those based on established reference works are used to examine the representation of ethnic groups (see the Appendix). The representation scores compare the proportion of ethnic minority groups in the population and the legislature. Formally, ethnic representation scores Q_E are calculated as the difference between the proportion of each ethnic group in the population ($\Pi_{Z,i}$), and the equivalent in the representatives ($\Pi_{R,i}$). The measure used is a generalised form of the one used for gender representation: $Q_E = 1 - \frac{1}{2}\sum_{i=1}^{n}\left|\Pi_{Z,i} - \Pi_{R,i}\right|$. It is suited for all countries, regardless of the size of the minority groups in the population. This measure corresponds to the *Rose Index* (Mackie and Rose 1991), and representation scores theoretically range from 0 to 1. A representation score of 1 is achieved in a country where the proportions of the different ethnic groups are perfectly reflected in the legislature. For example, in 2006, the proportion of whites in the population in the UK was 93 per cent, whilst the proportion of whites in parliament was 98 per cent. The difference between the two values is 0.05. At the same time, the proportion of ethnic minorities in the population was 7 per cent, with 2 per cent in parliament. The difference between values in this case is 0.05. The values are added up, divided by two, and then subtracted from 1 to give a representation score $Q_{E,UK}=0.95$.

Rather than focusing on a single ethnic minority group, the measure Q_E allows an assessment of how well the legislature reflects all the ethnic groups found in the population. In this sense, the measure is concerned with the normative claim that legislatures should mirror the population overall. Rather than imposing external categories, the measure used caters for the most salient ethnic differences in each country. There is more than one estimate for many countries, although the different sources tend to agree on which ethnic divisions are salient in a country and how many citizens and representatives fall into each group. The approach used in this chapter means that, in a few countries immigrant groups are considered as relevant ethnic groups, whereas in other countries different divisions are salient.

A measure of relative representation can be calculated by dividing the proportion of ethnic minorities in the legislature ($II_{R,m}$) by the proportion in the population ($II_{Z,m}$): $R_E = II_{R,m}/II_{Z,m}$. The variable m in this case denotes all ethnic minority groups combined. Such R-scores are simply a statement of what proportion of the minority population is included in the legislature, irrespective of its size. The values range from zero, where ethnic minorities are absent in the legislature, to values greater than one, where they are numerically over-represented. The latter happens for some individual ethnic groups. While they are sensitive to measurement error and outliers, relative representation scores (R-scores) are insensitive to the heterogeneity of society overall, and are therefore useful in assessing the influence of heterogeneity on levels of representation measured by Q-scores.

Findings

Using the data available, levels of ethnic group representation can be calculated for 101 countries; for 115 countries, there is information on whether or not ethnic minorities are present in the legislature. Figure 3.1 reproduces the distribution of representation scores in graphical form; the representation scores for all countries are included in the Appendix. The levels of ethnic group representation are generally considerably higher than the levels for women. However, in contrast with gender, there are many countries where the population is ethnically relatively homogeneous. Sensitivity analysis suggests that the skew visible in Figure 3.6 is not problematic: The more homogeneous countries do not drive the results reported in this chapter. The distribution for countries that are more heterogeneous than average is somewhat similar to the overall distribution: values are concentrated towards the upper end of the scale, but the distribution is flatter. As discussed below, the representation scores will invariably be comparatively high in relatively homogeneous societies, but a control for heterogeneity will be used to cater for this characteristic of the measurement. The nature of the measurement means that a direct comparison of representation scores is of limited value.

In 77 per cent of the national legislatures covered in this chapter, there is at least one member of an ethnic minority group present. In the countries that are more heterogeneous than average, this value is 94.7 per cent. This indicates that in most countries, members from ethnic minority groups are in one way or another present in the legislature, particularly in countries where they form a more substantial part of the population. In some of the more homogeneous countries, ethnic

Figure 3.1: Levels of ethnic group representation

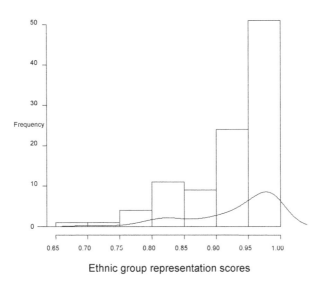

Ethnic group representation scores

Notes: The distribution (frequency and density) of levels of ethnic group representation as found in 101 national legislatures. The level of representation considers multiple ethnic groups at once. These values do not take into consideration the make-up of society (heterogeneity).

minority groups appear to be too small to claim even a single seat. Despite un-der-representation, it is possible to interpret the presence of a single minority rep-resentative in a positive way, i.e. minority voices are not entirely absent. In many cases, minority groups managed to break into the territory of decision making and power, perhaps legitimising the legislature and state. However, it is possible that a single representative or small number of representatives are admitted only to symbolically include the minority group, without efforts to work further towards equality and justice.

Representation of individual ethnic groups

A more detailed approach is possible when considering individual groups, rather than the situation at the national level. By comparing the proportion of a specific ethnic group in the legislature with the equivalent in the population, the level of relative representation of individual groups can be enumerated. Such a comparison approaches each ethnic group individually, and provides an insight into the nature of political representation of different ethnic groups. In the remainder of this section, I examine the representation of individual ethnic groups, but the main part of this chapter is concerned with levels of representation at the national level.

In a few cases, individual minority groups are over-represented numerically, because the single seat they gained in the legislature leads to greater representation in the legislature than in the population. This can be observed, for instance, for Africans in Australia, Arabs in Belgium, Jews and Poles in Latvia, Hungarians in Slovenia, and Chinese in Trinidad and Tobago. Some of these groups may not be over-represented when the level of representation is averaged over a number of elections, but other cases are likely to reflect historical reasons. An interesting problem may be observed in Denmark and Slovenia, where there are specific provisions for minority groups. In Denmark, the two seats for the Faroe Islands and Greenland are over-proportional in relation to the population, but a single seat would lead to a more significant under-representation. In Slovenia, it is similarly a question of including or excluding the Hungarian minority.

In a few countries, only one of the multiple minority groups is included in the legislature. For example, in Georgia, the Adkhars, being the largest minority group, are the only group included. In proportion to their population size, they are over-represented, but the majority population is more significantly over-represented in parliament. Similar cases can be found in Macedonia where Albanians are the only minority group in the *Assembly*, or Slovakia where Hungarians are included in the legislature, but no Roma. In some instances, only certain ethnic minority groups are officially recognised as such, which leaves others out of consideration for inclusion in the legislature. This may be particularly significant where reserved seats are in place for ethnic minority groups, and the lack of official recognition means lack of reservation for some of the groups.

In both Canada and the Ukraine, one of the ethnic minority groups is over-represented in the legislature: the Chinese in Canada, and the Russians in the Ukraine. It seems likely in both cases that the ethnic groups in question are disproportionately found in those parts of society that representatives are often drawn from – the highly educated. In South Africa, the white minority are over-represented, for historical reasons (Reynolds 2006).

It is also the case that some ethnic minority groups are well-represented. In Slovenia, Italians are present in parliament, although this is helped by special provisions. No such provisions are found in Trinidad and Tobago, where Africans are present in parliament in proportion to their population size, or for Hungarians in Romania. The most common occurrence for individual groups, however, is under-representation of the minority group. A complete absence in the legislature is common; however, it would be unwieldy to list all cases in a world where under-representation of minority groups is the norm.

Using relative representation scores to examine the representation of individual ethnic groups presents a rich and detailed picture. It appears that the representation of particular ethnic groups in the legislature is largely intrinsic to the countries. Compared to the analyses in this chapter – which are based on the representation score Q_E – no additional insights can be gained as to which variables influence overall levels of ethnic representation in national legislatures.

Representation at the national level

In a first step, I examine bivariate associations using the full sample of free and partly-free countries. To some extent, this allows a comparison between the findings of single-country studies and the cross-national design used here. One factor suggested as a significant correlate with levels of ethnic group representation is the electoral formula. However, no significant difference can be determined: levels of ethnic group representation achieved in countries with majoritarian systems are comparable to those with PR ($p>0.1$). This lack of association is also found with different and more elaborate operationalisations of the electoral formula. Similarly, no significant association can be determined for related factors that capture the proportionality of the electoral system and its key institutions. There is no significant association for the district magnitude ($p>0.1$), the effective number of parties ($r=0.16$, $p>0.1$), the presence of preferential voting ($p>0.1$), or effective thresholds ($r=0.05$, $p>0.1$). No apparent correlation exists between the level of vote–seat proportionality and that of ethnic group representation ($r=0.12$, $p>0.1$). It therefore appears that the nature of the electoral system has little direct impact on the level of ethnic group representation.

The presence of statutory provisions for ethnic minority groups as such is not associated with higher levels of representation ($p>0.1$). At first sight, this might be surprising, since quotas are implemented precisely for improving representation. However, as aforementioned, the salience and politicisation of ethnic divisions may differ from country to country. The perception is that in countries that are more heterogeneous, ethnic divisions are more salient. Indeed, when only looking at the countries that are more heterogeneous than average, the difference between countries with and without quotas increases. Whilst the difference is still not statistically significant, countries with statutory provisions for ethnic minorities seem to avert the worst cases of under-representation. What is more, as discussed in more detail below, quotas do not always reflect the proportion of ethnic minorities in the population, and quotas are frequently applied to only some minority groups in society. Consequently, the overall effect of quotas at the national level is reduced – even when quotas are enforced. This does not mean that quotas are necessarily ineffective for those groups they are designed for.

In terms of how well a democracy is established, differences in political rights are not significantly associated with levels of ethnic group representation ($p>0.1$). Similarly, little difference can be determined between old and new democracies ($p>0.1$). Whilst the worst cases seem to be exclusive to new democracies, the level of ethnic group representation achieved in some of the more established countries – such as the US – is significantly lower than that achieved in many new democracies.

The influence of cultural factors on ethnic group representation appears complex. For some of the underlying influences identified in the theoretical framework, no clear pattern can be recognised. The predominant religion of a country is not associated with differences in the level of representation ($p>0.1$), while regional differences are associated with significant differences ($p<0.05$). However, when only looking at countries that are more heterogeneous, differences between regions are no longer significant (p>0.1). The difference between industrial and post-industrial countries appears to have little impact on the representation of ethnic groups (p>0.1). In contrast, turning to directly measured attitudes towards marginalised groups in society, attitudes that are more positive are associated with higher levels of representation in the legislature (r=0.46, p<0.01). When looking only at heterogeneous countries, this association is stronger (r=0.75, p<0.01).

The actual make-up of society is of interest when considering levels of ethnic group representation. The measure of political representation used in this chapter does not include aspects of the heterogeneity of society and for this reason, on one level, this variable is required as a control. However, there is more to ethnic group representation than just this. Many countries with high heterogeneity manage to include ethnic minorities in the legislature more or less in proportion. Some countries may be so divided that ethnic divisions become highly politicised, which may be reflected in the level of representation. The high correlation between the level of heterogeneity and the level of ethnic group representation means that a study not considering the actual make-up of society may seriously misinterpret the relevant factors (r=0.51, p<0.001). A different aspect is the geographical concentration of minority groups, a variable that is significantly associated with levels of ethnic group representation. Lower levels of ethnic group representation are found in countries where minorities are geographically concentrated, although substantive differences may be small (p<0.05). This result may indicate that the geographical concentration of groups is a sign of marginalisation rather than improved mobilisation for minority groups.

Following the theoretical framework, significant influences from the electoral system and cultural variables are likely for levels of ethnic group representation. However, the bivariate analyses suggest that institutional factors are perhaps secondary in the case of ethnic group representation, although these bivariate results do not control for the make-up of society. Based on the associations outlined above, it appears that cultural aspects – approximated by region and measured as attitudes – may be the most significant covariates for ethnic group representation. As in the previous chapter on the representation of women, I start with multivariate analyses, including as many cases as possible. In a second step, the use of variables that measure attitudes towards marginalised groups in society invariably reduces the number of countries.

The second model in Table 3.1 introduces a control for the ethnic make-up of society. Whilst this increases the model fit substantially, the other variables are not substantively affected. The premise that the age of democracy may be a substantively significant factor, however, now looks implausible. One possible interpretation is that ethnic heterogeneity somehow acts as an impediment to establishing democracy (Lijphart 2004).

Table 3.1: Multivariate models of ethnic group representation I

	Model 1			Model 2			Model 3		
	B	SE	p-value	B	SE	p-value	B	SE	p-value
Constant	0.88	0.04	0.000*	0.95	0.04	0.000*	0.90	0.05	0.000*
Electoral formula									
Mj/MMM (Base)									
PR/MMP	−0.02	0.02	0.359	−0.02	0.02	0.242	−0.02	0.02	0.263
Quotas									
No quotas (Base)									
Statutory quotas	−0.01	0.02	0.810	0.02	0.02	0.404	0.03	0.02	0.101
Political rights	0.01	0.01	0.276	0.01	0.01	0.432	0.01	0.01	0.249
Age of democracy	0.02	0.02	0.337	−0.00	0.02	0.815	−0.03	0.03	0.243
Heterogeneity				−0.20	0.04	0.000*	−0.20	0.04	0.000*
Regions									
Eastern Europe (Base)									
Western Europe							0.05	0.03	0.070[+]
Nordic Countries							0.10	0.04	0.016*
Asia and Pacific							0.05	0.03	0.078[+]
Middle East							0.01	0.04	0.738
Sub-Saharan Africa							0.06	0.03	0.029*
Latin America							0.04	0.03	0.147
R^2	0.04			0.27			0.37		

Notes: Three multivariate models (OLS) with ethnic group representation scores as the dependent variable are displayed.
*Significant at p<0.05. +Significant at p<0.1. N=101.

In a first step, the modelling is designed to maximise the number of cases in the multivariate analyses. Model 1 in Table 3.1 performs poorly. With only institutional variables, the age of democracy and the level of political rights, the model fit is low and none of the variables appears to be a significant covariant. On average, statutory provisions for ethnic groups seem to make no difference, but although statistically insignificant, it can be speculated that more established democracies come with higher levels of ethnic group representation.

Adding considerations of geographical concentration to Model 2 – or any subsequent model – does not increase the model fit significantly. The variable itself is not statistically significant ($p>0.1$). This finding contradicts a strong theoretical case, where geographical concentration and levels of representation are expected to go hand in hand. It is conceivable that effects of geographical concentration are limited to majoritarian systems. However, no significant interaction between the electoral formula and the concentration of ethnic groups can be found, and the model fit is not significantly increased by the inclusion of such an interaction term. As in the other empirical chapters, I have tested various interaction terms, but with no significant results. In particular, no significant interaction could be observed between institutional and cultural factors.

The final model in Table 3.1 introduces regional differences. Almost all other regions fare better when compared to Eastern European countries, ($p<0.1$). Some differences between other regions are also significant ($p<0.1$). Perhaps the worst cases in regions outside Europe have not yet made the transition to democratic rule and therefore not available for consideration. Using the *Human Development Index* (HDI) as an indicator of cultural differences instead, the model fit is lower ($R^2=0.32$), but the variable is a significant correlate. Religious differences, in contrast, seem insignificant ($p>0.1$).

The results outlined in Table 3.1 suggest that there is an association between differences in regions and levels of ethnic group representation. Oddly enough, when considering regions, the age of democracy is a substantive significant factor, although the direction of the sign is unexpected. The result suggests that ethnic representation scores are higher in newer democracies. It is sometimes argued that in new democracies, effects of international tutelage and diffusion from neighbouring countries may positively influence the level of ethnic group representation (Bennett 1991; Stone 2001; Viterna and Fallon 2008). In other words, it is conceivable that levels of ethnic group representation are higher in new democracies, contrary to the expectation outlined in Chapter One.

In an additional model (not shown in Table 3.1), only cultural heterogeneity and regional differences were considered. This parsimonious model performs relatively well ($R^2=0.35$). This suggests that regional factors are dominant for ethnic group representation. The fact that different variables – regions and the level of development – perform slightly differently suggests that it may be worth pursuing cultural attitudes in more detail.

Table 3.2: *Multivariate models of ethnic group representation II*

	Model 3 (reduced sample)			Model 4			Model 5		
	B	SE	p-value	B	SE	p-value	B	SE	p-value
Constant	0.82	0.09	0.000*	0.75	0.11	0.000*	0.93	0.05	0.000*
Electoral formula:									
Mj/MMM (Base)									
PR/MMP	−0.02	0.03	0.418	−0.03	0.03	0.238	0.00	0.02	0.881
Quotas:									
No quotas (Base)									
Statutory quotas	0.02	0.03	0.514	0.02	0.03	0.526	0.03	0.02	0.116
Political rights	0.02	0.02	0.210	0.02	0.02	0.183	0.01	0.01	0.275
Age of democracy	−0.04	0.03	0.186	−0.03	0.03	0.324	0.03	0.03	0.203
Heterogeneity	−0.18	0.07	0.024*	−0.20	0.07	0.012*	−0.27	0.05	0.000*
Region: not Eastern European	0.08	0.03	0.021*						
Attitudes: marginalised groups				0.03	0.01	0.031*	0.02	0.01	0.026*
R²	0.50			0.52			0.32		

Notes: Three additional multivariate models (OLS) with ethnic group representation scores as the dependent variable are displayed. *Significant at p<0.05. Model 3 is identical to the one used in Table 3.1, but only includes the cases also used in Model 4; N=33. For presentational reasons, only the difference between Eastern European countries and all other countries is shown. Model 4 includes measured attitudes; N=33. Model 5 includes predicted attitudes for the countries where measured attitudes are unavailable; N=101.

In order to capture cultural attitudes directly, it is necessary to replace the regional variable because of issues concerning collinearity. As outlined in Table 3.2, the replacement of the variable on regional differences with the more direct attitudinal counterpart leads to a slightly better model fit. The other variables, however, are not substantively affected. Institutional factors, such as the electoral formula, still appear to have little influence on levels of ethnic group representation. The magnitude of the control for ethnic heterogeneity is similar in Models 3 and 4. Whereas the coefficient for regional differences refers to a binary variable, the corresponding coefficient for cultural attitudes stands for the average number of neighbours mentioned as unacceptable. The magnitude of the standardised estimates is similar.

The addition of geographical concentration was more successful in Model 3 using the subsample. This variable is a significant correlate ($p<0.05$), and when added to Model 3, the model fit increases ($R^2=0.59$). This suggests that in some countries where ethnic minorities are concentrated in certain areas, the level of ethnic group representation is higher, contrary to the bivariate findings above. This discrepancy in the full sample is probably due to the nature of the reduced sample, although the fact that the smaller sample includes many Eastern European countries cannot account for the difference. As in the full sample, the interaction between geographical concentration and the electoral formula is not significant in the subsample ($p>0.1$). This casts doubt on the suggestion that geographical concentration is important only or mostly in majoritarian systems. No equivalent effect can be observed when adding geographical concentration to Model 4. Similarly, adding other variables to Model 4 or Model 5 – such as religion – does not increase the model fit significantly, and the variables are not significant ($p>0.1$).

In Model 5, a different approach to the limited coverage of the measured attitudinal question was employed: based on the theoretical framework, the expected attitudes for countries not covered by the WVS were predicted. Using these predicted values makes it possible to utilise the full sample of free and partly-free countries. The substantive results are unchanged in Model 5 and the only clear difference is that, although statistically insignificant, the sign of the age of democracy has changed. It might be that the age of democracy picks up some cultural differences not covered in the regional variable and the reduced sample. Adding the variable on geographical concentration is not significant in Model 5 ($p>0.1$).

In order to test the robustness of the results, a sub-sample of OECD countries, as well as sub-samples that remove countries with small populations were considered – and the reported results can largely be replicated. In an additional test of robustness, I removed countries with an ethnically relatively homogeneous population from analysis, which excludes the cases where levels of ethnic group representation are invariably high. The results are substantively unchanged.

Implementation issues and backlashes

Following the framework of political representation in Chapter One, levels of ethnic group representation should resemble those of gender representation. The relevant hypotheses are formulated largely without regard to group size, focusing on marginalisation and positions of power instead. In this sense, both institutional and cultural factors can be expected as correlates for levels of ethnic group representation. The results of the empirical analyses, however, suggest that the key covariates differ to some extent from those of gender representation. For this reason, the study of the representation of ethnic groups in legislatures merits more attention than is currently found in the literature. Contrary to the expectation, none of the institutional factors seems to be significantly associated with the level of ethnic group representation. This is the case not only for the electoral formula and its related measures of proportionality, but also for the provision of quotas.[1]

In the case of quotas, implementation issues may be a problem since most measures for ethnic minority groups are, by nature, enforced. For example, in Croatia, 3.3 per cent of the seats are reserved for ethnic minority candidates – in a country where nearly 20 per cent of the population belong to ethnic minority groups. In New Zealand, 5.8 per cent of the seats are reserved for the Maori – they make up 12 per cent of the population – but relative to their proportion in the population, they managed to win more seats. This means that the relatively small quotas do not appear to be a problem in practice. In this case, the provision of quotas may have acted to overcome a representational blockage. At the same time, there are no provisions for Pacific Islanders – 5 per cent of the population. Given their numerical under-representation in parliament, there may be a strong case for quotas. In Serbia and Montenegro, there were special provisions for Albanians – 3.2 per cent reserved seats, 11.1 per cent of the population – but other minority groups had no such provisions, including Hungarians, Croats, and Roma. In Colombia, the 3 per cent of seats reserved for Afro-Columbians and other indigenous groups stand in contrast with at least 8 per cent of the population falling into this category – depending on the way 'indigenous' is understood.

In some instances, only certain ethnic minority groups are officially recognised, which means that other groups may not be considered for the legislature or special minority rights. This may be significant where reserved seats are in

---

1. The presence of statutory provisions for ethnic groups is uncommon in comparison to the occurrence of gender quotas, for example. To cater for the small number of cases, and thus possible sampling bias, I used propensity score matching to examine the role of quotas in the case of ethnicity. There is very little indication in the literature as to which factors influence the propensity of implementing measures for ethnic groups, and I used a model including the *Human Development Index*, the age of democracy, political rights, as well as the level of ethnic heterogeneity (R^2=0.18). The reported finding of no overall association was confirmed (p>0.1), indicating that on average provisions for ethnic groups seem ineffective at the national level.

place for ethnic minority groups, and lack of official recognition means a lack of reservation. The lack of official recognition means invisibility: absence in official statistics and possibly absence in political discourse. Particularly affected are Roma and Jews – such as in Hungary or Bosnia and Herzegovina – or ethnic minority groups with an immigration background, such as Turks in Austria. The consequence of such practices is that the overall effect of quotas – where these are in place – is reduced, despite being enforced measures. At the same time, it is important to bear in mind that quotas may be effective for the groups the quotas are designed for.

A different explanation for the lack of association is the blockage argument, and the implication that quotas may already have worked to break through a barrier in the levels of ethnic group representation. With the cross-sectional analysis in this chapter, this possibility cannot be ruled out. However, if this is correct, the quotas do not appear to have a significant impact beyond advancing past the barrier. In contrast, the lack of association may stem from the limited use of quotas and implementation issues: in countries where quotas and related provisions are used, often only a single or a few ethnic minority groups are covered. The under-representation of other groups means that overall little difference can be observed in these cases.

Enforced approaches clearly work, as illustrated by the quotas used in many countries. In this case, it is possible to achieve levels of descriptive representation that would not be expected based on the prevalent attitudes in the wider population. However, such enforced measures come with two drawbacks. First, they may be removed by future members of the elite, as was the case with quotas in countries previously associated with the Soviet Union, or in Egypt and Pakistan (Paxton *et al.* 2010). In this sense, their impact may be temporarily limited. Secondly, forced changes may lead to backlashes in the population (Ramet 1997). Smaller groups not covered by such quotas may also challenge rigid quota systems since they may be effectively excluded.

The role of potential backlashes is important when considering the actions of the political elite. Whilst the elite may talk about improving levels of representation, in most places, they do not appear to be actively engaged to this end. This may be understood when considering the fact that both the citizens and the elite are embedded in the same cultural context. Given that a part of the attitudes is shaped by this environment, it seems unlikely that the elite will enforce quotas or similar measures ahead of what the population is willing to support. The same conclusion can be drawn when arguing that many politicians are primarily motivated by being re-elected (Manin *et al.* 1999; Stimson 1999). In this case, members of the elite supportive of enforced measures to increase the level of ethnic group representation may reconsider their actions: enforced measures may lead to backlashes, with potentially negative consequences for the elite at the polls. In other words, the possibilities of the elite are restricted unless the population is either neutral or positive towards the inclusion of more representatives from ethnic minority groups. In this case, only strong members of the elite will press for enforced measures, whilst for other members of the elite, concerns for re-election might be more pressing.

Enforced quotas may be an option, but such quotas are rare, indicating that awareness of under-representation and politicisation of ethnic differences may be low – often because of historical reasons. Furthermore, quotas are restricted to the political realm, meaning that integration in other aspects of life is not necessarily linked. As an alternative option, there may be attempts to influence the attitudes of the public, such as by strengthening civil society actors. On the one hand, this step may be necessary to implement quotas successfully – assuming the political elite is not too detached from the voters and their opinions. On the other hand, once attitudes have changed to this extent, the implementation of measures to ensure representation may no longer be so pressing. It is sometimes argued that this is what happened with gender quotas in the Nordic countries (Freidenvall *et al.* 2006; McAllister 2006).

In the United States, redistricting was used in an attempt to increase the legislative representation of black people. Whilst such minority-majority districts are associated with increased numbers of black representatives, there is evidence that an unintended consequence may be a decrease in support for minority-sponsored legislation. This may happen if representatives of districts with a black minority become less responsive to the concerns of the black community (Lublin 1997; Cameron *et al.* 1996; Overby and Cosgrove 1996).

In contrast to quotas, regional and cultural variables proved more successful in predicting the level of ethnic group representation. In particular, significant regional differences could be identified, suggesting that different historical experience may be a significant factor for ethnic group representation. However, as was the case with gender representation, the more directly measured variable of attitudes towards marginalised groups in society fared better. In places where the population is more open towards marginalised groups, ethnic minorities are more likely to be included in national legislatures.

The measurement of attitudes towards marginalised groups in society correlates highly with the cultural variable used in Chapter Two: attitudes towards women as political leaders ($r=0.73$, $p<0.001$). In fact, attitudes towards marginalised groups in society are associated with levels of gender representation ($r=0.56$, $p<0.001$), in a similar way that the HDI or the predominant religion are significant covariates. In contrast, the specific variable on women in politics used in Chapter Two does not correlate significantly with the level of ethnic group representation ($r=0.04$, $p>0.1$). This probably indicates that the measurement in this chapter is a more generic measure of attitudes towards minorities – reflecting sociological liberalism – whilst in the previous chapter a measure more specific to gender representation is used.

Given that ethnic minorities make up different proportions in different countries, controlling for the ethnic heterogeneity proved a necessary step. In countries where the ethnic minority population is large, the scope to exclude or under-represent a significant part of the population is greater than in countries that are more homogeneous. However, it is not the case that countries with a more heterogeneous make-up necessarily exclude a larger proportion of the minority population. In some places where ethnic minorities form a considerable proportion of the population, they are included in the legislature accordingly. Sensitivity analysis was carried out to ensure that homogeneous societies do not drive the results presented.

This chapter fails to provide evidence that the electoral system and other institutional factors are significant influences for levels of ethnic group representation. This is true for all the factors tested, irrespective of ethnic heterogeneity as the control. For the factors related to the proportionality of the system, it can be speculated that the political elite learns to cope with the particularities of the system over time (Anderson 2007). In other words, the political actors might be able to adapt to the system, a point also highlighted by the discussion of the change of the electoral formula in New Zealand and its impact on levels of gender representation in Chapter Two. At the same time, the lack of significant association in this chapter should not distract from the fact that electoral systems can – and in some cases clearly do – affect levels of ethnic group representation. One example is Bosnia and Herzegovina with its rigid quota system.

Unfortunately, the lack of appropriate data means that we can say little about the role of ethnic minority candidates. It is conceivable that in some places, members from ethnic minorities do not come forward as candidates for election in sufficient numbers and, for this reason, ethnic minorities are under-represented in legislatures. However, a similar argument is often made for the representation of women, and this was not supported by the multivariate analyses in Chapter Two. To some extent, the inclusion of cultural factors may deal with arguments of supply.

Whilst there is a strong theoretical case to expect higher levels of ethnic group representation in places where ethnic groups are geographically concentrated, the analysis in this chapter could find no consistent support. However, there may be different effects of concentration occurring simultaneously that the analysis is unable to differentiate. On the one hand, geographical concentration means that ethnic minority groups find it easier to mobilise and support candidates from their own group, which would suggest higher levels of representation in countries where minorities are concentrated. On the other hand, in some cases, geographical concentration might be an indication of marginalisation and, with that, a sign of a relative lack of civic engagement. In other words, being marginalised, the voters and candidates might lack the necessary experience needed for higher levels of ethnic group representation.

In contrast to institutional factors, there is further evidence for the effects of cultural factors, both when approximated using regional differences and when measured directly as attitudes towards marginalised groups in society. Taken together, this chapter appears to indicate that cultural factors dominate in the case of ethnic group representation. I argued that strong leadership might be the only measure to improve the situation of ethnic minority groups in society in the short term. This is the case because representatives have incentives not to force higher levels of ethnic group representation in places where the population is not supportive of such a move. In the long term, changes towards more positive attitudes may be reflected in higher levels of ethnic group representation. Given the purported partial link of attitudes towards marginalised groups in society to human development, attitudes do appear to change in many places as the level of development increases. What is more, the suggestion that representative gains for women influence levels of ethnic group representation, and vice versa, may give hope to groups currently absent or grossly under-represented in national legislatures.

This page is intentionally blank

| the representation of issue positions

This chapter asks: are there systematic differences across countries in the degree to which the issue positions of citizens are reflected in national legislatures? Whilst descriptive representation may be essential in terms of legitimacy, substantive representation captures the concerns along which most, if not all, political systems are organised. Substantive representation covers political views, policy preferences and issue positions, and I use the terms *'policy representation'* and *'substantive representation'* interchangeably. In Chapter One, I argued that both descriptive and substantive forms of representation are necessary for a full understanding of political representation. This chapter introduces policy representation and adds a different form of political representation. It is also an essential step in preparation for the next and final empirical chapter, where levels of descriptive and substantive representation are compared. Again, the focus is on the macro level, and the analyses are comparative in order to pick out significant patterns.

The political representation of views and issue positions is much studied. This section of the book focuses on the compilation of different components, bringing together factors commonly studied in isolation. In this chapter, I consider multiple domains of policy representation that address both specific issue domains, as well as the more generic ideological space (left-right positions). In addition, there is new data that benefits from both better estimates of party positions and a larger sample compared to many previous studies. With a focus on representational outcomes, the main concern in this chapter is with the representation of policy preferences; the substantive representation of specific groups is not examined.

A great deal of research concentrates on the proportionality between votes cast and seats gained. The underlying question in these studies is somewhat different from the concerns of this chapter, focusing on how votes translate into the legislature or government being created. I start with the views held by the citizens and consider the collective representation of issue positions (see also Golder and Stramski 2010). However, vote-seat proportionality is thought to be a key factor in this collective relationship and much of the research on vote-seat proportionality is thus relevant to the analysis in this chapter. Most previous work identified a certain discrepancy between the issue positions of the citizens and representatives (e.g. Converse and Pierce 1986; Thomassen and Schmitt 1997, 1999a; Powell 2000; Budge *et al.* 2012), with the degree of difference varying significantly from study to study. Most studies focus on representation in the left–right domain, often because data for other domains are unavailable. Where other domains are considered, the economic issues domain and the left–right domain are often found to be strongly represented (Birch 2000; Dalton 1985; Pierce 1999). The left–right domain is also chosen because of its role as a summary scale. Even though the meaning of what the positions *left* and *right* stand for is not constant over time or across countries (Fuchs and Klingemann 1989; Sanders 1999), it is frequently argued that left–right is an appropriate way to summarise the political space. Interestingly, maybe, even where the concepts of left and right are actively rejected – such as by certain Green parties in Europe – they remain meaningful (Kitschelt and Hellemans 1990; Knutsen 1995). Defining left and right in different countries is not a problem in this chapter: here policy positions are compared only within countries.[1]

The choice of data allows this chapter to explore policy representation more thoroughly than most previous studies. In particular, going beyond the left–right notion is important because citizens are arguably more able to express their views and positions in more concrete domains, as opposed to these abstract constructs (Thomassen and Schmitt 1997). Moreover, in the domain of political left and right, a larger number of countries are covered than most previous studies, where sample sizes of fewer than two dozen are commonplace. Consequently, the number of countries with single-member districts (SMD) is often very small. To counter the problem of small numbers, data from multiple elections are often pooled, which may be problematic in some cases (Jenkins 2002).

By its nature, the electoral system has an impact on the proportionality between the votes cast and the seats gained, and thus affects levels of substantive representation. Until recently, almost all studies found that levels of substantive representation are higher in countries with proportional representation (PR) systems. The role of political rights and the age of democracy are often implicit in studies of substantive representation, when the impact of the political context or the party landscape on levels of representation is considered. In both cases, more rights and a more established system are thought to be associated with higher levels of representation. The role of cultural attitudes on the substantive representation of issue positions is not often tested, although the shift towards post-material values in more developed countries in particular is recognised to increase the salience of social issues or issues of the environment. As outlined in Chapter One, all these factors are considered in the analysis of substantive representation in the different issue domains covered in this chapter.

The policy representation scores utilise data by Benoit and Laver (2005), as further outlined in the Appendix. Based on a large survey, the data allow a reliable placement of parties in multiple domains (Benoit and Laver 2006, 2007). The weighted averages of party positions are taken as approximations for the positions

---

1. The assumption remaining is that both the citizens and the elite share the same conceptions of the ideological concepts in question. Anchoring vignettes (King *et al.* 2004) could offer a solution for this problem, but this clearly addresses a different research question and is beyond the scope of this book. Using anchoring vignettes, positions such as *very left* and *centre* could be anchored. Similarly, tests of measurement equivalence could explore this question empirically (Steenkamp and Baumgartner 1998; Davidov *et al.* 2010), but both approaches would require additional data on the elite.

of representatives. This approach seems acceptable, particularly when looking at the legislature as whole, rather than at individual representatives. One problem with Benoit and Laver's data is that the different domains sometimes cover different countries. The key domains of left–right, social issues, and environmental issues, however, all include a wide range of countries. What is more, the fact that some countries are absent in some domains is largely a reflection of the salience of these issues. Consequently, the party positions that are included in the analyses are more reliable and less likely to stand for non-positions. Further, the argument that citizens may be poorly informed on some issues carries less weight. This selection bias may mean that for each domain, representation scores for the countries included may be higher than for those absent. However, since the differences between citizens and representatives are approached within each country, rather than being compared across countries, the analyses are unaffected.

The policy representation scores in this chapter are based on a comparison of mean positions, possibly the most common measurement in the literature.[2] Assuming that citizens are unable to make very detailed distinctions on many political issues – some of which may not be readily formulated – this approach deals with the political space in a realistic manner: for example, citizens largely identifying as *left* or *right* (Aldrich and McKelvey 1977; Rabinowitz 1978; Alvarez and Franklin 1994). The measurement based on mean positions can be thought to mimic the proportional approach used in Chapters Two and Three. However, being based on mean positions, the measure is unable to address the question of whether any particular view is represented in the legislature. This measure can be expected to correlate with measures based on proportions (see Chapter Five). However, with the data used in this book, a measure based on the mean is the only viable approach.

Formally, policy representation scores for a particular issue domain are calculated by taking the difference between the mean position of the citizens ($\overline{Z}_k$) and the mean position of the parties, weighed by party strength in the legislature ($\overline{R}_k$): $Q_k = 1 - |\overline{Z}_k - \overline{R}_k|$. The policy positions in each domain k are measured on scales ranging from 0 to 1. As with the measures of descriptive representation,

2. Powell (2000) is sceptical of using mean positions, defending the median position as theoretically more significant, in both majoritarian and PR systems. This concern with the median voter is goes back to Black (1948), popularised by Downs (1957). The mean and median position reflect vaguely different concerns. Whereas minimising the distance to the median citizen minimises the size of the opposition, minimising the distance to the mean reduces the distance to the policy preferences (Achen 1978; Powell 2000). To some extent, this difference reflects different starting points: from the parties in the case of the median, from the citizens in the case of the mean. Whilst a competitive party system may lead to representation of the median voters, representation of the mean voter might be considered a fairer outcome. In practice, however, for the countries covered in this book, the differences between the two measures are insignificant, and none of the results reported is affected.

a subtraction from 1 is used so that higher values reflect higher levels of representation. The measurement does not include a salience component; this maintains comparability to measures of descriptive representation as much as possible. Salience is considered separately in Chapter Five.

Findings

A noticeable variance can be observed in the levels of policy representation found in different countries and across domains. Substantive representation is approached in eight domains: a generic left–right, a social scale measuring liberalism on matters such as homosexuality or euthanasia, views on privatisation, protection of the environment, the promotion of nationalism and cultural consciousness, the role of religion in politics, immigration policies, and views on the deregulation of the market (for more information, see the Appendix). The highest levels of left–right representation are found in Latvia and Slovakia, but they are also present in most Western European countries, the United States and Japan. At the other end of the scale are the Philippines and the Ukraine. In the social domain, levels of representation are generally slightly lower. The highest levels occur in Bosnia and Herzegovina, the United Kingdom and Iceland; the lowest levels are in Albania, the Ukraine and Denmark. In the environmental domain, levels of representation are noticeably lower. They are highest in Turkey and Australia; they are lowest in Serbia and Montenegro and Hungary. The representation scores for all countries are included in the Appendix. The variance across domains is summarised in Table 4.1. In all of the domains examined, levels of representation differ significantly across countries, but levels of representation tend to be highest in the left–right domain.

As shown in Figure 4.1, the representation scores for the left–right domain are concentrated at the higher end of the scale, with values close to 1 being more common. This indicates generally high levels of representation in terms of political left and right. For social issues, most representation scores are at the upper end of

Table 4.1: Policy representation in different domains

	Left–Right	Social	Environ.	Privatise	National	Religion	Immigr.	Deregul.
N	49	41	30	17	17	18	17	19
Mean	0.94	0.87	0.76	0.89	0.89	0.84	0.80	0.83
Std. dev.	0.05	0.06	0.08	0.09	0.07	0.10	0.10	0.06
Range	0.22	0.31	0.30	0.31	0.26	0.32	0.32	0.20

Notes: Descriptive statistics for the levels of policy representation in different domains: a generic left–right measurement, economic issues, social issues, positions on privatisation, environmental issues, nationalism, role of religion in politics, immigration, and market deregulation. Values of the representation scores theoretically range from 0 (perfect discrepancy) to 1 (perfect match).

the scale, but in contrast to political left–right, the highest values are not the most common ones. The outlier with the lowest score is Albania, but outlier and residual analysis was carried out for all domains to test the robustness of the reported findings for outliers. In no case could a substantively or statistically significant difference be observed.

Figure 4.1: Distributions of policy representation scores in different domains Domains

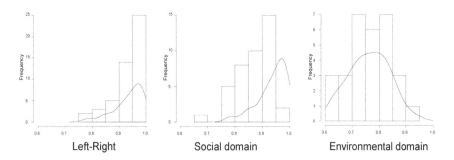

| Left-Right | Social domain | Environmental domain |

Notes: The distribution (frequencies and densities) of levels of representation in the key policy domains as examined in this chapter. The distributions for the other domains are described in the main text. The number of cases in each domain is apparent in Table 4.1.

In contrast with the previous two domains, levels of representation of environmental issues are significantly lower. Looking at the remaining domains, the distribution of representation scores regarding views on immigration and the role of religion in politics are both characterised by higher variance than for the left–right domain. Very different levels can be found in the countries covered, which might be a reflection of the different salience of the domains. The distribution of representation scores in the domain of deregulation appears to be similar to that of social issues. Also absent in Figure 4.1 is the distribution of representation scores in the domains of nationalism and privatisation. The distribution of the representation scores in these domains resembles that of the social domain, with the exception of the outlier: a concentration towards the upper end of the scale. In none of these additional domains are the highest levels of representation the most common ones, although there is a concentration towards the upper end of the scale. This might indicate that left–right representation is somewhat prioritised, perhaps at the cost of levels of representation in other domains.

Compared to levels of gender and ethnic group representation outlined in the previous two chapters, it seems that levels of policy representation are generally higher than levels of descriptive representation. The relationship between levels of representation in different forms will be examined and discussed in Chapter Five. The remainder of this chapter focuses on the variance within policy domains.

To begin with, bivariate associations are examined as a form of initial hypothesis testing. In the literature, the difference between countries with PR systems and countries with majoritarian systems is often highlighted, but no association can be found in the rich sample used in this chapter. This is the case for all the different domains, including left–right, the social domain and environmentalism. For none of the domains are the observed differences substantively or statistically significant (p>0.1). For some of the domains, the range of representation scores is noticeably larger in PR systems than in majoritarian systems. These results indicate that the lack of difference found in the left–right domain by Golder and Stramski (2010) applies equally to other issue domains. The results outlined here are not substantively different when classifying the electoral formula into majoritarian, mixed and proportional systems; although in this case, the small number of countries in some of the cells becomes problematic.

Looking at the level of vote–seat proportionality, rather than the difference in electoral formulas, does not substantively change the result. Statistically, most of the associations are insignificant (p>0.1). The exception is the left–right domain, where an association can be observed, and higher levels of representation in more proportional systems (r=0.51, p<0.05). The correlation between the two variables is stronger for new democracies (r=0.59) than for older democracies (r=0.50). In fact, the result for old democracies is driven by one country, and removing France from consideration, the association is no longer significant (r=0.10, p>0.1). This might indicate that in new democracies, the proportionality of the system is important, whereas in more established democracies, there are other factors that ensure higher levels of representation.

In contrast to the representation of women and ethnic groups, quotas are not used for issue positions. The aim of quotas is to increase levels of descriptive representation without affecting levels of substantive representation in unrelated domains. Indeed, there are no significant correlations between quotas for women or ethnic groups and levels of substantive representation for any of the domains (p>0.1) between the presence of quotas for women or ethnic groups and levels of substantive representation. The generic nature of the issue domains covered in this chapter means that the representation scores are unable to pick up the assumed higher levels of substantive representation of women and ethnic groups in issues that directly affect them. Though there is little agreement on what such issues might be, questions that are more specific would have to be covered to note such differences.

A correlation can be observed between political rights and the level of substantive representation for political left–right (r=0.42, p<0.01), and the social domain (r=0.29, p<0.1). There is no apparent association for the environmental domain (p>0.1). For the nationalism domain, the correlation is relatively strong (r=0.38, p>0.1), whilst for all the other domains there is no clear association (p>0.1). Treating the *Freedom House* rankings of political rights as a binary variable, only differences in the social and left–right domain are significant (p<0.05). Substantively, in the left–right domain the mean representation score in free countries is 0.95, as opposed to 0.90 in partly-free countries. Together with the difference in vote-seat proportionality, these results indicate that the degree to which a political system is established plays a significant role for levels of substantive representation. This role, however, is not a universal one, in the sense that not all issue domains are affected in the same way or to the same extent.

One way to capture cultural aspects and their influence on the salience of issue domains is by looking at the level of development. There is no clear pattern of association between the *Human Development Index* and most issue domains (p>0.1), with the exception of the left–right domain (r=0.53, p<0.001). This indicates higher levels of policy representation in more developed countries. Regional differences may also approximate cultural differences, and a significant difference can be found once again only in the left–right domain. Compared to the base category of Western Europe, the United States, Canada, Australia and New Zealand, countries in most regions fare worse in terms of left–right representation (p<0.05, ΔQ=0.04 to 0.06). In this case, regional variables may pick up differences in development or the prevalence of post-material values in certain regions. For the other domains, no significant association can be observed (p>0.1).

Some of the bivariate associations seem to differ from domain to domain, but both institutional and cultural variables appear significant covariates in some instances. Next, I use multivariate regression analyses to identify correlates for the different levels of policy representation in different domains. Because of the small number of cases in some of the domains, the focus remains on representation in three domains: left–right, social issues, and the environment. As in the previous chapters, I summarise the effects of the electoral system into the electoral formula. Given that the bivariate analyses yielded few significant associations, further distinctions seem unnecessary. In addition, I include variables on political rights and the age of democracy. The addition of regional and religious dummy variables is tested for all the models, and reported where significant.

Predicting levels of policy representation using the theoretical framework in Chapter One appears to be more difficult than predicting levels of descriptive representation. Even though modelling is conducted in parallel to Chapter Two and Chapter Three, the tables in this chapter do not include cultural variables. This is done to save space, as the variables are often not statistically significant, as outlined below, and because their exclusion has no significant bearing on the other variables in the models. For political left–right, the electoral system appears to be of little significance, a result that reflects the lack of bivariate association above. The level of political rights is a significant factor, as is the age of democracy. Higher levels of left-right representation can be found in older democracies and countries with more developed political rights (Table 4.2). Again, these results tell the same story as the bivariate associations. Replacing the variable on the electoral formula with one capturing vote–seat proportionality does not change the reported findings substantially, nor do different operationalisations of the electoral formula.

The addition of regional and religious variables to the model for left–right reported in Table 4.2 does not increase the model fit significantly, and the added variables are not statistically significant (p>0.1). A model including the *Human Development Index*, rather than the age of democracy, leads to a significantly

Table 4.2: Multivariate analyses for left–right, social issues, and the environment

	Left–Right			Social issues			Environment		
	B	SE	p-value	B	SE	p-value	B	SE	p-value
Constant	0.82	0.05	0.000*	0.81	0.08	0.000*	0.77	0.11	0.000*
Electoral formula									
Mj/MMM (Base)									
PR/MMP	0.00	0.01	0.864	−0.01	0.02	0.654	0.01	0.03	0.762
Political rights	0.02	0.01	0.048*	0.02	0.02	0.342	−0.01	0.02	0.690
Old democracy	0.03	0.01	0.019*	−0.01	0.02	0.749	0.06	0.03	0.049*
R^2	0.25			0.07			0.19		

Notes: Multivariate models (OLS) with representation scores in three different policy domains as dependent variables. *Significant at $p<0.05$. N=49 for left–right; N=41 for social issues; N=30 for environment. An old democracy was established at least 20 years earlier lower model fit for levels of left–right representation and the variable is not significant ($p>0.1$). In contrast, replacing the variable on the age of democracy with the difference between industrial and post-industrial countries increases the model fit significantly ($R^2=0.35$). The variable is significant, with the other factors in the model not noticeably affected ($p<0.05$). Taken together, this suggests that the bivariate association between the level of development and the policy representation score for the left–right domain may reflect differences in how well a democracy is established. The relevant cut-off between new and established democracies, however, may be somewhat different from the twenty years stipulated in the variable on the age of democracy. In none of these additional models does the electoral formula appear to be a significant or substantively noteworthy factor. The interaction between the age of democracy and vote–seat proportionality is not a significant factor in multivariate models that consider vote–seat proportionality rather than the electoral formula. This contrasts with the results of the bivariate analyses above.

With regard to the social issues domain, political rights and the age of democracy initially appear as insignificant as the electoral system. The model fit of such a model is low ($R^2=0.07$), but adding the variable on the predominant religion increases this significantly ($R^2=0.23$). When controlling for the predominant religion of the country, political rights also appear to be a substantive factor ($p<0.1$). Higher levels of representation can be found in countries where the development of political rights is greater. In terms of religion, the level of representation in the social domain is lower in predominantly Catholic countries than in predominantly Protestant countries or predominantly Muslim countries ($p<0.05$), although the number of the latter is very small. The difference between the predominantly Catholic and Protestant countries is in line with the expectation outlined in Chapter One, where I stipulate that in the affected countries, citizens may vote for certain parties despite disagreeing with their position on social issues.

The effects of religion on representation in the social domain are difficult to disentangle, because – for the countries covered by the data – all predominantly Protestant countries are also democracies established over twenty years ago. Using the age of democracy in a continuous sense does not substantively affect the results reported in Table 4.2, although multicollinearity may still be an issue. Looking only at countries that are predominantly non-Protestant, the difference between old and new democracies is statistically insignificant and substantively very small ($p>0.1$). The interaction between the age of democracy and a country being predominantly Catholic is statistically insignificant; neither does it improve the model fit ($p>0.1$). It can be speculated that the difference between Protestant and Catholic countries is a relevant factor for policy representation in the social issues domain, but the relative lack of variance in Protestant countries is an issue that cannot be resolved with the data used.

Turning to predictions of the level of policy representation in terms of environmental issues, the bivariate analysis suggests the age of democracy as a significant covariant. This is confirmed in the multivariate analysis, where more established countries tend to demonstrate higher levels of representation. Regional and religious variables do not add significantly to the model reported in Table 4.2, and they are not statistically significant (p>0.1). This finding contrasts with the expectation that levels of environmental representation might be associated with religious differences. Because the number of cases is small, it is not possible to examine regional and religious differences beyond the difference between Western and non-Western countries, or Christian and non-Christian countries.

Table 4.3 outlines the results for further policy domains. The table does not show the domain of privatisation because it appears to be difficult to predict. None of the variables tested was significant. The best model fit was achieved when including a variable on whether or not the countries are predominantly Christian ($R^2=0.25$), although substantively the difference between Christian and non-Christian countries is negligible. As outlined in Table 4.3, political rights are associated with higher levels of representation in terms of nationalism. This effect is robust against the addition of further variables – regional or religious – although these additional factors are neither statistically significant (p>0.1), nor do they add substantively to the model fit.

Table 4.3 shows policy representation in the domain of the role of religion in politics. Views on whether religion should play a significant role in politics appear to be better represented in countries with majoritarian systems, although the association is not statistically significant (p>0.1). The key factor seems to be the age of democracy: older democracies are associated with higher levels of representation. It should be borne in mind that the sample of countries for this particular domain includes only democracies established within the past twenty years. This may explain the size of the predicted effect, and it seems reasonable to assume that the effect of the age of democracy wanes over time. The addition of further variables does not improve the model fit and such variables are not statistically significant (p>0.1).

Policy representation in the deregulation domain appears to be dominated by the country's predominant religion, although substantively political rights also appear to be significant. Analysis not shown in Table 4.3 suggests that levels of representation are lower in predominantly Protestant countries than in predominantly Catholic or other countries (p<0.05). Controlling for political rights, the electoral system and the age of democracy, the difference in representation scores between predominantly Catholic and non-Catholic countries is 0.05. The difference in representation scores between predominantly Catholic and Protestant countries is 0.03. Whilst in both cases the population appears to be more liberal than the representatives, the difference between citizens and representatives is more marked in predominantly Catholic countries. This finding is in line with the expectations outlined for the corresponding hypothesis. Adding regional variables to the model does not improve the model fit, and the variables are not statistically significant (p>0.1).

Table 4.3 does not show results for the domain of immigration. Questions of immigration were mostly asked in Western European countries. Because of the lack of variance, the corresponding model cannot include variables on political rights. The predicted effect of PR is negative, but statistically insignificant (p>0.1). Similarly, the age of democracy appears to be of little importance. The

Table 4.3: Multivariate analyses for nationalism, religion in politics, and deregulation

	Nationalism			Religion in politics			Deregulation		
	B	SE	p-value	B	SE	p-value	B	SE	p-value
Constant	0.68	0.12	0.000*	0.72	0.17	0.001*	0.70	0.19	0.002*
Electoral formula									
Mj/MMM (Base)									
PR/MMP	0.02	0.05	0.758	−0.09	0.07	0.168	−0.05	0.04	0.162
Political rights	0.05	0.03	0.094+	−0.003	0.03	0.921	0.03	0.03	0.292
Age of democracy	0.03[a]	0.08	0.748	0.02[b]	0.01	0.059+	0.00[b]	0.00	0.194
R^2	0.25			0.33			0.19		

Notes: Multivariate models (OLS) of three additional issue domains, with representation scores as the dependent variable. *Significant at $p<0.05$, + significant at $p<0.1$. [a] Age of democracy measured as the contrast between old and new democracies as in Table 4.2. [b] Age of democracy measured in years, because all countries covered are new democracies. N=17 for nationalism and deregulation; N=18 for religion in politics.

addition of regional variables does not change the picture (p>0.1). With variables differentiating between different predominant religions, the model fit rises (R^2=0.20), but no variable is a significant covariate (p>0.1). In order to test the robustness of the findings reported in this chapter, I have analysed sub-samples and used different estimates for the left–right domain; however, no substantive difference to the reported results can be observed.

Beyond the electoral system

In this chapter, I have examined levels of policy representation in order to complement the analysis of descriptive representation in the previous chapters. For almost half of the domains, it proved impossible to identify clear covariates in the multivariate analyses. Perhaps the causes of high levels of representation are unique to each country and are more complex than anticipated; perhaps a key variable was missing. However, it may be possible to identify a more coherent story by changing perspectives and looking at the role of individual variables.

The electoral system appears to be a statistically insignificant factor when it comes to high levels of policy representation: the proportionality between votes cast and seats gained seems to be of little importance for the collective representational outcome. Given that this book does not consider party representation, it is unable to comment on the role of vote–seat proportionality in this case. The conclusion that there appears to be no association between the electoral system and levels of substantive representation is reflected in recent findings by McDonald *et al.* (2004) and Golder and Stramski (2010). Perhaps the individual voters and parties involved have developed suitable heuristics to work with the levels of disproportionality found in any particular electoral setting. This explanation would fit well with the association between the age of democracy and the proportionality of systems identified in the bivariate analysis, but no such effect was found in the multivariate analyses.

Powell (2007) argues that in some majoritarian systems, levels of representation have increased in the past decade, meaning that the difference to proportional representation (PR) systems has recently declined. Such explanations do not suggest that political institutions as such are irrelevant, but rather that their impact is not overriding, as often seems to be implied. Looking at the stability of new democracies, Cheibub (2007) comes to a similar conclusion. The results in this chapter, however, go beyond recent studies finding little influence of the electoral system on left–right representation by showing that the electoral system also appears to be of little significance in other domains. With the cross-sectional data used, it is not possible to test whether this lack of association now differs from the past, as Powell argues is the case for the left–right domain.

The electoral system may not be a significant explanatory factor of levels of policy representation, but three other variables proved useful in predicting the levels of policy representation: political rights, the age of democracy and – in some cases – the predominant religion of a country. All these factors are predicted by the theoretical framework. The age of democracy may be a significant factor as it takes time for the involved actors to familiarise themselves with the democratic setting. It is the time needed to learn about the political rhetoric and to develop heuristics to gauge the policy positions of the parties – or, conversely, the time needed to judge the views of the population. This factor appears to be important for the role of religion in politics, but also, more crucially, for the left–right domain. If the involved actors can adjust to the particularities of the electoral system, it becomes possible to explain why there is a correlation between vote–seat proportionality and levels of left–right representation in new democracies, while the same association is less clear in more established democracies.

Although attitudes relevant to policy representation may be difficult to capture directly, underlying factors and attitudes in society seem to matter for a number of domains, including the predominant religion. The predominant religion of a country is a significant factor for the domains of deregulation and social issues, and a possible factor for the domain of privatisation, as well as for views on immigration. The importance of attitudes and values established for descriptive representation is reflected here for policy representation, although in a less direct manner. Whilst religion is often linked to attitudes and views in society (Eposito and Watson 2000; Norris and Inglehart 2004), it may not always be clear how it affects the levels of representation.

Political rights – the freedom and ability to express views and participate in politics – are a factor linked to high levels of representation in the political left–right, social issues and nationalism. It may be that political rights are more significant than outlined because the sample of countries included in this chapter is relatively homogeneous in terms of political rights. In contrast with the other two factors that seem useful to explain levels of substantive representation, political rights seem more suitable for electoral engineering with the aim of increasing levels of substantive representation. Further research is needed to establish whether improved political communication between the representatives and the citizens leads to higher levels of representation, or whether a different factor influences levels of representation.

This list of factors that are most significant for high levels of policy representation, however, does not appropriately take into account the different levels of salience the various policy domains have in each country (Klingemann *et al.* 1994). That it is difficult to predict high levels of representation in some of the domains may be a reflection of the fact that the issues examined are less salient in some of the countries. Where issues are less salient, it is probable that many citizens lack crystallised views, which makes matching these views difficult for the representatives. The data used in this chapter mean that all domains included are relatively salient for the countries covered. However, if the salience of issues and policy domains is an explanation for levels of substantive representation, the implications for electoral engineering might be somewhat different from those outlined above. In this case, the role of the media, civil society organisations and interest groups in influencing the salience of issues are of interest. A difference also exists regarding levels of descriptive representation – these levels appear to increase over time. Regarding substantive representation, it seems difficult to maintain high salience for all issues, which probably leads to fluctuations in the levels of representation achieved in different domains over time. The only domain that might be exempt from such fluctuations is the left-right domain, where levels of representation are associated with the age of democracy, and it can be speculated that this also reflects changes over time.

chapter five | the relationship between different forms of representation

In this final empirical chapter, the focus is on the relationship between different forms of political representation. It addresses the question whether there are factors associated with high levels of political representation generally. Is it the case that some countries or systems are simply 'better' at representing the citizens in national legislatures? Whereas the previous chapters looked at underlying covariates for different forms of representation in turn, I now examine the association between levels of different forms of representation; in particular, the question of whether different forms of representation are linked. To this end, both substantive and descriptive forms of representation are considered.

The chapter is structured into three major sections. First, the links between different descriptive dimensions are addressed, then the next two sections examine associations between different issue domains and between descriptive and substantive forms of representation, respectively. The nature of the data used means that it is not possible to examine the substantive representation of women or ethnic groups: the extent to which their interests are represented in legislatures. This chapter analyses descriptive and substantive representation more generally – with the focus firmly on the second research question: *how are levels of representation in different forms linked?*

Levels of descriptive representation appear to be studied in isolation: studies concerned with the political representation of women do not directly address the representation of ethnic minority groups or vice versa. Some of the comprehensive studies on legislatures (Ross 1943; Converse and Pierce 1986; Copeland and Patterson 1998; Norris 2004; Kostadinova 2007) consider multiple dimensions – gender, ethnicity, age, education – but no attempt is made to compare the differences in levels of representation. Htun (2004) considers both gender and ethnicity, but focuses entirely on the nature of quotas rather than questions of political representation. She highlights that gender differences necessarily cut across parties, whilst ethnic differences may coincide with parties. Similarly, Bird (2003) includes both women and visible minorities, while Norris (2004) treats the representation of women and ethnic minorities, but neither provides a comparison. Norris draws on Taagepera (1994) and Lijphart (1999), who argue that the under-representation of women and ethnic minorities can be understood as two sides of the same coin. They argue that the level of representation in one dimension may be used to approximate the other. Walby (2009) takes a quite different approach, highlighting the uniqueness and complexity of inequalities, implicitly suggesting that we should not expect a relationship between representational outcomes in different forms. The results in the empirical chapters, however, suggest that a direct relationship should not be dismissed.

A limited number of studies consider multiple issue domains, and thus indirectly address the relationship between different domains. Birch (2000) examines policy representation in the Ukraine and finds the highest levels of political representation in economic issues. She argues that this reflects the importance people attach to these issues compared to others. This infers that the salience of issue domains may be a key factor shaping the relationship between levels of representation in different domains (see also Lutz 2003). Dalton (1985) looks at the link between party voters and representatives in the European Parliament. The smallest differences can be observed in terms of left–right rather than the more specific scales. Pierce (1999) and Thomassen and Schmitt (1997) also find the highest levels of representation in the generic left–right domain. Similar levels of representation to the left–right domain can only be found in terms of views on unemployment, although with much greater variance (Schmitt and Thomassen 1999).

Studies tend to focus on these different forms of representation in isolation. This is not entirely surprising, given that studies on descriptive representation are often rooted in questions of social justice and legitimacy, whilst studies on substantive representation usually take policy making as the starting point. Thus, when it comes to directly comparing levels of descriptive and substantive representation, there are no real empirical precedents. The closest the literature comes is asserting that individuals perceive politics primarily in terms of issues and policies rather than demographic aspects (Dalton 1985; Darcy et al. 1994).

In order to examine the relationship between different forms of political representation, I test the hypothesis that because of the shared covariates and underlying factors involved in shaping political representation, similar levels of representation can be expected in different forms of representation. Such shared covariates include the electoral system and candidate effects, as well as the influence of cultural attitudes. I test the relationship between different descriptive dimensions, between different policy domains, as well as the relationship between descriptive dimensions and policy domains. Consideration is given to the salience of demographic divisions and policy domains. As outlined in the theoretical framework, the salience of divisions is understood to mean the awareness and politicisation of under-representation in the case of gender and ethnic group representation, as well as the importance assigned to different domains in the case of policy representation. The salience of divisions may play a key role in voters making up their minds. Voters are thought to (have to) do many things, including considering different forms of representation or holding the legislature to account. This process may well lead voters to compromise between different considerations.

In Chapters Two and Three, I identified factors associated with higher levels of representation for ethnic minorities and women, such as the age of democracy or cultural attitudes. This suggests that shared factors for levels of gender and ethnic group representation exist. The expectation is then that levels of gender representation are positively correlated with levels of ethnic group representation. In Chapter Four, no such underlying variable was identified for levels of representation in different issue domains, meaning that this hypothesis is unlikely to hold for all forms of representation. Focusing on the salience of different forms, however, it may be that the relationship between levels of representation in different forms is shaped by considerations that cut across shared covariates.

The analysis in this chapter utilises the same representation scores as the previous chapters on descriptive and substantive representation. Descriptive and substantive forms of representation are compared with the theoretical framework as the basis. The task of the third section is to compare levels of representation with respect to an essentially categorical concept (demographic group membership) to levels of representation with respect to an essentially continuous concept (issue positions). In theory, this could be resolved by measuring substantive representation in a categorical way. Such a measure would be closely associated with the one based on the mean used in this book. With the data available, only the mean-based measure is attainable. In a categorical approach, the simplest case is to consider the proportions left and right of the mid-point. If the proportion of citizens on the left is larger than the corresponding group of representatives, for example, the representation score is lower. At the same time, the mean position of the citizens is further to the left: a larger difference in means. Where the proportions of citizens and representatives on the left differ significantly, the distance of the means is also larger. This means that the measurement based on mean positions is likely to be associated with a hypothetical measurement based on categories. This is also case for hypothetical measurements using a larger number of categories. Where the proportions differ more in each category, the difference between means is also larger.

The basic assumption behind this argument is that the distributions of issue positions for citizens and representatives are somewhat similar. Following Galtung (1967) and Holmberg (1999), I checked the distributions of all policy domains using the AJUS system as far as possible with the data. No problem cases could be identified in which the shapes of the distributions of the population and the representatives differ in an obvious way. This would be the case, for example, if the distribution was polarised in the population and concentrated around the mean for the representatives. The lack of obvious disparity means that the differences picked up by the mean positions are unlikely to stem from distributions that vary significantly between citizens and representatives.

The argument of correlation means that the representation of issue positions is measured in a way likely to approximate approaches that treat issue positions in a categorical sense, just as ethnicity or gender. Consequently, the relationship between levels of descriptive and substantive representation can be evaluated. Since the comparability between levels of descriptive and substantive representation cannot be resolved completely, the analyses employed are not sensitive to a precise measurement of representation. The main conclusions of the chapter can also be drawn solely on the sections that compare different descriptive dimensions and different policy domains respectively, two sections where comparability is clear.

Dimensions of descriptive representation

In this section, I examine whether there is link between the levels of descriptive representation in different dimensions (see also Chapters Two and Three). Commencing with shared covariates and explanatory factors, the expectation is that there will be a positive correlation between levels of gender representation and levels of ethnic group representation. The perception is that the same explanatory variables are associated with high levels of representation in both cases. However, voters may not have the option to vote for both descriptive dimensions at the same time. This would occur if they were compelled, more often than not, to choose between either women or candidates from an ethnic minority group. Where levels of gender representation are directly traded off against ethnic group representation, a negative correlation between the different representation scores can be expected. The salience and politicisation of demographic cleavages in society may play a role in shaping this trade-off between different forms of representation. The argument is that representation scores are higher in dimensions that are more salient.

The actual make-up of society may be an indicator of the salience and politicisation of demographic differences. For instance, in countries that are ethnically more heterogeneous, the salience of ethnic divisions may exceed that of gender differences.[1] The expectation in this case is that levels of ethnic group representation exceed levels of gender representation. Presumably, the reverse is also the case. However, it needs to be borne in mind that in relatively homogeneous countries in terms of ethnicity, high representation scores necessarily follow. Consequently, relative representation scores (R-scores) are used to examine this proposition. These relative scores are not affected by the size of the minority group.

In addition to gender and ethnicity treated in Chapters Two and Three respectively, other descriptive dimensions can be considered. For instance, divisions along the lines of linguistic and religious differences are in some places fundamental aspects of ethnic identity. However, both language and religion can be understood as descriptive dimensions in their own right (Lijphart 1979). Given that the theoretical framework was formulated for all kinds of representation, the hypothesis of shared covariates can be reformulated into the expectation that levels of representation in all dimensions are positively correlated, including levels of linguistic and religious representation. This widens the scope of the analysis in this section. The sample for religious and linguistic representation is too small to treat these forms of representation separately in a systematic manner. Nonetheless, they remain of interest for the relationship between different forms of representation.

---

1. I do not measure the salience of gender divisions in this chapter directly. The makeup of the population is unsuited in this case, but different measures are potentially available. None of these are included, both because I was not completely convinced by the validity of the measures and because of data availability issues. Nonetheless, indicators in the direction of wage gaps, women's health, or the strength of the women's movement are worth investigating in further research.

Exceptionally high refusal rates during data collection and the lack of secondary data meant the sample (N=13) for religious group representation is very small. The key covariates appear to be the presence of parties with a religious focus as part of their manifesto, and possibly attitudes towards marginalised groups. In the case of religious representation, there is only one country in the sample with a majoritarian electoral system, and it comes with lower levels of representation than in any of the countries with proportional representation (PR) systems. Older democracies may have slightly higher levels of religious representation, whilst there is a substantive association between the presence of religious parties and the level of representation. Given the small sample, none of the associations is statistically significant (p>0.1). In most places, religious minorities are underrepresented. Analyses on the representation of language groups are based on a larger sample (N=30). In contrast with the other descriptive dimensions, the representation of linguistic groups seems unaffected by either the electoral system or cultural aspects. The level of representation is higher in countries where minority groups are geographically concentrated (p<0.01). In a multivariate analysis, only geographical concentration, the age of democracy and the control of cultural heterogeneity are statistically significant (p<0.05, R^2=0.74). Cultural heterogeneity incorporates considerations of linguistic similarity when determining the value of heterogeneity (Fearon 2003).

In order to address the hypothesis of shared covariates, Table 5.1 summarises the key explanatory factors for the representation of all four descriptive dimensions considered in this section. Significant factors are indicated with one or two asterisks. Cultural attitudes appeared to be the key covariates in the analysis of gender and ethnicity. The same is also true for the smaller sample available for religious representation, together with the presence of religious parties. For linguistic representation, in contrast, the geographical concentration of minority groups seems to be the most significant factor. Similarly, the age of democracy may be associated with levels of gender, ethnic and linguistic representation. It appears, therefore, that the hypothesis of shared covariates has some merit, as there are shared covariates for three of the descriptive dimensions. However, the argument that levels of representation are linked within countries appears unsubstantiated by the actual representation scores, as these scores for gender and ethnicity do not correlate significantly (r=0.05, p>0.1). The shared underlying factors outlined in Table 5.1 are not reflected in correlations between levels of descriptive representation, therefore the hypothesis of shared covariates cannot be supported.

A different explanation is based on the view that higher levels of representation in one form may come at the cost of another form; direct trade-offs between different forms of representation. In the case of descriptive representation, this would occur if voters were more often than not forced to choose between either women or ethnic minority candidates, because the available candidates would mean that it was impossible to vote for both. If the voters (on average) deal with such cross-pressures in a similar manner, and levels of gender representation are directly traded off against the level of ethnic group representation, the outcome is a negative correlation. The expectation therefore is that levels of gender

Table 5.1: Explanatory factors across four descriptive dimensions

Variable	Gender	Ethnicity	Religion	Language
Electoral formula	Yes*			
Quotas	Yes*	(Yes)		
Specific parties[†]			(Yes)	
Age of democracy	Yes	Yes*		Yes**
Development	Yes			
Ethnic heterogeneity (Control)		Yes**		Yes**
Concentrated minorities		—		Yes**
Predominant religion	Yes	Yes		
Cultural attitudes[‡]	Yes**	Yes**	(Yes)	

Notes: Given is a summary of bivariate associations for the different descriptive dimensions. Factors that appear to be associated, but where the association is not statistically significant are given in brackets. *Factor remains significant in a multivariate analysis; other factors are only significant in bivariate associations. **Factor still remains significant when considering cultural attitudes measured directly. †Specific parties refer to linguistic and religious parties respectively. ‡Cultural attitudes refer to attitudes towards women in politics in the case of gender representation, and attitudes towards marginalised groups in society in the case of ethnicity, religion and language.

representation are negatively correlated with levels of ethnic group representation (Banducci *et al.* 2004; Grey 2006; Holmsten *et al.* 2010; Shella 2011a, 2011b). Given that attributes of gender and ethnicity are not exclusive, there is little reason to assume voters are frequently forced into such a direct trade-off, and this proposition seems less likely than one where a positive correlation is predicted.

The lack of association outlined above equally means that there is no negative correlation. Given that, there is no evidence of a direct trade-off between the two dimensions of representation. Moreover, there are no significant correlations with the other descriptive dimensions of religious and linguistic representation ($p>0.1$). Thus, the proposition that all forms of descriptive representation are linked – including language and religion – cannot be supported for any of the forms of representation considered.

In order to address the nature of a possible trade-off between levels of gender and ethnic group representation, it is necessary to look at the difference between representation scores. In many countries, the difference between levels of ethnic group representation and gender representation is large, although there are also countries where levels of representation in the different dimensions largely coincide. Overall, levels of gender representation tend to be lower than in the other dimensions, often significantly lower. The mean representation score for gender representation is 0.66, whereas for ethnic groups the corresponding value is 0.93

Table 5.2: Comparison of representation scores

	N	Mean	Min	Max	Range	Std. Dev.
Gender	131	0.66	0.49	0.95	0.46	0.10
Gender (Sub-sample)	101	0.66	0.49	0.95	0.46	0.10
Ethnicity	101	0.93	0.69	1.00	0.31	0.07
Language	30	0.92	0.69	0.99	0.30	0.08
Religion	13	0.87	0.78	0.95	0.17	0.06

Notes: Given are the number of cases, the mean scores and the range for the four different dimensions of descriptive representation. The gender sub-sample includes the countries for which there is also an ethnic representation score.

(see Table 5.2). This difference might be a reflection of the fact that, in terms of gender, all countries are necessarily highly heterogeneous, a fact that is addressed in the subsequent analysis, where the salience and politicisation of different dimensions is considered.

The relationship between levels of gender representation and levels of ethnic group representation may be characterised by the salience of the corresponding division rather than a direct trade-off. In the context of this section, the salience of social divisions refers to the awareness and politicisation of under-representation of women and certain ethnic groups. Of interest is the salience of ethnic divisions relative to the salience of gender divisions in society. This factor of salience is highlighted in the scant literature on the relationship between different descriptive dimensions, and it was introduced in the theoretical framework. The premise is that where divisions are more politicised, it can be assumed that parties are more likely to mobilise on that basis, and that voters are more likely to vote on the division in question (Birch 2000; Mateo Diaz 2005). The relationship between levels of ethnic and gender representation may thus be affected by varying awareness: divisions that are more salient can be expected to lead to higher representation scores.

Empirically, the salience of divisions and awareness of under-representation is difficult to attain. With regard to ethnic divisions, in this chapter it is assumed that such differences are more politicised in societies that are more heterogeneous (Milne 1981). Consequently, in this section the ethnic heterogeneity of a society is understood as a proxy of salience. This measure is not perfect because there are other influences, e.g. historical, on the salience of ethnic divisions in a country. However, ethnic heterogeneity scores are probably the best available data for the cross-national analyses in this chapter. Given that the proportion of women is relatively constant across societies, no equivalent measurement of gender heterogeneity can be included. For the purposes of examining the impact of salience, the level of ethnic heterogeneity is used as an approximation of the relative salience of ethnic divisions. The argument follows that where ethnic heterogeneity is high, ethnic representation scores are expected to be relatively high compared to gender representation scores. By extension, where ethnic heterogeneity is low, levels of gender representation are expected to be relatively high compared to levels of ethnic group representation.

The focus on relative representation means that R-scores are used to examine this proposition instead of the representation scores used elsewhere in this book, because R-scores are not affected by the heterogeneity of the population (see Chapter Three for the concept of relative representation). These R-scores simply state what proportion of women or the ethnic minority population is included in the legislature, irrespective of the size of the group. R-scores greater than one correspond to a numerical over-representation. However, because relative representation scores are based on ratios, outliers may affect the findings a great deal; therefore, median values are compared in the analysis that follows.

Table 5.3: Relative ethnic and gender representation in high and low ethnic heterogeneity

	High ethnic heterogeneity	Low ethnic heterogeneity
Gender (R-scores, median)	0.30	0.34
Ethnicity (R-scores, median)	0.63	0.28

Notes: This table compares median values of relative representation scores (R-scores) by level of ethnic heterogeneity. The level of ethnic heterogeneity is used as a proxy of the relative salience of ethnicity rather than gender. Differences of median values are significant at the 0.01 level. High heterogeneity means more heterogeneous than average, low heterogeneity means less. N=101.

Table 5.3 shows that both the propositions outlined above are supported. In places where ethnic heterogeneity is higher, the relative level of representation of ethnic minority groups is higher than that of women (0.63>0.30). At the same time, in places where the ethnic makeup of society is more homogeneous, the level of gender representation is higher (0.34>0.28). The salience of demographic divisions appears to be associated with the levels of descriptive representation achieved ($p < 0.01$). I have checked the robustness of this result by removing Nordic countries from consideration, as well as removing outliers where ethnic R-scores are greater than one because a minority group is considerably over-represented, but the reported relationship is not significantly affected.

To provide more detail, the correlation between ethnic heterogeneity and relative representation scores for gender and ethnicity were examined. Levels of ethnic heterogeneity are positively correlated with the difference between relative levels of ethnic representation and relative levels of gender representation ($r=0.41$, $p<0.001$). Levels of ethnic heterogeneity are positively correlated with relative levels of ethnic group representation ($r=0.40$, $p<0.001$), whilst they are negatively correlated with relative levels of gender representation ($r=-0.25$, $p<0.01$). This indicates that, in practice, higher levels of relative gender representation are traded off against higher levels of relative ethnic group representation, in accordance to the relative salience of divisions – as measured by the level of ethnic heterogeneity. The reported relationship is not entirely driven by the association between levels of ethnic heterogeneity and relative levels of ethnic group representation.

In this section, I examined the relationship between levels of ethnic and gender representation. Even though some of the underlying factors are shared, overall, no significant association can be determined. I also examined cases where levels of ethnic and gender representation may differ, illuminating the relationship between different descriptive dimensions. It appears that, where levels of ethnic heterogeneity are higher – and with that, the salience and politicisation of difference presumably increased – the level of relative ethnic group representation is greater than that of women. The opposite is also the case: where levels of ethnic heterogeneity are lower, the level of relative gender representation is higher than that of ethnic groups. Levels of representation appear to be higher in dimensions that are more salient and politicised.

Considering that in many places representation scores for ethnicity are higher than those for gender, it is possible to speculate about the order of events over time. It may be that in many places, relatively high levels of representation of ethnic groups precede higher levels of gender representation. Other forms of representation, such as religion and, by extension, the representation of sexual orientation, toward (post-modern) lifestyle choices, may follow suit. Included in these considerations is the observation of increased demands for descriptive representation in legislatures on grounds of justice: success in one dimension may lead to demands in another (Allwood and Wadia 2004).

The order of events may differ depending on the salience of divisions in society. In some divided societies, the cleavage of religion, for instance, has led to parties adding religion to their programmes and thus increasing levels of representation. The elite may play a role in politicising a certain division, although the results above suggest that the actual make-up of society may be the prevalent factor. This means that the historical aspects of nation-building may affect present-day representation in national legislatures. High levels of descriptive representation may also be achieved in a country where one of the dimensions is a non-issue and the salience of a division approaches zero, in the sense that members of different groups are treated the same. Consequently, and purely based on probability, the legislature would be mirroring the population nearly perfectly. However, this probably does not apply to the divisions examined in this book.

Domains of policy representation

In this section – having looked at the relationship between different descriptive forms of representation – I consider the relationship between levels of representation in different policy domains. Once again, the logic of shared covariates can be applied. The argument is that because of shared underlying factors, the levels of representation in different domains should be positively correlated. Given the results in Chapter Four, however, such an association seems unlikely.

As outlined above, and following the results of the previous section, a different view can be justified when looking more closely at the nature of the left–right domain. This argument is based on the view that the level of representation can be expected to be higher in more salient domains. Because the left–right scale is a summary of political issue positions, the representation scores in the left–right domain ought to be more salient and thus exceed the levels of representation achieved in other domains. This expectation is particularly applicable to more established democracies in which the positions of left and right have become more solidified and meaningful over time.

The hypothesis tested in this section, however, is concerned with a positive correlation between different domains owing to shared underlying factors. The relationship between different issue domains indicates that there are no significant positive correlations between different domains (Table 5.4). For instance, levels of representation in the social domain appear independent from political left–right scores ($r=0.21$, $p>0.1$). The lack of positive correlations means that the hypothesis of shared covariates cannot be supported. Levels of representation in different domains do not appear to be positively associated with each other. To some extent, this finding is consistent with Shafer and Claggett's (1995) presentation of politics as an essentially multi-dimensional space (see also Kitschelt and Hellemans 1990, Norris and Lovenduski 1995).

One possible explanation for this lack of positive association is that higher levels of representation in one domain come at the direct cost of representation in another form. This argument emerges when considering the choices of voters during elections. Political parties offer certain policy positions, but voters are required to choose a package (Roemer 2009). For example, it is impossible to choose the economic policies of party *A* and the foreign policies of party *B*, assuming that the policies of the parties diverge in the different domains. If the voters, on average, trade off one issue domain directly against another, the expectation is that levels of policy representation in different domains are negatively correlated.

This argument of direct trade-offs between different domains of policy representation does not fare much better than the argument of shared covariates and underlying factors. As visible in Table 5.4, most of the correlations are not significant. High levels in the left–right domain are most closely associated with low levels in the domains of deregulation and the domain of the role of religion in politics. Both these correlations are negative, indicating that voters on average are likely to trade off one against the other. Similarly, where views on social issues are well represented, this is not the case for views on immigration.

Table 5.4: Correlations between domains of policy representation

	LR	Social	Privat.	Environ.	National	Religion	Immigr.
Social issues	0.21						
Privatisation	0.19	0.02					
Environment							
Nationalism	0.15	−0.03	0.10	0.29			
Religion in politics	−0.49*	−0.28	0.07	0.32	0.31		
Immigration	0.06	−0.52*					
Deregulation	−0.51*	0.33		−0.29			0.05

Notes: Given are the correlations between representation scores in eight policy domains. *Significant at p<0.05. N ≥ 11; correlations for cells with fewer cases are not shown.

The three negative correlations in Table 5.4 might indicate that for some of the domains the proposition of direct trade-offs has some merit. Perhaps the results are a reflection of the fact that issue positions are generally combined within parties. For instance, if there is no party offering left-wing politics and the view that there should be an increased role of religion in politics, some voters are probably forced to trade off one against the other. Where such a combination of views is offered, a trade-off is not necessary. In places where such a combination of views is offered, a trade-off is not necessary. With the results in Table 5.4, it can be speculated that voters are trading off levels of representation in the most salient domain at the cost of representation in certain other domains, but it is unclear why the significant correlations observed are the ones where a trade-off is observed.

One explanation for the different correlations is that voters are constrained by the political system. In a country where the number of parties is larger, voters are more likely to find a party that fits their views across a range of different policy domains. On average, voters are thus less likely to have to trade off issue domains against each other. The effects regarding the number of parties were tested by regressing levels of representation in one domain on levels of representation in others, whilst controlling for the number of parties. Once the effective number of parties is controlled, the associations between levels of left–right representation and deregulation, and the social domain and immigration are no longer significant (p>0.1). Only the association between levels of left–right representation and religion in politics remains significant (p<0.05). For other domains of policy representation, no significant difference could be determined. This finding is in line with the argument presented.

A different explanation for the lack of association with levels of left–right representation may be the substantive meaning of left and right in different countries. This argument is linked to the argument of salience outlined at the beginning of the chapter. In Chapter Four, I argued that it lies in the nature of the left–right domain to soak up meaning from various other domains. The positions of left and right then become summary or shorthand positions for other political divisions. What follows is that the left–right domain becomes the dominant or most salient of the policy domains (Fuchs and Klingemann 1989; Knutsen 1997). This is probably the case in older democracies, where the positions of left and right have become solidified and meaningful enough to facilitate political communication. Because of the higher salience of the left–right domain, the expectation is that levels of left–right representation are higher than levels of other policy domains. In other words, levels of left–right representation may be associated with different issue domains in different countries, and this could explain the lack of overall association in Table 5.4. It is unclear whether there is a pattern to these differences. The correlations between levels of representation in different domains do not vary significantly between old and new democracies, or predominantly Protestant and Catholic countries (p>0.1).

Perhaps the first indication that the proximity between the positions of citizens and representatives may be closest in the left–right domain was Figure 4.1. The left–right domain is where citizens seem to be represented best in most countries: in twenty-seven out of forty-nine countries the highest level of policy representation is achieved in the left–right domain. Similarly, paired sample t-tests indicate that the left–right representation scores are significantly higher than in any other domain (p<0.05). This fits well with the argument that political left and right operates as a summary or shorthand scale. Political left and right appears to be the dominant domain when it comes to policy representation, enabling effective political communication. The fact that most correlations in Table 5.4 are statistically insignificant, however, suggests that the left–right domain is not a simple summary scale of the more concrete issue domains. The meaning of left and right may be more on how citizens perceive politics: a form of shorthand that refers to specific issue domains.

The relationship between different policy domains may also be shaped by their relevant salience: higher levels of representation in the issue domains that are more salient. To this end, the relationship between the domain with the highest level of representation and the most salient domain is examined, based on a question included in both the Comparative Study of Electoral Systems (CSES) and the *World Values Survey*. It lies in the nature of the measurements that there is a degree of uncertainty inherent in the variables of *highest score* and *most salient*. Neither the removal of uncertain cases nor their reclassification changes the overall pattern reported. Respondents are asked which political issue they consider to be the most pressing. Issues revolving around the state of the economy include concerns over economic stability and unemployment; social issues in most countries relate to the healthcare system.

Given the view that the left–right scale takes on meaning from other domains, it might be expected that it takes time for the involved actors – parties and citizens – to develop this meaningful summary or shorthand scale. Consequently, in new democracies the expectation is that the domain with the highest representation

Table 5.5: Highest level of representation in old and new democracies

	Old democracy	New democracy
Left–Right domain	22	4
Other domains	3	13

Notes: Given is the domain with highest levels of policy representation in old (left) and new democracies (top). Included are the left–right domain and all other domains combined. $\chi^2=17.83$, p<0.001. The result can be replicated when more policy domains are considered rather than combined.

score is more likely a domain other than left–right (compare Walczak and Van der Brug 2012). The intuition is that, initially, the political system focuses on a small number of issues and that consequently initial representation is highest in the corresponding domains. Over time, other issues are increasingly politicised and incorporated into positions of left and right. The result is not necessarily high representation scores in all domains, both because of contradictory positions and because some issue domains will be less salient. Following this argument, it can be expected that there is a positive correlation between the age of democracy and the level of left–right representation being higher than any other policy domain.

As outlined in Table 5.5, it seems very likely that the association between left–right being the domain with the highest score and old democracies holds (p<0.001). Whilst the results presented in this table are unable to say much about how the variables affect levels of representation, they clearly demonstrate that the age of democracy may be a significant factor when it comes to high levels of representation in the left–right domain. It might be that over time the involved actors find ways to create high levels of policy representation irrespective of the electoral formula. The actors involved seem to be able to adjust to the system, and on average – in the sense of left–right – the representational outcome seems reasonably high. Although speculative in nature, this argument would explain why the electoral institutions seemed to be of such little importance to explain the levels of policy representation in Chapter Four.

Table 5.6: 'Most important issue' in old and new democracies

	Old democracy	New democracy
Security	4	1
Economy	9	15
Social	10	0

Notes: Given are the issues considered the most important in old (left) and new democracies (top). $\chi^2=12.44$, p<0.01. If security is excluded as a possible issue, the differences are more marked (p<0.001).

Differences in representation can be understood as a reflection of development, rather than time passing. Although it is reasonable to think that overall development does not occur in a linear fashion (Sachs 1992), the following argument does fit a linear account. In terms of development, the issue citizens consider most important commences with security. The presentation in Table 5.6 might be misleading in this regard since in 2006 terrorism-related security was a highly salient issue in some of the established democracies, such as the United States or Spain. However, this illustrates the fundamental need for security: only when security is achieved are other concerns considered pressing. As a next step, the stability of the economy and issues of employment might be considered – issues of economic management and political stability. For the post-communist countries included in the sample, issues concerning the privatisation of key industries and deregulation of markets are in many cases highly salient. Similarly, issues of political stability reflect concerns over corruption in Romania, or the role of religion in politics in the Ukraine. Across countries, the economy is the most frequently mentioned of the most pressing issues. With increasing development, social issues become more prominent: in most cases, the healthcare system. This may occur once economic stability is taken for granted (see also Dalton *et al.* 1984). To a certain extent, these concerns are reflected in the domain with the highest score, but over time, the positions of political left and right take on a more encompassing meaning. Thus, the underlying factor driving changes in salience and the domain with the highest representation scores is how well the system is established – not necessarily the age of democracy in years to which the factor is closely associated.

Descriptive and substantive representation

This section attempts to bring together the dimensions of descriptive representation and different policy domains outlined above. This novel approach compares different forms of representation at the level of representative outcomes rather than the substantive representation of specific groups in society. The conclusions drawn from this section hinge on the assumption that levels of descriptive and substantive representation are somewhat comparable. I argued that even though the measurement of policy representation is based on mean positions rather than categories, it is likely that the observed patterns of associations are correlated to hypothetical associations based on a categorical measurement. Operating with the data available, the analysis in this section is the best possible with regard to comparisons between levels of descriptive and substantive representation in national legislatures.

The hypothesis of shared underlying variables is tested. On a theoretical basis, the same covariates were identified for both descriptive and substantive forms of representation. Consequently, levels of the two can be expected to be linked. This contrasts with the view that high levels of descriptive representation may come at the cost of high levels of substantive representation, reflected in a negative correlation. It is often asserted that voters perceive politics primarily in terms of issues and policies. Therefore, it can be expected that substantive differences

Table 5.7: Correlations between levels of descriptive and substantive representation

	Left–Right	Social issues	Environment
Gender	0.35*	0.10	0.28
Ethnicity	−0.03	−0.04	0.01

Notes: Given are the correlations between representation scores for gender and ethnicity (left), and three domains of policy representation (top). *Significant at p<0.05

are more salient than their descriptive counterpart, which is probably translated into the levels of representation achieved. The result is that substantive representation scores are expected to exceed those based on demographic characteristics.

Beginning with the argument of shared covariates, Table 5.7 outlines the correlations between levels of descriptive and substantive forms of representation. The table includes gender and ethnicity on one hand, and left–right, social issues, and the environment on the other. Not included in the table are the dimensions of linguistic and religious representation, as well as a number of issue domains because of the small number of cases in each cell. The only statistically significant correlation is that between gender representation scores and the levels of left–right representation (r=0.35, p<0.05). On close examination, it becomes clear that this effect is largely due to the difference between old and new democracies in the countries covered. In old democracies, gender representation tends to be relatively high regardless of the level of policy representation; in new democracies, levels of left–right representation tend to be lower in all cases. Their shared association with the age of democracy shapes the association between levels of gender representation and levels of left–right representation. Essentially, the same result can be replicated when regressing levels of left–right representation on levels of gender and ethnic group representation: only levels of gender representation are significant (p<0.05). There are no significant associations for ethnic group representation or the domains of social and environmental issues (p>0.1). The lack of significant positive correlations between the levels of representation in different forms means that the hypothesis of shared covariates can only be supported for the relationship between levels of gender representation and levels of left–right representation.

Proportional representation (PR) systems are often seen as a means of increasing both the levels of descriptive and substantive representation. Although in the chapter on ethnic group representation and policy representation no such association could be determined, the expectation would be that the associations outlined in this chapter are stronger under PR. Not surprisingly, there is no support for such interaction effects (p>0.1).

A different explanation is the argument of direct trade-offs between different forms of representation (Overby and Cosgrove 1996; Cameron *et al.* 1996; Bühlmann *et al.* 2010). When studying a particular form of political representation, it is often forgotten that citizens normally only have a single vote with which they are expected to achieve a number of different things, including expressing preference in terms of descriptive and substantive representation. Consequently, a direct trade-off between different forms of representation is a likely outcome. For example, if voters emphasise ethnic differences, candidates may be chosen based on their ethnicity rather than their ideological views or policy preferences. If the voters on average trade off representation in demographic terms against representation in terms of ideology and policy preferences, a negative correlation between descriptive representation scores and levels of substantive representation can be expected. The lack of a significant negative correlation in Table 5.7 however, means that the argument of direct trade-offs cannot be supported. There is no indication that higher levels of descriptive representation come at the direct cost of higher levels of substantive representation, or vice versa. Likewise, at the level of representative outcomes, higher levels of descriptive representation are not associated with higher levels of substantive representation.

Focusing on the differences between substantive and descriptive representation scores highlights the salience of social divisions. Based on the argument that divisions that are more salient lead to higher levels of representation, the expectation is that substantive representation scores exceed their descriptive counterparts. In most countries, the political space is primarily organised based on substantive rather than descriptive differences. Voters are equally thought to perceive politics principally in terms of issue positions, and vote on that basis. What follows is that, generally, ideological differences are likely to be more salient than their descriptive counterparts. Consequently, substantive representation scores should be higher than in any of the descriptive domains. This is probably particularly the case for left–right scores.

Overall, in 60 per cent of the countries studied, substantive representation scores exceed their descriptive counterparts. However, representation scores will be invariably high in a country with a homogeneous population. This affects levels of ethnic group representation in particular. One way to consider this is by restricting the view to gender representation. In this case, the relationship is very clear: levels of left–right representation exceed levels of gender representation in every case (100 per cent).

The role of ethnic group representation merits further investigation. This can be done by removing countries with an ethnically-homogeneous population, which excludes the cases where levels of ethnic group representation are invariably high from analysis. In this case, the percentage of countries with higher policy representation scores increases from 60 per cent to 70 per cent. However, the proportion of countries where ethnic divisions are relatively salient may in this case also be larger; thus, places are included where, to a certain degree, voters are more likely to vote based on ethnicity. Rather than dividing countries into ethnically heterogeneous and homogeneous, an alternative measurement can be used. Table 5.8 utilises the proportion of ethnic minorities as part of the total population. The table indicates for which form of representation the highest levels were achieved, grouped by the proportion of ethnic minority population. In this case, in all of the most homogeneous societies, the level of ethnic group representation is higher than levels of left–right representation. This is an artefact of the measure of representation used: the level of representation is necessarily high, since the proportion of the population not represented is small. Consequently, very high levels of left–right representation would be necessary for the left–right score to exceed the level of ethnic group representation.

In countries where the proportion of minority groups is larger, but is still under 10 per cent, the picture is mixed: in some countries, left–right representation scores are higher; in others, the representation scores for ethnic groups are higher. Looking at countries with a proportion of ethnic minority population of 10 per cent to 30 per cent, levels of left–right representation increasingly exceed those of ethnic group representation. In this group, 88 per cent of the countries' left–right representation scores are the highest of any form. In the most homogeneous countries, it is often the case that no member of an ethnic minority group is present in the legislature; in this group of countries, there is at least one minority member present in all the countries. However, it appears that in contrast to the more homogeneous countries, the presence of a single representative from an ethnic minority group in many cases is no longer sufficient for high levels of ethnic group representation.

At the end of the scale with more heterogeneous societies, the picture again becomes mixed. In two of the countries, left–right representation scores are higher; in two countries, ethnic representation scores are higher. A larger proportion of ethnic minorities in the population may increase the salience and politicisation of ethnic differences – and with that a sensibility for political integration. At the same time, if such integration does not occur – or only to a limited extent – the scope for lower levels of ethnic group representation is large in these countries.

Table 5.8: Highest level of representation by proportion of ethnic minority population

Ethnic minority population	Left–Right highest	Ethnic representation highest	N
0%–3%	0%	100%	9
3%–10%	38%	62%	16
10%–30%	88%	12%	17
30%	50%	50%	4

Notes: This table presents the proportion of countries where representation scores are highest in the left–right domain and the dimensions of ethnicity respectively (top), given at different levels of ethnic minority population (left). The categories chosen reflect the distribution of the values.

What emerges is that once the level of ethnic heterogeneity is considered, the argument of salience also supports the ethnic representation scores. In other words, discounting countries where levels of ethnic group representation are high because of the relative homogeneity of the society, left–right representation scores tend to be the highest scores achieved. The story is slightly different in countries that are more homogeneous, where ethnic representation scores are high in any case, or where a single representative from an ethnic minority group can make a difference. In countries that are more heterogeneous, a single representative is no longer enough for high levels of ethnic group representation, leading to the under-representation outlined in Chapter Three. Unfortunately, I do not have policy representation scores for the most heterogeneous countries considered in this book. With that, it would be possible to test the suggestion that in the most heterogeneous countries, ethnic differences become so salient and politicised that left–right scores are overshadowed. It is also possible to envisage the same relationship as observed in the medium heterogeneity groups if despite the high salience of ethnic divisions, some ethnic groups are under-represented – be it for historical reasons or issues of power.

A further consideration is that it is likely that the difference between substantive and descriptive representation scores is larger in countries that are more homogeneous. This argument follows the discussion on the make-up of society above, although the size of the observed effect may not be linear because of measurement issues in the case of policy representation. The intuition is that in societies that are more homogeneous, descriptive differences are less salient and thus the corresponding representation scores are comparatively lower. Similarly, in countries that are more heterogeneous the level of descriptive representation is assumed to be relatively high. At the same time, for the purposes of this argument, the salience of left–right is assumed to be independent of the make-up of society. Thus, the difference from policy representation scores is larger.

There are multiple ways to conceptualise differences between substantive and descriptive representation. I considered all of the following; highest scoring policy domain versus highest scoring descriptive dimension; highest substantive versus lowest descriptive, lowest substantive versus highest descriptive; and the lowest level achieved for each form.

Comparing the highest representation scores in each case leads to a relatively clear pattern: the difference between descriptive and substantive representation scores is largest in countries that are more heterogeneous than average. The association is strong and statistically significant (r=0.64, p<0.01), but the sign of the association is counter to the expectation outlined. This might be a result of the strong negative association between ethnic heterogeneity and levels of ethnic group representation. Excluding the ethnically more homogeneous countries from analysis demonstrates this, suggesting that the strong positive correlation is mainly driven by the measurement used. In the more heterogeneous countries – where levels of ethnic group representation are not necessarily high – the result is different. In countries that are more homogeneous than average, the difference is slightly larger, as stipulated by the argument. However, the effect is small and with the small sample not statistically significant ($r=-0.05$, $p>0.1$; $N=11$). Unfortunately, in contrast to the section above, where I compared levels of gender representation with levels of ethnic group representation, R-scores for policy domains cannot be calculated in a meaningful manner, and are thus unavailable to test this argument.

When focusing on differences that involve the lowest scoring descriptive dimension, no clear pattern of association can be determined. This appears to be the case because levels of gender representation tend to be significantly lower than levels of representation in other forms of descriptive and substantive representation. Whilst the highest policy representation scores are higher than the lowest descriptive representation scores in all countries, the opposite is not always the case. In 10 per cent of the cases, the lowest performing policy domain still exceeds its highest descriptive counterpart. If anything, this can be taken as support for the suggestion that voters primarily make sense of politics in terms of issues and policies. In none of the comparisons, however, did the proposition of larger differences in more homogeneous societies appear to have much merit. This was the case for the reported results, as well as for sub-samples of established or ethnically-heterogeneous countries, amongst others. Whilst the counter-intuitive positive correlation presented can be explained with the measurement of ethnic group representation, the sub-sample of ethnically-heterogeneous countries failed to provide a significant relationship, albeit hampered by a small sample size.

Salience and politicisation

This chapter has examined the relationship between different forms of political representation: between the representation of women and ethnic groups, between different policy domains, as well as between substantive and descriptive forms of representation. These considerations complement the other empirical chapters, where different forms of representation were approached in isolation. In the section on the relationship between levels of descriptive and substantive forms of representation, the comparability of measures is not immediately apparent – although I defended the position of different representation scores being comparable in a meaningful sense. This does not affect the other two sections, from which the substantive results of this chapter can be drawn: the results from the different sections are mutually supportive.

Throughout the chapter, I tested the hypothesis of shared covariates and underlying factors, but also paid attention to different explanations in order to illuminate the relationship between different forms of representation. These different explanations are:

> there are direct trade-offs between levels of representation in different forms; and the salience of divisions and awareness of under-representation may account for differences in representation scores.

The hypothesis based on the premise of shared underlying variables and correlates was rejected in almost all cases. The exception was the relationship between levels of gender representation and levels of left–right representation. Both these variables are positively associated with the age of democracy. Given the small size of the effect, relying on the age of democracy does not appear to be a good strategy with regard to increasing levels of representation more generally (see Chapter Two). In the other cases, however, the presence of shared explanatory factors does not directly translate into similar representational outcomes. This finding contradicts expectations that certain institutional settings – such as proportional representation systems – are associated with higher levels of representation in general.

Similarly, there is no clear evidence for the proposition that levels of representation in one form are directly traded off against levels of representation in another, as apparent in the lack of negative correlations between levels of representation in different forms. There are some significant negative correlations between levels of policy representation in different domains, but it is unclear why the particular correlations are significant and some disappear when controlling for the number of parties. For the relationship between levels of gender and ethnic group representation, or descriptive and substantive forms of representation, no significant negative correlation can be observed. This is encouraging for proponents of electoral engineering: there is no evidence that increasing levels of descriptive representation – for example by means of enforced quotas – would compromise levels of policy representation. At the same time, there is no indication that increasing descriptive representation increases substantive representation of the population as a whole. With the focus on representative outcomes, this chapter is unable to comment on the substantive representation of specific groups, such as women or ethnic minority groups.

An important influence on the relationship between levels of representation in different forms is the salience and politicisation of different political divisions. Throughout this chapter, the argument linked to the salience of different factors proved much more successful than those based on shared covariates or direct trade-offs. These findings are in line with studies that argue that salience is a key factor for policy representation (Birch 2000; Wlezien and Soroka 2007). I demonstrated that this appears to be the case not only for differences in policy representation, but also for differences in descriptive representation, which affects the relationship between different forms of representation. Particularly in the section on the relationship between different descriptive dimensions, it was possible to ascertain that demographic differences that are more salient seem to lead to higher representation scores. I approached this using ethnic heterogeneity as a proxy of the relative salience of ethnic divisions. The result is that, where ethnic divisions are thought to be more salient and politicised relative to gender divisions, levels of ethnic group representation tend to be higher than levels of gender representation. The inverse case – lower salience and lower representation scores – tends also to be the case.

The argument of salience was applied equally to policy preferences, in addition to demographic differences. In older democracies, left–right positions seem to have developed into more meaningful or useful shorthand positions, leading to higher representation scores in left–right relative to other policy domains. In most cases, levels of policy representation are higher than levels of descriptive representation. I argued that this is a reflection of the higher salience of ideological differences. This result fits well with the proposition that voters and other political actors perceive the political system primarily in terms of ideological differences and policy issues. The argument of salience crosses the division between substantive and descriptive representation. Higher levels of representation seem to be achieved in the forms of representation that are more salient, whether the underlying divisions are of descriptive or substantive nature. In many cases, the most salient division is the left–right domain, but the make-up of society means it is likely that ethnic differences dominate the political landscape in some countries.

This chapter addressed the second research question in this book – regarding the relationship between levels of representation in different forms – and the results suggest that levels of substantive and descriptive representation are not inherently linked. Based on the theoretical framework, I suggested that the salience of political issues and awareness of under-representation might influence the relationship between levels of representation in different forms. The key finding in this chapter, however, is that in most cases, the levels of representation in different forms are not associated. In particular, there is no evidence that higher levels of descriptive representation necessarily come at the cost of levels of substantive representation. With that, electoral engineering, in the name of group justice, may become viable.

chapter six | political representation between institutions and cultural attitudes

The variables associated with different levels of political representation were addressed in four empirical chapters (Chapters Two – Five); this chapter now brings the findings together. Not only are the main findings reviewed and discussed, but also additional factors that might influence the levels of political representation are addressed. It was not possible to consider adequately all potential factors that might influence levels of representation in legislatures. This is the case where no data are available or where measurement is inadequate. Some factors are highly context-dependent and not measurable as country variables – something that is necessary for inclusion in the cross-national comparison in this book.

I revisit Chapters Two to Five (the empirical chapters) in turn, summarising each and discussing the main findings, and then addressing additional influences on levels of political representation. This discussion includes the role of political parties, the supply of candidates, the implementation of quotas, as well as the role of the elite and individual voters. The consideration of additional factors provides a better and more complete understanding of political representation in general; it also helps identify areas worthy of further investigation. Not only does this discussion enable the research questions of this book to be addressed in a more nuanced way, but it also leads to a consideration of how levels of representation could be improved. The viability and effectiveness of electoral engineering – often suggested in the literature – are discussed in light of the findings in this book.

Chapter Two, focuses on the political representation of women. The strong bivariate effects of the electoral system and voluntary gender quotas were reduced once controls for regional differences and attitudes towards women as political leaders were introduced. While broadly consistent with the literature that considers the impact of cultural and institutional factors, the extent to which attitudes towards women in politics proved dominant contrasts with many previous studies. The results outlined regarding free and partly-free countries in Chapter Two suggest that cultural factors, particularly attitudes towards women as political leaders, dominate in the case of gender representation. The electoral formula may also play a role, although it cannot account for changes over time.

In line with all the literature concerning political culture in one form or another, issues of causal direction could not be resolved completely in this book (Fuchs 2007). In Chapter Two, I used a limited analysis over time to demonstrate that cultural attitudes may be closely associated with changes in the levels of gender representation. In addition, I highlighted that there are many factors shaping cultural attitudes, which makes it unlikely that the presence of women in legislatures has a significant influence on attitudes towards women in positions of power. Chapter One outlined a number of these factors, including the predominant religion of a country and the status of women as role models in public positions other than in the legislature, and I showed that these factors are statistically associated with variables that capture cultural attitudes. Whilst a certain degree of reverse causality cannot – and based on the framework presented in Chapter One, should not – be ruled out, I argued that the main direction of influence is from attitudes to levels of representation, rather than the other way around.

One factor that might affect levels of gender representation, but was largely absent in the empirical analysis, is the role of political parties. Political parties are major political actors, and their role in the recruitment of candidates can affect political representation (Leijenaar 1993; Simms 1993; Bystydzienski 1995; Allwood and Wadia 2004). The variables of candidate supply and voluntary quotas addressed this factor to some extent, but not sufficiently. Given that there are multiple parties to consider in each country, the cross-national perspective makes it difficult to account for the influence of individual parties and their actions.

Political parties influence political representation by their choice of candidates presented to the voters. Parties are important because they can set the rules and procedures of recruitment. To some extent, political recruitment is framed by the political system. The political culture and the key institutions of a country shape the norms and rules within parties, which in turn influence the way the recruitment process works (Skjeie 1993; Matland 2006; Schwindt-Bayer *et al.* 2010). Female candidates and minorities may be disadvantaged during recruitment due to the selection and nomination rules in place, particularly choices over what is considered relevant political experience. This makes selection and nomination more difficult for women and ethnic minorities in cases where they are also under-represented at lower levels of the political system. Norris (1993) identified party ideology as one factor as to why parties differ in their approach to candidate selection: left-wing parties often adopt a more egalitarian approach. Such differences in party culture may lead to unconscious and unintended discrimination towards certain aspirants (Appleton and Mazur 1993; Leyenaar 2004).

Quotas and affirmative action are often suggested as means to overcome recruitment issues within parties, forcing them to find suitably qualified aspirants (Bystydzienski 1995), but without diligent implementation such actions may remain ineffective (Paxton *et al.* 2010). In fact, when it comes to the successful implementation of gender quotas, the support for these quotas in the wider population may also play a role (Mueller 1988; Gray 2003). Contrasting quota regulations in Argentina and Chile, Gray (2003) argues that broad support for quotas in Argentina ensured diligent implementation, which in turn led to more women in the *Congress*. In Chile, support for quotas in the wider population was largely absent, resulting in unenforced regulations and no significant gain for women in politics. Rather than focusing on the institutional element as Gray does, it may be more appropriate – based on the results in the empirical chapters – to consider the incentives of the elite.

I argued that the political elite is influenced by the same political environment as the wider population (Anderson 2007; Peffley and Rohrschneider 2007). However, even if the selectors were completely detached from the cultural influences outlined, and assuming that the representatives are interested to stay in power, it would be in their rational interest not to be too much out of step with the demands of the electorate (Braud 1988; Laver 1997; Driscoll and Krook 2012; but see Kunovich 2012). Thus, in a country where a female candidate is unlikely to gain more votes than a man, the parties have little incentive to actively encourage women to come forward. In some instances, women candidates are considered an electoral risk (Rule and Zimmerman 1994; Norris and Lovenduski 1995). This means that although the actual implementation of procedures can encourage better representation within parties, the parties are unlikely to make use of such potential beyond what they consider beneficial for electoral success. However, Kunovich (2012) examines the role of preferential voting in Poland and concludes that the elite seem to consistently underestimate the extent to which voters support women.

Even if enforced quotas are used to increase the number of women in legislatures, they are unlikely to substantively shape attitudes towards women in politics. Chapter Two notes that when considering regional differences or the level of development, the share of women in legislatures in the past is not a significant covariate for attitudes towards women in politics in the present. This finding is in line with the argument that there are many other influences on cultural attitudes than the number of women in legislatures, such as the predominant religion of a country. Thus, whilst enforced quotas could increase the number of female representatives, the resulting impact on the status of women in society would probably be limited. Schwindt-Bayer (2010) studied women's representation in Latin America and she concludes that while women are now present in increased numbers across Latin America, they largely remain marginalised. Women tended to end up in the least powerful positions, and they did not gain substantial political power as the proportion of women in parliaments increased. More research of this kind is necessary beyond Latin America when assessing the impact of quotas on political representation and women's everyday life.

The experience of countries in Eastern Europe raises further doubts on the ability of quotas to shape cultural attitudes in any lasting manner. In these countries, enforced quotas ensured relatively high levels of gender representation during communist rule. However, with the fall of communism, not only did the quotas disappear, but the number of women in legislatures also dropped markedly (UN 1992; Dahlerup 2006). In these countries, the presence of women in legislatures during communist rule did not substantially increase support in the wider population for the inclusion of more women in legislatures.

Having considered additional influences on the representation of women, the role of parties in the recruitment of candidates is useful in explaining differences within countries. For the cross-national comparison in this book, however, the overall picture of the empirical chapter should remain unaffected. Attitudes towards women in politics are the strongest correlate for levels of the representation of women. The discussion of political parties highlights the potential of the party elite to influence overall levels of representation, particularly through quotas. However, considering incentives of electoral success, I argued that cultural factors are likely to remain dominant.

Chapter Three examines the representation of ethnic groups. The results in this chapter cast doubt on the suggestion that institutional factors are the main factors shaping ethnic group representation. When the control for the ethnic make-up of society is applied, the significant covariates are cultural factors rather than institutional aspects. However, when quota regulations were looked at more closely, it became clear that the role of institutional factors could not be ignored in individual cases. The manner in which quotas for ethnic minority groups are implemented seems of great importance. Across countries, the lack of diligent implementation seems to be the reason why ethnic quotas are an insignificant factor in the cross-national comparison, despite being enforced measures. Whilst cultural aspects – measured as attitudes towards marginalised groups in society – appear to be the key driver of ethnic group representation, it seems that strong leadership in conjunction with adequately implemented quotas could equally work to increase the level of ethnic group representation. Indeed, the lack of overall association does not mean that institutions and electoral systems never matter. In individual cases, institutional arrangements certainly can affect levels of representation – a clear case is Bosnia and Herzegovina with its strict ethnic quotas in national politics. In this case, cultural attitudes do not appear dominant in shaping the level of representation.

The role of political parties in selecting candidates was considered above. Unfortunately, no appropriate data could be found for ethnic minority groups that would allow analysis at the national level. Compiling such data would be an area of further research, notwithstanding the separate need to consider aspects of supply at the party level. However, as outlined in the context of the representation of women, it seems unlikely that the absence of supply effects significantly impinge on cross-national models where cultural attitudes are incorporated.

Although quotas and related measures on the representation of ethnic groups are covered in Chapter Three, issues of implementation merit further consideration. In the empirical analysis, the provision of quotas did not appear to be associated with higher levels of representation. In this section, however, I attempt to combine these findings with considerations at a more individual level. The presence of quotas is controversial in any case, even if they may be an effective means of increasing the number of representatives from ethnic minority groups. The preferential treatment underlying such measures is at odds with principles of equality and meritocracy (Miller 1999; Mansbridge 2005), but is sometimes defended as unavoidable to reach a fairer outcome. There is always the possibility of a backlash because of the controversial nature of quotas (Jones 2005; Ayata and Tütüncü 2008), but further research is needed to understand the longer-term consequences, including whether citizens adjust to the changed setting. Strong quotas may be rare because although politicians may be willing to implement changes, the will to stay in power is stronger.

It is often argued that a successful implementation of quotas requires enforcement on behalf of the elite or the state (Stanley 1995; Gray 2003; Matland 2006). This argument is compatible with the findings in the empirical chapters, where quotas did not appear to be associated with higher levels of representation, possibly because of the lack of such enforcement. The elite may use enforced quotas or other forms of political engineering to increase the level of descriptive representation of specific groups. There may be international pressure to deal with under-representation, meaning that the elite considers quotas (Bennett 1991; Stone 2001; Paxton *et al.* 2006). However, as in the case of candidate selection, the cultural environment and incentives to stay in touch with the wider population may limit the impact of such external influences. In order not to alienate (potential) voters, measures may be chosen that technically address issues of under-representation without actually affecting the levels of representation.

The implementation of quotas and affirmative action go beyond the selection of candidates – parties often assign candidates to their respective seats. Fair rules of selection or diligently implemented measures may still fail at this stage; for example, women may be assigned seats that have little chance of success while more men end up in safe seats (Norris 1993). What may be at play here are attitudes at the micro-level – the attitudes of individuals. Where the party elite does not wholeheartedly embrace the rules and selection procedures, this can be problematic for newcomers, for example recent immigrants. For this reason, Norris argues that affirmative action is most effective when formalised and used in centralised parties, where it cannot be easily undermined by local branches. For example, the recent introduction of parity laws in France affected the selection of women candidates in all parties. Whilst the consequence was a significant increase in female candidates, women disproportionally ended up in unwinnable seats, greatly reducing the impact of the new legislation (Karp and Banducci 2007; Murray 2007). The same may happen with unenforced quotas for ethnic groups (Htun 2004). The outlined consequences can probably be best understood in terms of the incentives of the political elite seeking electoral success. The overall results are therefore unaffected: cultural factors remain the strongest correlates for differences in the representation of ethnic groups.

The third empirical chapter introduces considerations of substantive representation. Looking at different domains of policy representation, one can see that the electoral system again appeared to be of little significance for high levels of representation. This finding contradicts many previous studies, but it might reflect the time frame of the data, in line with some recent studies (Powell 2007). Powell argued that, in terms of policy representation, the differences between countries with majoritarian systems and countries with PR have largely disappeared. The analysis in Chapter Four is compatible with this view. No significant association between the electoral system and levels of left–right representation can be found – in this case, using a larger sample than Powell did. What is more, the results suggest that this lack of difference also applies to other policy domains, further supporting the argument of diminishing differences. More research is needed to explain the trend outlined by Powell, and also to investigate the findings of previous studies where levels of representation were found to be associated with the electoral system. The fact that the system remained and the associated effect seems to disappear probably indicates that the electoral formula on its own is the wrong variable. The operationalisation of the variable does not appear to be the reason for the reported lack of association.

No clear pattern could be determined across levels of representation in the different domains considered in Chapter Four. Different levels of left–right representation are closely associated with the age of democracy and political rights. Political rights are also associated with higher levels of representation in the domains of social issues and nationalism. The implication is that levels of representation are higher in more established systems, and that levels of representation could probably be increased by expanding political rights. The role of religion came to the fore in the domain of social issues, and perhaps on immigration. This is in line with expectations that the dominance of Catholicism influences the relationship between individual attitudes and the votes cast. Although religion is often linked to attitudes and values in society, it may not be entirely clear how exactly it influences levels of representation, but the results in this chapter suggest further research along this line is warranted.

Beyond the representation in legislatures, the actual power of and within national legislatures may affect policy outcomes (Gallagher *et al.* 2001; Heath *et al.* 2005). Such considerations of policy making are largely beyond the scope of this book, where representation is approached with questions of justice in mind and the analysis did not take account of policies. As will become apparent, adequate considerations of power within the legislature are difficult to implement in cross-national approaches. Powell (2000), for instance, argues that in terms of policy making, it is the government (rather than the legislature) that has the strongest influence. Powell demonstrates that in committee systems, where the opposition plays an active role in policy making, higher levels of substantive representation are the consequence. Such considerations of power require further research along the lines of Powell's work (2000). A full consideration would take into account a greater number of influences, including the strength of the opposition, involvement in committees, ad-hoc committees created for single issues, or the different status and power of different ministries (Gallagher *et al.* 2001; Escobar-Lemmon and Taylor-Robinson 2005). Additionally, representatives are usually active in only a limited number of issue domains, those in which they are relatively influential (Hall and Wayman 1990).

It is also important to recognise that national legislatures are not the sole actors in policy making (Diamond 2002). The influence of representatives on policies should be seen in relation to the power of external consultants, the power of a possible president, or the role of supreme courts. The influence of commissions and external experts appears to be growing as policy decisions become increasingly complex (Gallagher *et al.* 2001). Other influences stem from international pressure, which can limit the actual policy options available to representatives (Paxton *et al.* 2006). Additionally, there are the fiscal realities: policy making is caught between public demands and economic constraints (Bosanquet 1996, Page and Wright 1999), factors that may shift the focus of representatives and reduce levels of substantive representation. If one regards the role of legislatures solely as policy making, the influence and the power of (and within) legislatures undoubtedly merits investigation to establish to what extent representatives are able to represent the electorate in the face of such pressures.

In contrast with many previous contributions, Chapter Four could not confirm that the electoral formula is the strongest covariate for differences in levels of policy representation. On the contrary, and in line with some recent contributions, there appears to be a lack of association between the electoral formula and levels of left–right representation. The chapter demonstrated that this lack of association is found in all the policy domains considered, not just the left–right domain. Instead, it appears that other variables may be more significant for levels of policy representation, such as the age of democracy for levels of left–right representation.

Chapter Five, the final empirical chapter, focuses on the relationship between different forms of representation. It tested the hypothesis that shared covariates lead to a positive correlation between levels of representation in different forms. At the same time, attention was paid to the arguments that there might be a direct trade-off between levels of representation and that the salience of political divisions may shape levels of representation. The chapter suggests that neither shared covariates nor direct trade-offs directly shape the relationship between different forms of representation. In contrast, the suggestion that the salience of issue domains and descriptive divisions might account for differences in representation scores proved successful. It seems that more salient issue domains and an increased awareness of demographic differences translate into higher levels of representation. In most cases, policy differences remain dominant over demographic divisions.

With reference to the representation of ethnic groups, the elite had been already mentioned in the context of the implementation of quotas. In this section, a broader definition of elite is used so as to include members of the economic and social elite and prominent members of civil society (Etzioni-Halevy 2004; Blondel and Müller-Rommel 2007), in order to examine the influence of their actions on levels of representation. Empirically, it is difficult to determine who should be counted as a member of the elite (Becker 1983; Yach and Bettcher 2000; Givel and Glantz 2001). Therefore, the empirical chapters ignored whether the elite is able to influence levels of political representation. In this section, I consider agenda setting, as well as the motivations and incentives of the elite – both factors that may influence levels of representation and the relationship between levels in different forms.

By means of press releases and public statements, the elite and interest groups may be able to influence the political agenda. For example, they are able to draw attention to certain issues or to certain aspects of an issue (Smith 1995; Nestle 2002). Pressure groups, are often providers of information, both to the public as well as the more generalist representatives (Heclo 1978; Browne 1990). In terms of the relationship between different forms of representation, influence over the political agenda includes the ability to draw attention to the under-representation of women and ethnic minority groups.

The mass media play an important role in shaping and maintaining the political stories and the way issues are presented (Cohen and Young 1973; Bartels 1993; Iyengar and Reeves 1997; Kellstedt 2000; Soroka 2003). In practice, however, the power of the media is reduced since many news stories are reproduced without much mediation (Bryant and Thompson 2002; Lewis et al. 2008). Rather than playing an active role in shaping the views of the public, the media often release public relation statements, which may originate from companies with a particular agenda, interest groups, civil society organisations, government, or political parties. For the elite, the media can play an important function as a campaign tool, disseminating information that links the elite and the masses (Mainwaring and Scully 1995; Norris *et al.* 1999; Semetko 2007). Of course, the media may work for the citizens, acting as a watchdog that monitors political leaders and evaluates the performance of representatives.

The impact of the media on voters will vary according to context and there is disagreement in the literature over the extent to which the media affect citizens (Thompson 1995; Crigler 1996). If people have well-formulated preferences on political issues, it is likely the media have a relatively insignificant impact. In contrast, for new and unknown areas, the media are thought to be powerful, especially in terms of agenda setting, but this will vary dependent on context and those concerned. Only further research will establish whether the discernible nature of the mass media in a country has a effect on political representation at the national level.

The motivation of individuals to become representatives must also be considered; how they see their roles will affect their behaviour once elected into the legislature (Blondel 1973; Wessels 1999b). It is difficult to incorporate such considerations into a cross-national research design. However, it may be constructive to assume a certain degree of self-interest as this helps assess the possible incentives of the political elite to emphasise high levels of representation. For example, a representative or political party interested in re-election may be expected to emphasise representation and responsiveness to the citizens, but only to the degree that this goal is achieved. Consequently, higher levels of representation can be expected in the most salient issues: both the parties and the representatives are likely to focus on the issues they will be held to account for.

This argument fits with the findings in Chapter Five, where I show that levels of representation are higher in the forms of representation that are thought to be more salient. I argued that this is not only the case for different policy domains, but also for demographic differences. This assumption of self-interest has implications for political reform: should the political elite decide to include more women or minority candidates, or emphasise representation in a less salient policy domain on their own accord, the payoff in terms of electoral success may be limited, if not absent. Without demand for change in the population, the incentive to change the current state of affairs by the political elite is limited, i.e. change to the status quo is costly to the elite.

Individual voters might influence levels of representation. It is argued that voters perceive politics primarily in terms of issues and policies. Therefore, it seems reasonable for citizens to invest more effort into ensuring that their vote goes to the right candidate in this regard rather than any other aspect that an individual might also support. Mueller (1988) is clear that although many citizens are concerned about women's equality, when it comes to voting, the state of the economy and national security overshadow such concerns for social justice. This primacy of concern for issue positions means that men and women do not differ significantly in their support for women candidates (Dolin 2004). It also means that in places where the electorate are neutral towards the gender of a candidate, the elite can select an increased number of female candidates without affecting the electoral success of the party. This might have happened in Nordic countries, where parties included more women on closed lists.

It is likely that voters, as opposed to non-voters, shape levels of representation, for two reasons: first, they make their views known through the votes that are counted; and, secondly, representatives interested in re-election have a clear incentive to reach out to those who are likely to cast votes. Looking at policy representation in the United States, Griffin and Newman (2005) report that the views of voters are significantly better represented than those of non-participants. The result in the United States is a conservative bias.

Where the views and opinions of citizens are poorly articulated, it is difficult for representatives to meet expectations. However, the lack of crystallised views can be largely compensated for by means of heuristics and information shortcuts, such as party recommendations (Converse 2000; Kuklinski 2002; Schläpfer et al. 2004). Indeed, using experiments, Schläpfer and Schmitt (2005) have demonstrated that many voters are largely unable to formulate coherent preferences without such guidance, especially on issues that are less salient. However, citizens who simply lack clearly formulated preferences should not be regarded as irrational voters. Political views can be complex and, at times, contradictory, making it difficult and costly for citizens to formulate clear views on many issues. Unfortunately, considerations of the voting behaviour of individuals are difficult to incorporate in cross-national analyses. Further research in this area is warranted to establish whether patterns of individual voting behaviour differ significantly across countries, thus affecting overall levels of representation.

In this section, I have considered agenda setting and the actions of the elite, but these factors do not appear to influence in any significant way the relationship between levels of representation in different forms. If anything, the discussion helped to underline the importance of salience and awareness. The elite is in a position to influence levels of representation, such as the introduction of more women candidates, but self-interest with regard to re-election means this potential is rarely exploited.

Electoral engineering

In the remainder of this chapter, I discuss the viability of electoral engineering, together with intervention in the electoral system and the introduction of quotas referred to in the literature. Such steps are attempts to accommodate differences in the population when other approaches are either unsuccessful or too slow. Electoral engineering is put forward as a means of increasing the representation of parties – as was the case with the referendum on changing the electoral system in Britain in 2011.[1] It is also put forward as a way to increase levels of representation for

---

1. The final result of the UK-wide referendum was declared by the Electoral Commission on 7 May 2011, delivering a 'no' to changing the UK Parliamentary voting system.

women and ethnic minorities. In this section, I focus on the effectiveness of such intervention compared with the proportionality between votes and seats, for which changes in the electoral system have a relatively clear and predictable impact.

In Chapter Five, I established that there is generally no direct trade-off between levels of representation in different forms. In particular, higher levels of descriptive representation do not appear to come at the cost of high levels of substantive representation. This makes it worth considering forms of electoral engineering that attempt to increase levels of descriptive representation – which may be sought for multiple reasons. A key argument centres on group justice: because women and ethnic minorities are equal citizens, they have an equal right to sitting in legislatures. Suggestions that descriptive under-representation may be linked to substantive under-representation of particular issues make a more utilitarian case for focusing on the inclusion of ethnic minorities and women. The key argument is that the social, economic, and political environment affects different groups in society in different ways. Because of these different experiences, men and women may differ in some of their policy preferences. The same argument applies to ethnic minority groups.

From a justice point of view, some forms of electoral engineering may fall short of achieving their aims. Interventions such as reserved seats or enforced quotas may increase the number of women in legislatures, but that is as far as they go. It is conceivable that where women enter legislatures by means of quotas, rather than wider support in both the parties and population, women are omitted from the actual decision making processes (Schwindt-Bayer 2010). Powell (2000) highlights the need to consider the composition of governments and cabinets, in addition to legislatures. However, the proportion of women in legislatures is probably the single most significant factor predicting the number of women appointed as cabinet ministers (Escobar-Lemmon and Taylor-Robinson 2005; see also Högström 2012; Krook and O'Brien 2012). The proportion of women in the legislature is a good indicator of their involvement in policy making. Focusing on the representation of women in Mexico, Zetterberg (2008) finds no indication that women who entered the congress by means of quotas are marginalised more than any other woman in the legislature (see also Murray 2010; Schwindt-Bayer 2010). Generally, representation in legislatures can be regarded as valuable in itself, notwithstanding the actual involvement in policy making. The association between increased minority representation and perceived legitimacy, however, is not straightforward and linear (Scherer and Curry 2010). Increasing levels of descriptive representation do not always reduce the political alienation of minority groups and tensions around social cohesion, or increase levels of political and social participation.

Different methods of intervention to increase the number of women and members of ethnic minorities in legislatures are considered. The obvious relationship between votes cast and seats gained means that the electoral system itself is often considered. Perhaps the most drastic action is a change of electoral formula towards a more proportional variant (Lijphart 1977; Sartori 1997; Sisk and Reynolds 1998). Although such interventions are rare, there are examples, such as the recent switch to proportional representation in New Zealand (Zimmerman and Rule

1998). In France, a change in the electoral system was tried, but withdrawn later, whilst in Japan the change was from a majoritarian to a mixed system (Colomer 2004). Substantive changes to the electoral institutions influence the incentive structure, and therefore have an effect on voting behaviour. However, the consequences of such changes may be difficult to predict because many other factors influence both voting behaviour and the manoeuvring of political parties. Further research is needed to assess the impact of changes to electoral arrangements. Given the relatively low frequency of such changes, certainty about the impact of some of the institutional changes may never be achievable.

Proportional representation (PR) systems are often suggested as a means to increase the number of women in legislatures (Rule 1987; Matland and Taylor 1997; Paxton 1997; Reynolds 1999). The argument is sometimes widened to the representation of minority groups in general (Hogan 1945; Reynolds 2006). Particularly, PR systems with closed lists are highlighted (Kenworthy and Malami 1999; Matland 2006), although other aspects of the electoral system are also considered (Lijphart 1994; Sartori 1997; Reilly 2002; Birnir 2004; Norris 2004; Taylor 2005; Van Cott 2005). In the case of closed lists, levels of representation are dependent on the political parties including an appropriate number of women and ethnic minority candidates. This makes it clear that individuals within the political institutions make representation work (Wessels 2007; Osborn 2012). For instance, despite an electoral context wherein the arrangements are unfavourable to women and ethnic minorities, they may be included as part of the mainstream parties. In the United Kingdom, for example, the electorate does not seem to discriminate against Labour's all-women shortlists (Cutts and Widdop 2012). By contrast, there are countries where most parties exclude (specific) minority candidates, for example Russians in Estonia. In such cases, the electoral system in itself is unable to ensure adequate representation of minority groups in the legislature. The results in the empirical chapters suggest that changes in the electoral system are unlikely to affect levels of descriptive representation directly. Likewise, changes with the aim of increasing party representation (such as the one discussed in Britain) are unlikely to affect levels of descriptive representation negatively.

When it comes to levels of substantive representation, suggestions for higher levels of representation often depend on the focus of the individual study. The actions of the representatives are sometimes highlighted, although in line with the suggestions for descriptive representation, PR systems are frequently suggested for better congruence between citizens and representatives (Rae 1967; Lijphart 1994; Huber and Powell 1994; Powell 2000). Powell (2007) argued that, whilst PR systems were associated with higher levels of policy representation in the past, in recent years the difference from majoritarian systems has largely disappeared. This lack of association is reflected in the results presented in Chapter Four.

In contrast to changes in the electoral system, changes within political parties require the agreement of a significantly smaller number of people – often like-minded people – which can provide immediate results. When considering electoral engineering, the immediacy of change is of interest for political reasons (Engstrom and McDonald 1982; Jones 2005), although from the point of view of social justice, sustainable change is preferred. Institutional changes may have immediate effects, but these changes are not necessarily sustained over time. For example, the change in the electoral formula in New Zealand was associated with an unprecedented increase in the number of women elected to parliament. However, in subsequent elections, this increase could not be repeated and the long-term trend seems to be unaffected by the change of electoral formula. In the section on gender representation, I argued that, although the adoption of quotas is frequently put forward as a means of increasing the number of women and ethnic minorities in legislatures, quotas might not be associated with higher levels of representation because they are not implemented diligently. I also argued that members of the elite are unlikely to force quota regulations where it is clear that the population is averse to such interventions.

Importantly, quotas appear to be ineffective at the national level, and the analysis in the empirical chapters does not make claims about the effectiveness of quotas within parties. Comparisons between before and after the introduction of quotas indicate that they generally work within parties (Ballington 1998; Childs 2000; Yoon 2004; Kang 2009), but such simple comparisons do not account for changed attitudes. Within parties, threshold effects may make the change in attitudes appear instantaneous. There are also effects that are seen as socially desirable, where quotas become associated with notions of progress (Baldez 2006; Schwindt-Bayer and Palmer 2007). The empirical chapters simply indicate that once cultural variables are taken into consideration, then in practice quotas are not associated with higher levels of representation at the national level. Further research is necessary to understand under which circumstances quotas and other institutional arrangements are conducive to higher levels of representation.

Despite the lack of association as outlined, apparently unsuccessful and unenforced quotas can be welcomed because they might raise awareness of the underrepresentation of women and ethnic minority groups. Taking this approach, the actual implementation of quotas, or the enforcement of voluntary party quotas, is no longer a central issue of concern. Instead, the focus is on the political integration of different groups in society. Bystydzienski (1995) argues that discussions about quotas and equality have the largest impact on levels of representation; not the unenforced quotas that are commonplace. In this case, however, quotas could be replaced by a different stimulus to encourage discussions of equality and justice. Indeed, it appears that the introduction of quotas do not affect attitudes towards women as political leaders. In a model with attitudes in 2006 as the dependent variable, unsurprisingly attitudes a decade earlier are clearly associated with attitudes in 2006 ($p < 0.001$), but the introduction of quotas in the meantime is not ($p > 0.1$) (see also Kittilson and Schwindt-Bayer 2010). This analysis does not capture the discussions about quotas and equality referred to by Bystydzienski, but highlights that the introduction of quotas does not appear to affect attitudes towards women in politics; perhaps introductions of quotas do not always stimulate the same level of political discussion.

Enforced measures work, but they may be removed by future members of the elite. This was the case with quotas in countries previously associated with the Soviet Union. In this sense, their impact may be temporary and limited. Drawing on evidence from India, however, Bhavnani (2009) demonstrated that quotas appear to work after they are abolished. The odds of women being elected remain higher for seats that formerly had quotas. It remains unclear how long such an effect lasts, or whether it simply describes incumbency effects or changed attitudes due to some other reason. The experience of countries in Eastern Europe suggests that quotas do not always have a significant impact beyond the time they are implemented.

Chafetz (1984) warns against losing sight of the aim of quotas – increasing the number of women in legislatures should not become an end in itself. Rather than trying to increase the number of women in legislatures, the government could focus on policies with a direct impact on the lives of women, such as the provision of childcare for women in paid work. Here Chafetz seems to imply that it is possible for men to represent the interests of women, and also that there are relatively clear interests shared by all or most women. Such governmental policies may lead to changes in work organisation, followed by changes in attitudes towards the role of women in society. The eventual outcomes in terms of both the lives of women and the proportion of women in legislatures may be similar to that of institutional interventions, but with the crucial difference that the more abrupt implementation of quotas risks backlashes and resistance.[2] Further research along the line of Koch and Fulton (2011) is needed to fully understand the influence of increased numbers of women in legislatures on policy making. With that, it would be possible to gauge the success of quotas vis-à-vis other policy interventions.

When only institutional factors are considered, individual interventions of electoral engineering appear to have potential. It becomes evident that the manner of implementation is crucial. The impact on attitudes may be the most sustainable contribution to levels of representation: not so much the intervention, but the accompanying increase in awareness of under-representation and injustice. When taking a more inclusive look, it becomes clear that there are other factors beyond electoral engineering that affect the level of representation. Thus, the impact of institutional interventions on levels of representation should not be overestimated.

---

2. What is more, quotas risk essentialism (Mansbridge 2005). For this reason, James (2011) argues for racial constituencies, although these can have unintended consequences (Lublin 1997; Cameron *et al.* 1996; Overby and Cosgrove 1996). The application to gender differences is unclear. Members of the elite may also invest in civil society; in this way, an issue can be kept on the agenda without the direct threat of a backlash from the electorate.

Throughout the book, I have considered an array of influences on levels of political representation. Some of these factors are small-scale in nature, affecting only parts of the processes that shape levels of representation (Chafetz 1984). Given that all these factors are embedded within the wider political system, the cross-national perspective chosen in this book is both useful and necessary. The aim is not to dismiss the smaller factors, but to concentrate on the factors with the largest impact. The discussion in this chapter, together with the results in the empirical chapter, highlights two factors: the role of the elite and cultural values. These are central to changes in levels of political representation because they are able to influence many of the other factors considered. For example, the elite may affect the level of development through policy decisions, influence the implementation of quotas, or affect the media and the actions of political parties. Thus, actions of the elite may act as a catalyst, invoking a series of other changes.

Changes in attitudes towards women and marginalised groups in society are important and enable substantial and sustainable changes in levels of representation because they affect most other variables. Consequently, even small changes in attitudes may lead to noticeable changes in levels of representation, probably reflecting changed status in society. However, given that values and attitudes are shaped by a great number of factors, including the level of development, the predominant religion and cultural history, a direct intervention on attitudes seems difficult. Continuous advocacy work to increase the awareness of inequalities might lead to long-term changes in attitudes – which, in turn, might affect levels of political representation.

It is in this context that civil society organisations could play a central role in influencing levels of political representation – albeit from the evidence, indirectly. Walby (2009), for example, highlights that civil society organisations in many places work towards deepening democracy – shifting the understanding of democracy from a purely electoral and institutional one to an insistence on the presence of different groups (see also Phillips 1995). Such organisations are central to political and public debates on inclusiveness, shaping and influencing the way meaning is created and transformed. At the same time, many civil society organisations lobby for and are active in the process of changes at the individual and collective level. The media may be invoked at both levels to increase the salience of inequalities and the under-representation of certain groups. While these actions may at times be largely symbolic, they certainly fulfil the observation by Chafetz (1984) that discussions about appropriate societal roles seem to be driving changes in attitudes.

Rather than acting as a call against institutional interventions, the argument presented here should be understood as highlighting the need for attitudinal changes for a sustainable increase in levels of representation. However, in order to make such changes, there must also be relevant adjustments in cultural attitudes. Without these, there is also a risk that progressive members of the elite will suffer at the elections, and the levels of representation may decrease. Thus, the elite is more likely to actively influence levels of descriptive representation in places where the electorate is either positive, or at least neutral towards an increased inclusion of women and ethnic minorities in legislatures, or assign little importance to descriptive representation – meaning that there is little electoral risk for the elite. At the same time, however, it seems that the actions of citizens and representatives are such that they can largely adjust to a given institutional reality. One implication is that any backlash to electoral engineering might be short-lived. It seems reasonable to assume that if the institutional setting becomes a real obstacle in a society where there is significant demand for more inclusion, then this demand translates into changes in the electoral institutions. The opposite – changes in the electoral system directly translating into substantial changes in cultural attitudes – does not appear to happen, probably because values and attitudes are only to a small part shaped by the electoral institutions in place.

At the beginning of this chapter, I emphasised that there appears to be no trade-off between high levels of descriptive and substantial representation. Efforts to include more women and ethnic minorities in positions of power do not come at the cost of levels of policy representation. If anything, levels of policy representation could increase through better representation of uncrystallised views and attitudes related to being a member of a minority group (although such an impact is difficult to measure). Better representation of uncrystallised views would not be reflected in the policy representation scores used in this book, which are based on more salient issues. Whilst electoral engineering is often suggested in the literature as a solution to increase the representation of women and ethnic minority groups, this chapter is more cautious. I argued that quotas and related measures cannot be ruled out as a solution, but they probably should be regarded as only part of a solution where changes in attitudes play a central role.

Conclusion

Democratic theory assumes that all humans are essentially equal. Despite advances in the last century, women and ethnic minority groups remain significantly under-represented in many societies. Rooted in questions of group justice, this book set out to explain the variables associated with different levels of political representation in a cross-national comparison. A theoretical framework integrated various factors as explanations for the different levels of representation found in countries around the world. By considering both descriptive and substantive forms of representation, this book treated political representation in a more comprehensive way than most previous studies. Moving towards questions of rectifying under-representation, this book also looked at whether there is a link between levels of descriptive and substantive representation. Four empirical chapters (Chapters Two – Five) examined two research questions.

The first research question asked: *How can we explain differences in the levels of political representation?* For the representation of women and ethnic groups, variables measuring cultural attitudes are the dominant factors explaining differences in representation scores. Where attitudes towards women and marginalised groups in society are more positive, women and ethnic minorities are more likely to be included in national legislatures. In the case of policy representation, the salience of the issue domain seems closely associated with the level of representation in the respective domain.

Chapter Two highlights the importance of cultural attitudes with regard to the representation of women, in terms of both regional differences and measured attitudes towards women in politics. In addition to cultural variables, only the electoral formula may be a significant correlate, although the evidence is mixed. In the bivariate analysis, the presence of gender quotas is associated with higher levels of gender representation, but once cultural differences are controlled for, voluntary party quotas appear unable to significantly affect levels of gender representation at the national level. This finding has significant implications for the literature on electoral engineering, where voluntary quotas are frequently suggested – yet the effectiveness of such quotas vis-à-vis cultural factors is not considered.

Chapter Three examines the representation of ethnic groups. Recent data on the ethnic composition of legislatures made it possible to demonstrate that cultural factors are the strongest predictors for levels of representation. This was the case for regional differences, particularly for measured attitudes towards marginalised groups in society. Whilst quotas and reserved seats for ethnic groups are generally enforced and thus, by definition, affect levels of representation, the analyses suggest the implementation of such measures might often be inadequate. This leads to the finding that, on average, ethnic quotas are not associated with higher levels of representation at the national level. For example, quotas may be implemented for only certain ethnic minority groups in a country while ignoring others.

Chapter Four introduces levels of representation in different issue domains. No clear overall pattern could be determined. Using new data, the chapter established that the electoral formula is not associated with differences in the levels of policy representation. This is the case for the left–right domain – where this lack of association was recently established with smaller samples – as well as in other domains, such as the representation of social issues and views on the environment. Differences in levels of policy representation might be explained with the salience of issue domains: Chapter Five demonstrates that levels of representation tend to be higher in the more salient domains.

In this Chapter, I complement the results of the empirical chapters with considerations of additional factors that for various reasons could not be included in the numerical analyses – including the role of political parties and incentives of the elite. With that addition, the range of factors shaping levels of political representation was widened. As in the empirical chapters, the importance of cultural attitudes in shaping levels of descriptive representation transpired as a key factor: positive views on the inclusion of women and marginalised groups in public life, and political office in particular. These are attitudes akin to sociological liberalism. Although on theoretical grounds institutional factors seem as relevant as cultural factors, it appears that the involved political actors are largely able to adjust to the specific political setting.

Contrary to expectations in much of the literature, institutional factors featured less significantly as explanatory variables than their cultural counterparts. In particular, the proportionality between votes cast and seats gained seems to be of little relevance to the representation of ethnic groups and different domains of policy representation. This finding might reflect a recent trend towards more centrist positions in majoritarian systems, which largely cancels out the advantage of proportional representation (PR) systems in terms of policy representation (Powell 2007). In terms of gender representation, the main advantage of PR systems is that the elite is empowered to select more women, which in turn provides the opportunity for the inclusion of more women in legislatures. Factors that shape today's cultural attitudes – such as the predominant religion of a country – may possibly have influenced the choice of electoral system in the first place. Whatever the case, the dominance of cultural factors is something the literature should focus on. Currently, these factors are often ignored as a specific variable or the literature treats them as an afterthought; the findings in this book suggest that cultural variables should be a central consideration.

The finding that cultural factors are the best predictors for levels of descriptive representation, however, does not mean that institutional and other factors are not influential. In the context of gender representation, the electoral system may be a significant covariate; for the representation of ethnic groups, diligently implemented quotas may have merit. In the case of policy representation, the age of democracy and political rights are significant covariates particularly with regard to levels of left–right representation. What is more, in terms of descriptive representation, enforced institutional intervention means that institutional factors have the potential to shape levels of descriptive representation. However, a look at the incentives of the political elite indicates that such enforced interventions are unlikely to become common practice where the electorate is not supportive of increased numbers of women and ethnic minorities in the legislature. Further research is necessary to understand how institutional factors shape levels of representation – they do not appear to do so in a universal way, as often assumed.

The second research question in this book asked: *How are levels of representation in different forms linked?* Chapter Five makes it clear that in most cases there is no evidence for a direct link between levels of representation in different forms, contrary to the many theoretical indications in the literature. Countries where levels of policy representation are high do not necessarily have high levels of descriptive representation. The only positive association is between levels of gender representation and levels of left–right representation, both influenced by the age of democracy. At the same time, there is no clear evidence for a direct trade-off between levels of representation in different forms, where higher levels of one form of representation would come at the direct cost of another. There are some negative correlations between levels of representation in different issue domains, but it is unclear why these particular correlations are significant relative to others. Instead, it seems that the salience of political differences might shape the relationship between different forms of representation. Levels of representation are associated with the salience of issues and the awareness of under-representation.

Chapter Five addresses the relationship between levels of substantive and descriptive representation empirically. It transpires that the salience of issues and the awareness of under-representation might be a factor to understanding the association between different forms of representation. Where political divisions are thought to be more salient, the corresponding levels of representation tend to be higher. This equally applies to cases where the underlying divisions are descriptive or substantive, although for the most part ideological differences are the most salient ones. The importance of salience means that advocacy work to increase the awareness of the under-representation of certain groups in society might prove to be just as useful as institutional interventions. It is in this context that civil society organisations can play an important role in informing and shaping public debates.

In this Chapter, I considered additional influences on levels of representation; however, cultural attitudes maintained their central role. This was particularly the case when considering the incentives of representatives to stay in power. For example, the scope of including more women – or significantly fewer – against a level that the general population would support is limited. Such actions come with considerable electoral risks, particularly in places where demographic divisions are more salient. The argument, however, is not one of cultural determinism. In individual cases, strong leadership by the elite or within political parties can lead to significant differences. This holds true where the citizens are neutral towards the inclusion of more women and members of ethnic minorities – or not strongly opposed to such undertakings. In these cases, cultural factors remain an important mediating factor, shaping the bounds within which changes are possible.

In terms of electoral engineering, the argument presented means that some institutional interventions, such as enforced quotas or registration requirements, can make a significant difference in levels of political representation. The key, however, is that such measures are implemented diligently. Whilst such enforced interventions may be required to prevent the complete exclusion of certain groups in society, such forms of electoral engineering require corresponding changes in attitudes to be effective in the long term. For new democracies, this means not only choosing the right institutions, but also recognising that without corresponding advocacy work on attitudes the outcomes may not be as intended. This is where the political elite can play a crucial role in diligently implementing an institutional setting.

The results reported in this book are compatible with modernisation theories, suggesting that in the established and more developed countries, levels of representation may be generally higher – as well as left–right representation, this includes women and ethnic minorities. It is not clear whether postmodern societies will witness increasing calls for representation of other demographic groups – and perhaps even groups defined by lifestyle choices. A tension remains between such theories that emphasise change over time and the empirical findings that largely relied on cross-sectional analysis. In any case, the empirical work in this book suggests that both cultural and institutional factors have the potential to shape levels of descriptive and substantive representation. Where the institutional setting is averse to the inclusion of women or minorities, positive cultural attitudes can often overcome such a hurdle – mediated by electoral success and failure. In contrast, where attitudes are averse to the inclusion of women or ethnic minority groups, institutional interventions may fail to rectify the situation. In such cases, there is a real possibility of insincere implementation that fails its intent, or that the level of descriptive representation increases without corresponding changes in status in society. Institutional interventions require corresponding cultural attitudes in order to be effective.

appendix

Representation scores for women
All data as of 2006

Albania	0.561	Democratic Republic Congo	0.614
Andorra	0.806	Denmark	0.863
Antigua and Barbuda	0.581	Dominica	0.632
Argentina	0.844	Dominican Republic	0.695
Armenia	0.540	East Timor	0.770
Australia	0.740	Ecuador	0.655
Austria	0.823	El Salvador	0.653
Bahamas	0.693	Estonia	0.649
Bangladesh	0.657	Fiji	0.621
Barbados	0.615	Finland	0.863
Belgium	0.836	France	0.608
Belize	0.569	Gabon	0.588
Benin	0.565	Gambia	0.632
Bolivia	0.668	Georgia	0.572
Bosnia and Herzegovina	0.671	Germany	0.805
Botswana	0.693	Ghana	0.606
Brazil	0.594	Greece	0.622
Bulgaria	0.708	Grenada	0.784
Burkina Faso	0.609	Guatemala	0.585
Burundi	0.801	Guinea-Bissau	0.625
Canada	0.603	Guyana	0.810
Cape Verde	0.637	Honduras	0.735
Central African Republic	0.599	Hungary	0.579
Chile	0.642	Iceland	0.834
Colombia	0.612	India	0.600
Comoros	0.526	Indonesia	0.614
Costa Rica	0.891	Ireland	0.629
Croatia	0.698	Israel	0.635
Cyprus	0.634	Italy	0.659
Czech Republic	0.642	Jamaica	0.616

Japan	0.579	Poland	0.689
Kenya	0.575	Portugal	0.696
Kiribati	0.541	Romania	0.599
Kuwait	0.618	Saint Kitts and Nevis	0.497
Kyrgyzstan	0.488	Saint Lucia	0.546
Latvia	0.670	St. Vincent & Grenadines	0.681
Lebanon	0.532	Samoa	0.561
Lesotho	0.623	San Marino	0.606
Liechtenstein	0.727	Sao Tome and Principe	0.566
Lithuania	0.687	Senegal	0.682
Luxembourg	0.726	Serbia and Montenegro	0.606
Macedonia	0.693	Seychelles	0.790
Madagascar	0.566	Sierra Leone	0.630
Malawi	0.630	Slovakia	0.646
Malaysia	0.596	Slovenia	0.610
Mali	0.591	Solomon Islands	0.517
Malta	0.588	South Africa	0.806
Mauritius	0.666	South Korea	0.637
Mexico	0.730	Spain	0.849
Micronesia	0.506	Sri Lanka	0.544
Moldova	0.696	Suriname	0.763
Monaco	0.684	Sweden	0.948
Mongolia	0.561	Switzerland	0.739
Mozambique	0.829	Tanzania	0.801
Namibia	0.757	Thailand	0.598
Nauru	0.505	Tonga	0.543
Netherlands	0.862	Trinidad and Tobago	0.707
New Zealand	0.810	Turkey	0.549
Nicaragua	0.706	Tuvalu	0.486
Niger	0.623	Ukraine	0.535
Norway	0.874	United Kingdom	0.683
Palau	0.546	United States	0.643
Panama	0.671	Uruguay	0.595
Papua New Guinea	0.522	Vanuatu	0.553
Peru	0.788	Venezuela	0.683
Philippines	0.660	Zambia	0.620

Representation scores for ethnic groups

Given in the following are Q-scores, with R-scores in brackets; 'present' means that ethnic minority groups are present in the legislature, but no detailed data are available. Of the free and partly free countries, no data could be obtained for the following countries: Austria, Dominican Republic, Gambia, Grenada, Indonesia, Jamaica, Kuwait, Mexico, Nicaragua, Saint Kitts and Nevis, Saint Lucia, Saint Vincent and the Grenadines, Sao Tome and Principe, Seychelles, Sierra Leone, and South Korea. For many of the countries there are estimates from different sources that largely agree. All data as of 2006.

Albania	0.980 (0.510)	Czech Republic	0.971 (0.030)
Andorra	0.980 (0.000)	Denmark	0.997 (1.170)
Antigua & Barb.	0.910 (0.000)	Dominica	0.989 (0.758)
Argentina	0.970 (0.000)	East Timor	Present
Armenia	0.979 (0.000)	Ecuador	0.770 (0.179)
Australia	0.968 (0.579)	El Salvador	0.990 (0.000)
Bahamas	0.948 (0.650)	Estonia	0.795 (0.310)
Bangladesh	0.990 (1.500)	Fiji	0.960 (0.900)
Barbados	0.900 (0.000)	Finland	0.997 (0.000)
Belgium	0.979 (0.721)	France	0.944 (0.143)
Belize	Present	Gabon	Present
Benin	0.904 (1.162)	Georgia	0.903 (0.450)
Bolivia	0.950 (1.111)	Germany	0.977 (0.233)
Bosnia & Herzegovina	0.994 (0.000)	Ghana	Present
Botswana	0.833 (1.795)	Greece	0.994 (0.351)
Brazil	0.967 (0.070)	Guatemala	0.689 (0.234)
Bulgaria	0.914 (0.464)	Guinea-Bissau	Present
Burkina Faso	0.950 (0.916)	Guyana	0.927 (1.180)
Burundi	Present	Honduras	0.933 (0.260)
Canada	0.877 (0.371)	Hungary	0.943 (0.000)
Cape Verde	0.990 (0.000)	Iceland	0.999 (0.000)
Central African Rep.	0.923 (0.649)	India	0.926 (0.787)
Chile	0.950 (0.000)	Ireland	0.995 (0.000)
Colombia	0.968 (0.360)	Israel	0.864 (0.420)
Comoros	0.977 (0.000)	Italy	0.982 (0.081)
Costa Rica	0.940 (0.000)	Japan	0.993 (0.060)
Croatia	0.861 (0.328)	Kenya	Present
Cyprus	0.958 (0.000)	Kiribati	0.982 (0.240)

Kyrgyzstan	0.809 (0.456)	Poland	0.998 (0.725)
Latvia	0.829 (0.620)	Portugal	0.950 (0.000)
Lebanon	0.819 (—)	Romania	0.985 (1.150)
Lesotho	0.985 (0.000)	Samoa	0.967 (0.552)
Liechtenstein	0.989 (0.000)	San Marino	1.000 (—)
Lithuania	0.867 (0.160)	Senegal	Present
Luxembourg	0.978 (0.427)	Serbia & Montenegro	0.813 (0.180)
Macedonia	0.885 (0.680)	Slovakia	0.910 (0.612)
Madagascar	0.956 (0.781)	Slovenia	0.835 (0.134)
Malawi	0.991 (10.00)	Solomon Islands	0.985 (0.727)
Malaysia	Present	South Africa	0.793 (1.850)
Mali	0.945 (0.635)	Spain	0.781 (0.292)
Malta	0.995 (0.000)	Sri Lanka	0.904 (1.591)
Mauritius	Present	Suriname	0.943 (1.176)
Micronesia	Present	Sweden	0.976 (0.820)
Moldova	0.723 (0.080)	Switzerland	0.961 (0.000)
Monaco	0.978 (0.000)	Tanzania	0.984 (0.688)
Mongolia	0.983 (0.712)	Thailand	0.812 (0.248)
Mozambique	Present	Tonga	0.988 (0.000)
Namibia	0.978 (0.640)	Trinidad & Tobago	0.853 (0.822)
Nauru	0.840 (0.000)	Turkey	Present
Netherlands	0.895 (0.450)	Tuvalu	0.960 (0.000)
New Zealand	0.928 (0.751)	Ukraine	0.943 (1.075)
Niger	Present	United Kingdom	0.948 (0.260)
Norway	0.986 (0.300)	United States	0.829 (0.472)
Palau	0.824 (0.415)	Uruguay	0.970 (0.253)
Panama	0.996 (1.068)	Vanuatu	0.977 (2.564)
Papua New Guinea	0.952 (8.340)	Venezuela	0.908 (0.165)
Peru	0.878 (0.631)	Zambia	0.988 (7.000)
Philippines	0.999 (1.017)		

Representation scores for issue positions

Given in the following are representation scores for political left–right, social issues, and the environment respectively. Data on countries marked with an asterisk (*) are taken from the CSES (2007) rather than Benoit and Laver (2005).

Albania	0.906, 0.681, 0.768	Luxembourg	0.976, 0.812, ——
Australia	0.963, 0.933, 0.865	Macedonia	0.928, 0.915, 0.832
Austria	0.976, 0.801, ——	Malta	0.923, 0.876, ——
Belgium	0.976, 0.865, ——	Mexico *	0.892, ——, ——
Bosnia and Herzegovina	0.929, 0.993, 0.756	Moldova	0.849, 0.838, 0.787
Bulgaria	0.906, 0.796, 0.744	Netherlands	0.955, 0.943, ——
Brazil *	0.859, ——, ——	New Zealand	0.959, ——, 0.805
Canada	0.970, 0.879, 0.864	Norway	0.961, 0.900, 0.833
Chile *	0.942, ——, ——	Peru *	0.938, ——, ——
Croatia	0.964, 0.923, 0.740	Philippines *	0.781, ——, ——
Czech Republic	0.862, 0.901, 0.779	Poland	0.899, 0.832, 0.820
Denmark	0.986, 0.782, ——	Portugal	0.977, 0.899, ——
Estonia	0.904, 0.933, 0.814	Romania	0.843, 0.896, 0.708
Finland	0.944, 0.907, 0.719	Serbia and Montenegro	0.955, 0.822, 0.627
France *	0.789, 0.800, ——	Slovakia	0.995, 0.859, 0.757
Germany	0.989, 0.848, 0.724	Slovenia	0.976, 0.945, 0.803
Greece	0.919, 0.926, ——	South Korea *	0.933, ——, ——
Hungary	0.974, 0.907, 0.650	Spain	0.937, 0.866, 0.783
Iceland	0.984, 0.949, ——	Sweden	0.990, 0.891, 0.857
Ireland	0.925, 0.882, ——	Switzerland	0.985, 0.783, 0.689
Israel	0.975, ——, 0.708	Turkey	0.993, 0.835, 0.924
Italy	0.950, 0.898, ——	UK	0.974, 0.982, ——
Japan	0.981, 0.912, 0.726	Ukraine	0.837, 0.779, 0.629
Latvia	0.999, 0.907, 0.654	US	0.995, 0.937, 0.819
Lithuania	0.890, 0.787, 0.686		

Data for the dependent variables

Representation of women: the proportion of women in legislatures is taken from the *Inter-Parliamentary Union* (IPU 2009), and is as of July 2006. Only single and lower chambers are covered, although upper chambers tend to be similar ($r=0.48$, $p<0.001$). Figures for the proportion of women in the population are taken from *Encyclopaedia Britannica* (2006b). Setting the proportion of women in the population to 50 per cent rather than taking more accurate estimates does not affect the results noticeably; the resulting representation scores correlate very highly ($r=0.99$, $p<0.001$).

Representation of ethnic groups: data on the representatives are based on newly-collected data. These data were obtained by approaching official contacts of the legislatures (overall response rate of 27 per cent). These data are as of 2006, and give the percentage of representatives in each ethnic group, whereas the ethnic groups recognised vary from country to country, according to which divisions are salient. A very small number of legislatures include the ethnicity of representatives in the respective biographies on their webpage, from which percentages can be calculated. The data for the legislatures were complemented with data by Alonso and Ruiz-Rufino (2007), Reynolds (2006, 2007), Latner and McGann (2005), Johnson (1998), as well information included in country reports published by the *US Department of State* (2006). Because of the multiple data sources, I have multiple data points for many of the countries. In almost all cases, the different sources agree on which ethnic groups are salient, and what proportion of the representatives belong to each group. The substantial results of the statistical calculations in Chapter Three can be replicated with sub-samples that remove any of the data sources.

The corresponding data for the population are taken from national statistics or, where unavailable, the *World Factbook* (2006), and crosschecked against *Britannica* (2006b) and Fearon (2003), and in some cases the *Ethnologue* (Raymond 2005) and the *Joshua Project* (2006). Where possible, I restricted the data to citizens of a country, because citizens may have a stronger claim to representation. I cannot determine a case where the difference between population and citizens is significant enough to affect the overall findings. In some cases, I had to combine ethnic sub-groups into larger groups to match the classifications used for the representatives. The representation scores used are insensitive to splitting and combining groups.

Representation of language groups: data on the representatives were collected by approaching official contacts of the legislature. The data are as of 2006. Data from Alonso and Ruiz-Rufino (2007), and Reynolds (2006, 2007) were used to complement the newly-collected cases. The linguistic composition of the population is based on national statistics or, where unavailable, the *Ethnologue* (Raymond 2005).

Representation of religious groups: data on the representatives were collected by approaching official contacts of the legislatures. The data are as of 2006. Data from Alonso and Ruiz-Rufino (2007), Reynolds (2006, 2007), and the

Congressional Quarterly (2007) were used to complement the newly-collected cases. The religious composition of the population is based on national statistics or, where unavailable, the *World Factbook* (2006).

The positions of representatives on different policy issues are approximated using weighted averages of party positions from Benoit and Laver (2005). The data were collected for 2002 and 2003. In order to increase the sample size, for the generic left–right scale, data from the *Comparative Study of Electoral Systems* (CSES, Sapiro and Shively 2007) were also used for countries not covered by the Benoit and Laver data. For the many countries where there are data in both data sets, the estimates correlate highly (r=0.68, p<0.01). In all cases, the positions of the citizens are derived from questions in the *World Values Survey* (2006). This data set includes variables that directly or very closely match the classification used by Benoit and Laver, as outlined in the following lines.

The domains covered in this book are set out below (each case provides the question used for the parties, the question used for the citizens, and the key aspects that are maintained):

Left–Right Parties: 'Please locate each party on a general left–right dimension, taking all aspects of party policy into account.' – Citizens: 'In political matters, people talk of "the left" and "the right"'. How would you place your views on this scale, generally speaking?' Key aspects: left, right, generally.

Social issues Parties: 'Favours/opposes liberal policies on matters such as abortion, homosexuality, and euthanasia.' – Citizens: a scale was constructed including a question on what kinds of neighbours the respondents would not tolerate ('On this list are various groups of people. Could you please mention any that you would not like to have as neighbours?' using the items: 'People with a criminal record,' 'Heavy drinkers,' 'Emotionally unstable people,' 'Homosexuals,' 'People who have AIDS,' and 'Drug addicts'.). The choice of items reflects issues included in the Benoit and Laver questionnaire, but for reasons of coverage in the WVS data, some closely related issues were also included. The question used by Benoit and Laver leaves much room to the experts to decide which social issues to consider; a comparison is thus complicated. However, the resulting scale for citizens has a Cronbach's alpha of 0.87, indicating that social issues may be less messy than feared. – Key aspects: issues of liberal policies, attitudes to non-traditional life-styles.

Environment Parties: 'Supports protection of the environment, even at the cost of economic growth. Supports economic growth, even at the cost of damage to the environment.' – Citizens: 'Here are two statements people sometimes make when discussing the environment and economic growth. Which of them comes closer to your own point of view? Protecting the environment should be given priority, even if it causes slower economic growth and some loss of jobs. Economic growth and creating jobs should be the top priority, even if the environment suffers to some extent.' – Key aspects: economic growth, environment, perceived trade-off.

Privatisation Parties: 'Promotes maximum state ownership of business and industry. Opposes all state ownership of business and industry.' – Citizens: 'Private ownership of business and industry should be increased. Government ownership of business and industry should be increased.' – Key aspect: state ownership of industry.

Nationalism Parties: 'Strongly promotes a cosmopolitan rather than a national consciousness, history, and culture. Strongly promotes a national rather than cosmopolitan consciousness, history, and culture.' – Citizens: 'We should emphasise high technology more than tradition.' – Key aspects: openness to non-traditional influences, perceived trade-off between progress and national history.

Role of religion in politics Parties: 'Supports religious principles in politics. Supports secular principles in politics.' – Citizens: 'How strongly do you agree or disagree with each of the following statement? Politicians who do not believe in God are unfit for public office.' – Key aspect: idea of separating religion from politics.

Immigration Parties: 'Favours policies designed to help asylum seekers and immigrants integrate into society. Favours policies designed to help asylum seekers and immigrants to return to their country of origin.' – Citizens: 'Immigrants and their customs and traditions: Maintain distinct customs and traditions. Take over the customs of the country.' – Key aspects: integration, assimilation and integration contrasted with isolationist multiculturalism.

Deregulation Parties: 'Favours high levels of state regulation and control of the market. Favours deregulation of markets at every opportunity.' – Citizens: 'Competition is good. It stimulates people to work hard and develop new ideas. Competition is harmful. It brings out the worst in people.' – Key aspects: markets, contrast between competition and the regulation of markets.

Data for the independent variables

Aspects of the electoral system are captured in a multitude of ways, but many approaches revolve around the proportionality between votes and seats (Farrell and Scully 2007).

Electoral formula: The classification of electoral formulas is taken from Colomer (2004). For the purposes of this book, the number of categories is reduced, because some electoral formulas are very rare. A distinction is made between PR system and majoritarian ones. Following Shugart and Wattenberg (2003), mixed systems were also classified as either PR or majoritarian, depending on their tendency.

Vote-seat proportionality: The proportionality between votes and seats is based on the *Gallagher Index* of least squares, a measure that is not based on an electoral formula (Gallagher 1991). Data are taken from Farrell (2001), based on averages for the 1990s. Whilst vote–seat proportionality might be a better measure of proportionality than the electoral formula, data are not available for all countries.

District magnitude: Based on Farrell (2001), district magnitude is conceptualised as a categorical rather than continuous variable: Countries are classified into single-member districts (SMD), multi-member districts (MMD), and national districts. Many majoritarian systems come with single-member districts; and national districts are only found in PR systems. The data were checked against Colomer (2004), and they include Croatia's change from mixed to proportional representation.

Number of parties: The number of parties was counted based on *Election World* for the most recent election before July 2006 (Derksen 2006). The *effective number of parties* weighs the parties by their size, and is preferred as a measurement of how fragmented a party system is (Laakso and Taagepera 1979). Data on the effective number of parties were taken from Farrell (2001), Lijphart (1999), and Norris (2004). These values are averages for the 1990s, or where available, the most recent election.

Quotas: The existence of gender quotas is documented by the *Institute for Democracy and Electoral Assistance* (IDEA) (2006). Coded as gender quotas were voluntary party quotas, statutory or legal quotas, and reserved seats.[1] For ethnic groups, I coded reserved seats, statutory arrangements, voluntary party quotas, and the appointment of ethnic minority representatives. Reserved seats mean separate rolls for specific groups: depending on the setup, the entire population or only members of the group are allowed to vote for these specific seats.[2] For both gender quotas and ethnic quotas, the coding is limited to interventions that are conceptually clear and for which reliable data are available.

I have cross-checked the presence of quotas and the respective year of introduction against Dahlerup (2006) and Derksen (2006), information provided by individual parties on their websites, as well as the literature on specific countries. Data on the presence of quotas and reserved seats for ethnic minority groups were taken from Htun (2004), IDEA (2006), and Norris (2004). I have cross-checked these against a number of sources, including Matland (2006), Bieber (2004), and Derksen (2006).

Supply of candidates: The percentage of girls in secondary education was taken from the World Bank (2006). The data are as of 2005 for most countries, but in a few cases up to 10 years previous than that. The data on economically least developed countries are recent, since the UN tracks progress as part of the *Millennium Goals*. Economic participation of women was operationalised as the percentage of women in paid work. The data are taken from the UNDP (2005), for the proportion of women in professional jobs from the UN Statistics Division (2006).

Composition of society: The extent to which a country is fractionalised into different ethnic groups is taken from Fearon (2003). Similar measures and data are available from Ordeshook and Shvetsava (1994) or Alesina *et al.* (2003). Fearon also offers an alternative set of heterogeneity data, by considering how different the various groups in a country are: cultural heterogeneity. This measure not only

---

1. A number of related actions are not considered: official aims of a party to include more women or ethnic minority candidates, the presence of women's sections, separate women's parties, and the appointment of women.
2. Not coded as ethnic quotas were exemptions from thresholds, and districting along ethnic divisions; specific ethnic parties were coded into a separate variable.

considers the number and size of different ethnic groups in a country, but also their cultural similarity by considering the linguistic difference between groups. The more distant two languages are in the linguistic tree, the larger the significance of the ethnic difference is assumed to be.

Geographical concentration: Data on the geographical concentration of ethnic groups is newly collected and based on whether concentration was mentioned in the country profiles in *Encyclopaedia Britannica*. For example in Austria the country profile mentions Hungarians 'living mainly in Burgenland', and Slovenes 'living mainly in Kärnten' (*Britannica* 2006c), which I coded as concentrated. The variable distinguishes between no concentration where none was mentioned, a tendency of concentration, and heavy concentration where the country is largely divided along ethnic divisions or ethnic minority groups are concentrated in certain areas. This classification is equivalent to the one used by Mozaffar *et al.* (2003) for countries in Africa. Whilst this measurement may be relatively crude, it covers all countries and offers a reasonable approximation in a systematic manner.[3]

Specific party: The presence of linguistic and religious parties was coded using party profiles on *Election World* (Derksen 2006). A party was coded as ethnic, linguistic or religious if it contained such a reference in its name, or if ethnic, language or religious rights were mentioned as a key policy.

Cultural attitudes: Attitudes relevant to gender representation and ethnic group representation are measured using questions from the *World Values Survey* (WVS). For gender representation, the national mean of responses to the statement 'Men make better political leaders than women' is used, because of its direct relationship to gender representation. Responses to this question correlate very highly with other questions related to women's status in society: agreement with the statement that 'a university education is more important for a boy than for a girl' ($r=0.80$, $p<0.001$), approval of the women's movement ($r=0.50$, $p<0.01$), or agreement that it is a problem if a woman earns more than her husband does ($r=0.49$, $p<0.001$).

For the analyses on ethnic groups, the focus is on attitudes towards marginalised groups in society. The *World Values Survey* asks respondents what kinds of neighbours the respondents would not tolerate ('On this list are various groups of people. Could you please mention any that you would not like to have as neighbours?'). One of the questions available specifically asks about people of a different race, but these estimates appear unreliable. Substantively higher values are obtained when people are asked about a specific ethnic group or race rather than others in general. For this reason, a ten-item scale was calculated, using a range of potential neighbours as the basis: people with a criminal record, people of a different race, heavy drinkers, emotionally unstable people, Muslims, immigrants or

---

3. There is a corresponding variable in the *Minorities at Risk* data set (Minorities at Risk Project 2008), but as acknowledged by the project, it suffers from internal inconsistencies and unreliability: the classification of groups seems to follow rather different reasoning in different countries.

foreign workers, people with AIDS, drug addicts, homosexuals, and Jews. This is not to imply that different ethnic minorities actually were criminals or otherwise deviant, but that there is a tendency to treat them in a similar manner. The scale in principle ranges from 0 to 10, depending on how many kinds of people were mentioned as unacceptable neighbours (Cronbach's $\alpha=0.93$). I have inversed the scale so that a higher score on this scale indicates that a respondent is more tolerant towards marginalised groups in society. The national means are used, ranging from just under 2 to about 6, meaning that there is significant variance between countries. In the absence of evidence to the contrary, it is assumed that these differences reflect cross-cultural variation and not measurement bias. Invariance tests could be applied to address this question empirically (Steenkamp and Baumgartner 1998; Davidov *et al.* 2010).

The predominant religion of a country was coded following the example of Inglehart and Norris (2003), based on information found in national statistics and *Britannica* (2006b). The measure distinguishes between predominantly Catholic and Protestant countries, as well as Muslim countries, with the remainder combined as *other*.[4] The category *other* also includes countries where no religion dominates, such as Germany.

The classification of different regions was taken from Kenworthy and Malami (1999). The regional boundaries are somewhat arbitrary: Western Europe, the US, Canada, Australia, New Zealand as one group of Western countries; Nordic countries; Eastern Europe; Asia and Pacific; Middle East and Northern Africa; Sub-Saharan Africa; and Latin America. Caribbean countries are classified as Latin American. No justification for regional codes is generally given, but very similar coding is used in other studies (e.g. Moore and Shackman 1996; Paxton 1997). A study of the historical influences to justify such regional boundaries is beyond the scope of this book. The use of regional variables as a measure of cultural attitudes can be justified on empirical grounds, however, because of their explanatory power for cultural attitudes. Positive attitudes towards women in politics can be explained statistically with the prevalent religion and whether a country can be classified as post-industrial or not ($R^2=0.69$).[5] Institutional variables, the age of democracy, and the level of political rights are not significantly associated with the attitudinal variable ($p>0.1$). Once adding regional variables, neither religious nor developmental differences remain significant ($R^2=0.85$), suggesting that regional differences may approximate these two factors. The story is very similar when statistically explaining attitudes towards marginalised groups in society: religion and

4.   Unfortunately, this commonly used variable of the predominant religion suffers from classification issues for some countries, as well as an inability to incorporate levels of religiosity. The substantive results in this book are unaffected by the exclusion of countries where classification was less certain.

5.   The difference between industrial and post-industrial countries is taken from Inglehart and Norris (2003), and Norris and Inglehart (2004).

post-industrialism are significant covariates ($R^2=0.67$), with other factors being insignificant ($p>0.1$). When adding regional variables, post-industrialism remains a significant covariate ($p<0.05$), suggesting that for the countries covered, regional differences also account for religious differences, but not entirely for developmental ones ($R^2=0.89$).

Established Democracy: Data on the age of democracy were taken from Colomer (2004), stating for how many years a democracy has existed. Where democracy was established multiple times in a country, the latest date of establishing the democracy is taken, such as after a spell of dictatorship. Following Farrell (2001) and Colomer (2004), a country where democracy was established in the 20 years before 2006 is considered a new democracy. Old democracies are countries where democracy was established before 1986. For the countries covered, Paxton's (2008) insistence on women's right to vote for a democracy to exist does not affect the definition of the age of democracy.

Data from *Freedom House* (2006) are used to capture influences of political rights. These data are based on expert judgements, but a rigorous and standardised approach is used to ensure comparability.

Most important issue: The political issue considered most important by the citizens was taken from the *World Values Survey* (2006). For some of the countries – where representation scores are calculated based on CSES data – the most important issues is also taken from the CSES (Sapiro and Shively 2007).

Further resources from the author can be found here: http://figshare.com/articles/Political_Representation_of_Women_Ethnic_Groups_and_Issue_Positions/675917

bibliography

Abou-Zeid, G. (2006) 'The Arab region: Women's access to the decision-making process across the Arab Nation' in D. Dahlerup (ed.) *Women, Quotas and Politics*, London: Routledge.

Achen, C. (1978) 'Measuring representation', *American Journal of Political Science* 22(3): 475–510.

Alba, R. and Moore, G. (1982) 'Ethnicity in the American elite', *American Sociological Review* 47(3): 373–83.

Aldrich, J. and McKelvey, R. (1977) 'A method of scaling with applications to the 1968 and 1972 presidential elections', *American Political Science Review* 71(1): 111–30.

Alesina, A., Devleeschauwer, A., Easterly, W., Kurlat, S. and Wacziarg, R. (2003) 'Fractionalization', *Journal of Economic Growth* 8: 155–94.

Allwood, G. and Wadia, K. (2004) 'Increasing women's representation in France and India', *Canadian Journal of Political Science* 37(2): 375–93.

Alonso, S. and Ruiz-Rufino, R. (2007) 'Political representation and ethnic conflict in new democracies', *European Journal of Political Research* 46(2): 237–67.

Alvarez, M. and Franklin, C. (1994) 'Uncertainty and political perceptions', *Journal of Politics* 56(3): 671–88.

Anderson, C. (2007) 'The interaction of structures and voter behavior' in R. Dalton and H.-D. Klingemann (eds) *The Oxford Handbook of Political Behaviour*, Oxford: Oxford University Press.

Anwar, M. (1994) *Race and Elections: The participation of ethnic minorities in politics*, Warwick: Centre for Research in Ethnic Relations.

Appleton, A. and Mazur, A. (1993) 'Transformation or modernization: the rhetoric and reality of gender and party politics in France' in J. Lovenduski and P. Norris (eds) *Gender and Party Politics*, London: Sage.

Arcenaux, K. (2001) 'The 'gender gap' in state legislative representation: New data to tackle an old question', *Political Research Quarterly* 54(1): 143–60.

Aroújo, C. and García, I. (2006) 'Latin America: the experience and the impact of quotas in Latin America' in D. Dahlerup (ed.) *Women, Quotas and Politics*, London: Routledge.

Arscott, J. (1995) 'A job well begun... representation, electoral reform, and women' in F. Gingras (ed.) *Gender and Politics in Contemporary Canada*, Oxford: Oxford University Press.

Ayata, A. and Tütüncü, F. (2008) 'Critical acts without a critical mass: the substantive representation of women in the Turkish Parliament', *Parliamentary Affairs* 61(3): 461–75.

Bacchi, C. (2006) 'Arguing for and against quotas: theoretical issues' in D. Dahlerup (ed.) *Women, Quotas and Politics*, London: Routledge.

Baldez, L. (2006) 'The pros and cons of gender quota laws: what happens when you kick men out and let women in?', *Politics and Gender* 2(1): 101–28.

Ballington, J. (1998) 'Women's parliamentary representation: the effect of list PR', *Politikon* 25(2): 77–93.

Banda, F. and Chinkin, C. (2004) *Gender, Minorities and Indigenous Peoples*, London: Minority Rights Group International.

Banducci, S., Donovan, T. and Karp, J. (2004) 'Minority representation, empowerment, and participation', *Journal of Politics* 66(2): 534–56.

Barber, B. (2003) *Strong Democracy: Participatory politics for a new age*, London: University of California Press.

Bartels, L. (1993) 'Messages received: the political impact of media exposure', *American Political Science Review* 87(2): 267–85.

—— (2005) *Economic Inequality and Political Representation*, Princeton: Princeton University. Online. Available http://www.princeton.edu/~bartels/economic.pdf (accessed 8 December 2011).

Becker, G, (1983) 'A theory of competition among pressure groups for political influence', *Quarterly Journal of Economics* 98(3): 371–400.

Benjamin, G. (1998) 'Systems of representation for legislatures in democracies' in G. Kurian (ed.) *World Encyclopedia of Parliaments and Legislatures*, Washington: Congressional Quarterly.

Bennett, C. (1991) 'What is policy convergence and what causes it?', *British Journal of Political Science* 21: 215–233.

Benoit, K. and Laver, M. (2005) *Party Policy in Modern Democracies Version: 1 Feb 2006* (computer file), Dublin: Trinity College (distributor).

—— (2006) *Party Policy in Modern Democracies*, London: Routledge.

—— (2007) 'Estimating party policy positions: comparing expert surveys and hand-coded content analysis', *Electoral Studies* 26(1): 90–107.

Berkman, M. and O'Connor, R. (1993) 'Do women legislators matter? Female legislators and state abortion policy', *American Politics Research* 21(1): 102–124.

Bhavnani, R. (2009) 'Do electoral quotas work after they are withdrawn? Evidence from a natural experiment in India', *American Political Science Review* 103(01): 23–35.

Bieber, F. (2004) 'Power sharing as ethnic representation in postconflict societies: the cases of Bosnia, Macedonia, and Kosovo' in A. Mungui-Pippidi and I. Krastev (eds) *Nationalism after Communism: Lessons learned*, Budapest: Central European University Press.

Birch, A. (1971) *Representation*, London: Pall Mall.

Birch, S. (2000) *Descriptive, Ideological, and Performative Representation in the Ukrainian Verkhovna Rada*, Colchester: University of Essex. Online. Available http://www.psa.ac.uk/cps/2000/Birch%20Sarah.pdf (accessed 15 December 2005).

Bird, K. (2003) 'The political representation of women and ethnic minorities in established democracies: a framework for comparative research', *Working Paper presented for the Academy of Migration Studies in Denmark (AMID)* No. 11 November.

— (2005) 'The political representation of visible minorities in electoral democracies: a comparison of France, Denmark, and Canada', *Nationalism and Ethnic Politics* 11(4): 425–65.

Bird, K., Saalfeld, T. and Wüst, A. (eds) (2010) *The Political Representation of Immigrants and Minorities: Voters, parties and parliaments in liberal democracies*, London: Routledge.

Birnir, J. (2004) 'Stabilizing party systems and excluding segments of society? The effects of formation costs on new party foundation in Latin America', *Studies in Comparative International Development* 39(3): 3–27.

Black, D. (1948) 'On the rationale of group decision-making', *Journal of Political Economy* 56(1): 23–34.

Blais, A. and Bodet, M. (2006) 'Does proportional representation foster closer congruence between citizens and policy makers?', *Comparative Political Studies* 39(10): 1243–62.

Blais, A. and Massicotte, L. (2002) 'Electoral systems' in L. LeDuc, R. Niemi and P. Norris (eds) *Comparing Democracies 2: New challenges in the study of elections and voting*, London: Sage.

Blondel, J. (1973) *Comparative Legislatures*, New Jersey: Prentice-Hall.

Blondel, J. and Müller-Rommel, F. (2007) 'Political elites' in R. Dalton and H.-D. Klingemann (eds) *The Oxford Handbook of Political Behaviour*, Oxford: Oxford University Press.

Blondel, J., Sinnot, R. and Svensson, P. (1997) 'Representation and voter participation', *European Journal of Political Research* 32: 243–72.

Bochsler, D. (2006) *Electoral Engineering and Inclusion of Ethnic Groups: Ethnic minorities in parliaments of Central and Eastern European countries*, Geneva: University of Geneva. Online. Available http://www.unige.ch/ses/spo/staff/corpsinter/bochsler/minorities (accessed 6 March 2007).

Bogaards, M. (2004) 'Electoral systems and the management of ethnic conflict in the Balkans' in A. Mungui-Pippidi and I. Krastev (eds) *Nationalism after Communism: Lessons learned*, Budapest: Central European University Press.

Bosanquet, N. (1996) 'Public demands and economic constraints: All Italians now?' in J. Hayward (ed.) *Elitism, Populism, and European Politics*, Oxford: Clarendon Press.

Bousetta, H. (2001) *Extending Democracy: Participation, consultation and representation of ethnic minority people in public life*, Bristol: Centre for the Study of Citizenship and Ethnicity. Online. Available http://www.international.metropolis.net/events/rotterdam/papers/14-Bousetta.pdf (accessed 9 February 2007).

Braud, P. (1988) *The Garden of Democratic Delights: For a psycho-emotional reading of pluralist systems*, London: Praeger.

Brennan, G. and Hamlin, A. (1999) 'On political representation', *British Journal of Political Science* 29(1): 109–27.

Britannica (2006a) *Representation*, Chicago: Encyclopædia Britannica. Online. Available http://search.eb.com/eb/article-9063230 (accessed 19 April 2006).

—— (2006b) *World Data* (computer file), Chicago: Encyclopædia Britannica (distributor).

—— (2006c) *Austria*, Chicago: Encyclopædia Britannica. Online. Available http://search.eb.com/eb/article-33395 (accessed 14 August 2006).

Brock, G. (2005) 'Can Kymlicka help us mediate cultural claims?', *International Journal on Minority and Group Rights* 12: 269–96.

Browne, W. (1990) 'Organized interests and their issue niches' in R. Alexander (2006) *The Classics of Interest Group Behavior*, Belmont: Thomson Wadsworth.

Bryant, J. and Thompson, S. (2002) *Fundamentals of Media Effects*, London: McGraw Hill.

Budge, I. and McDonald, M. (2007) 'Election and party system effects on policy representation: bringing time into a comparative perspective', *Electoral Studies* 26: 168–79.

Budge, I., McDonald, M., Pennings, P. and Keman, H. (2012) *Organizing Democratic Choice: Party representation over time*, Oxford: Oxford University Press.

Bühlmann, M., Feh Widmer, A. and Schädel, L. (2010) 'Substantive and descriptive representation in Swiss cantons', *Swiss Political Science Review* 16(3): 565–95.

Bühlmann, M. and Schädel, L. (2012) 'Representation matters: the impact of women's descriptive representation on the political involvement of women', *Representation* 48(1): 101–14.

Burke, E. (2004/1774) *Speech to the Electors of Bristol*, Indianapolis: Online Library of Liberty. Online. Available. http://oll.libertyfund.org/Texts/LFBooks/Burke0061/SelectWorks/HTMLs/0005-04_Pt02_Speeches.html#hd_lf5-.head.005 (accessed 24 January 2006).

Bylesjö, C. and Seda, F. (2006) 'Indonesia: the struggle for gender quotas in the world's largest Muslim society' in D. Dahlerup, D. (ed.) *Women, Quotas and Politics*, London: Routledge.

Bystydzienski, J. (1995) *Women in Electoral Politics: Lessons from Norway*, London: Praeger.

Cameron, C., Epstein, D. and O'Halloran, S. (1996) 'Do majority–minority districts maximize substantive Black representation in Congress?', *American Political Science Review* 90(4): 794–812.

Campbell, R., Childs, S. and Lovenduski, J. (2010) 'Do women need women representatives?' *British Journal of Political Science* 40(1): 171–94.

Cederman, L., Wimmer, A. and Min, B. (2010) 'Why do ethnic groups rebel? New data and analysis', *World Politics* 62(1): 87–119.

Chafetz, J. (1984) *Sex and Advantage: A comparative, macro-structural theory of sex stratification*, Totowa: Rowman and Allanheld.

Chaney, P. (2006) 'Critical mass, deliberation and the substantive representation of women: Evidence from the UK's devolution programme', *Political Studies* 54(4): 691–714.

Chaney, P. and Fevre, R. (2002) 'Is there a demand for descriptive representation? Evidence from the UK's devolution programme', *Political Studies* 50: 897–915.

Cheibub, J. (2007) *Presidentialism, Parliamentarism, and Democracy*, Cambridge: Cambridge University Press.

Cheibub, J. and Przeworski, A. (1999) 'Democracy, elections, and accountability for economic outcomes' in A. Przeworski, S. Stokes and B. Manin (eds) *Democracy, Accountability, and Representation*, Cambridge: Cambridge University Press.

Chen, L. (2009) 'Do gender quotas influence women's representation and policies?' *Research Papers in Economics* 2009(3).

Childs, S. (2000) 'The New Labour women MPs in the 1997 British parliament: issues of recruitment and representation', *Women's History Review* 9(1): 55–73.

— (2002) 'Hitting the target: are Labour women MPs "acting for" women?', *Parliamentary Affairs* 55: 143–53.

— (2006) 'The House turned upside down? The difference Labour's women MPs made' in M. Sawer, M. Tremblay and L. Trimble (eds) *Representing Women in Parliament: A comparative study*, Abingdon: Routledge.

Childs, S. and Krook, M. (2006) 'Should feminists give up on critical mass? A contingent yes', *Politics & Gender* 2(4): 522–530.

— (2008) 'Critical mass theory and women's political representation', *Political Studies* 56(3): 725–36.

Cohen, S. and Young, J. (eds) (1973) *The Manufacture of News: Social problems, deviance, and the mass media*, London: Constable.

Colomer, J. (ed.) (2004) *Handbook of Electoral System Choice*, New York: Palgrave Macmillan.

— (ed.) (2011) *Personal Representation: The neglected dimension of electoral systems*, Colchester: ECPR Press.

Congressional Quarterly (2007) '110th Congress: religions', *Congressional Quarterly* May.

Contreras, A. (2002) 'Minority voting issues', *Educational Policy* 16(1): 56–76.

Converse, P. (2000) 'Assessing the capacity of mass electorates', *Annual Review of Political Science* 3: 331–53.

Converse, P. and Pierce, R. (1986) *Political Representation in France*, London: Belknap Press of Harvard University Press.

Copeland, W. and Patterson, S. (1998) 'Parliaments and legislatures' in G. Kurian (ed.) *World Encyclopedia of Parliaments and Legislatures*, Washington: Congressional Quarterly.

Cox, G. (2006) 'Evaluating electoral systems', *Revista de Ciencia Politica* 26(1): 212–5.

Crigler, A. (ed.) (1996) *The Psychology of Political Communication*, Ann Arbor: The University of Michigan Press.

Crouch, C. (1999) *Social Change in Western Europe*, Oxford: Oxford University Press.

Curtin, J. (2008) 'Women, political leadership and substantive representation: the case of New Zealand', *Parliamentary Affairs* 61(3): 490–504.

Cutts, D., and Widdop, P. (2012) 'Was Labour penalised where it stood all women shortlist candidates? An analysis of the 2010 UK general election', *The British Journal of Politics & International Relations*. doi: 10.1111/j.1467-856X.2011.00494.x.

Dahl, R. (1985) *A Preface to Economic Democracy*, Cambridge: Polity Press.

— (1989) *Democracy and Its Critics*, London: Yale University Press.

Dahlerup, D. (ed.) (2006) *Women, Quotas and Politics*, London: Routledge.

Dahlerup, D. and Freidenvall, L. (2005) 'Quotas as a "fast track" to equal representation for women: why Scandinavia is no longer the model', *International Feminist Journal of Politics* 7(1): 26–48.

Dalton, R. (1985) 'Political parties and political representation: party supporters and party elites in nine nations', *Comparative Political Studies* 18(3): 267–99.

Dalton, R., Flanagan, S. and Beck, P. (eds) (1984) *Electoral Change in Advanced Industrial Democracies: Realignment or dealignment?*, Princeton: Princeton University Press.

Dalton, R. and Wattenberg, M. (eds) (2000) *Parties without Partisans: Political change in advanced industrial democracies*, Oxford: Oxford University Press.

Darcy, R., Welch, S. and Clark, J. (1994) *Women, Elections, and Representation*, London: University of Nebraska Press.

Darity, W. and Mason, P. (1998) 'Evidence on discrimination in employment: codes of color, codes of gender', *Journal of Economic Perspectives* 12: 63–90.

Davidov, E., Schmidt, P., and Billiet, J. (2010) *Cross-Cultural Analysis: Methods and applications*, New York: Routledge.

Delemotte, B. (2001) 'De la communauté à la commune', *Migrations société* 13(73): 35–40.

de Rezende Martins, E. (2004) 'History of parliaments' in N. Smelser and P. Baltes (eds) *International Encyclopedia of the Social and Behavioural Sciences*, Amsterdam: Pergamon.

Derksen, W. (2006) *Electionworld*, Nijmegen: Nijmegen University. Online. Available http://www.electionworld.org/ (accessed 1 September 2006).

Diamond, L. (2002) 'Thinking about hybrid regimes', *Journal of Democracy* 13(2): 21–35.

Dodson, D. (2006) *The Impact of Women in Congress*, Oxford: Oxford University Press.

Dolin, K. (2004) *Voting for Women: How the public evaluates women candidates*, Oxford: Westview Press.

Dovi, S. (2007) *The Good Representative*, Oxford: Blackwell.

Downs, A. (1957) *An Economic Theory of Democracy*, New York: Harper and Row.

Driscoll, A., and Krook, M. (2012) 'Feminism and rational choice theory', *European Political Science Review* 4(2): 195–216.

Dunn, J. (1999) 'Situating democratic political accountability' in A. Przeworski, S. Stokes and B. Manin (eds) *Democracy, Accountability, and Representation*, Cambridge: Cambridge University Press.

Duverger, M. (1955) *The Political Role of Women*, Paris: UNESCO.

Egan, P. (2012) 'Group cohesion without group mobilization: the case of lesbians, gays and bisexuals', *British Journal of Political Science* 42(3): 597–616.

EHRC (2008) *Sex and Power 2008*, Manchester: Equality and Human Rights Commission. Available http://www.equalityhumanrights.com/Documents/EHRC/sexandpower08.pdf (accessed 4 September 2008).

Eichenberg, R. (2007) 'Citizen opinion on foreign policy and world politics' in R. Dalton and H.-D. Klingemann (eds) *The Oxford Handbook of Political Behaviour*, Oxford: Oxford University Press.

Emerson, M., Tolbert, R. and Yancey, G. (2002) 'Contact theory extended: The effect of prior racial contact on current socialties', *Social Science Quarterly* 83(2): 745–61.

Engstrom, R. and McDonald, M. (1982) 'The underrepresentation of blacks on city councils: Comparing the structural and socioeconomic explanations for south/non-south differences', *Journal of Politics* 44(4): 1088–99.

Eposito, J. and Watson, M. (eds) (2000) *Religion and Global Order*, Cardiff: University of Wales Press.

Esaiasson, P. and Holmberg, S. (1996) *Representation from Above: Members of Parliament and representative democracy in Sweden*, Aldershot: Dartmouth.

Escobar-Lemmon, M. and Taylor-Robinson, M. (2005) 'Women ministers in Latin American Government: when, where, and why?', *American Journal of Political Science* 49(4): 829–44.

Etzioni-Halevy, E. (2004) 'Elites: Sociological aspects' in N. Smelser and P. Baltes (eds) *International Encyclopedia of the Social and Behavioural Sciences*, Amsterdam: Pergamon.

Eulau, H. and Wahlke, J. (eds) (1978) *The Politics of Representation*, London: Sage.

Fairlie, J. (1940a) 'The nature of political representation I', *American Political Science Review* 34(2): 236–48.

—   (1940b) 'The nature of political representation II', *American Political Science Review* 34(3): 456–66.

Farrell, D. (2001) *Electoral Systems: A comparative introduction*, New York: Palgrave.

Farrell, D. and Scully, R. (2007) *Representing Europe's Citizens? Electoral institutions and the failure of parliamentary representation*, Oxford: Oxford University Press.

Fearon, J. (1999) 'Electoral accountability and the control of politicians: selecting good types versus sanctioning poor performance' in A. Przeworski, S. Stokes and B. Manin (eds) *Democracy, Accountability, and Representation*, Cambridge: Cambridge University Press.

—— (2003) 'Ethnic and cultural diversity by country', *Journal of Economic Growth* 8: 195–222.

Fernández, R., Fogli, A. and Olivetti, C. (2004) 'Mothers and sons: Preference formation and female labor force dynamics', *The Quarterly Journal of Economics* 119(4): 1249–99.

Fiorina, M. (1976) 'The voting decision: Instrumental and expressive aspects', Journal of Politics 38(2): 390–413.

Forbes, H. (1997) *Ethnic Conflict: Commerce, Culture, and the Contact Hypothesis*, London: Yale University Press.

Ford, H. (1925) *Representative Government*, London: Sir Isaac Pitman and Sons.

Freedom House (2006) *Freedom in the World Comparative Rankings: 1973–2006* (computer file), Washington: Freedom House (distributor): FIWAllScores.

Freidenvall, L., Dahlerup, D. and Skjeie, H. (2006) 'The Nordic countries: An incremental model' in D. Dahlerup (ed.) *Women, Quotas and Politics*, London: Routledge.

Froman, L. (1961) 'Personality and political socialization', *Journal of Politics* 23 (2): 341–52.

Fuchs, D. (2007) 'The political culture paradigm' in R. Dalton and H.-D. Klingemann (eds) *The Oxford Handbook of Political Behaviour*, Oxford: Oxford University Press.

Fuchs, D. and Klingemann, H.-D. (1989) 'The left–right schema' in M. Jennings *et al.* (1990) *Continuities in Political Action*, New York: de Gruyter.

Furedi, F. (2005) *Politics of Fear*, London: Continuum.

Gallagher, M. (1991) 'Proportionality, disproportionality and electoral systems', *Electoral Studies* 10(1): 33–51.

—— (1992) 'Comparing proportional representation electoral systems: quotas, thresholds, paradoxes and majorities', *British Journal of Political Science* 22(4): 469–96.

Gallagher, M., Laver, M. and Mair, P. (2001) *Representative Government in Modern Europe: Institutions, parties, and governments*, New York: McGraw-Hill.

Galligan, Y. (2005) 'Ireland' in Y. Galligan and M. Tremblay (eds) *Sharing Power: Women, parliament, democracy*, Aldershot: Ashgate.

Galligan, Y. and Tremblay, M. (eds) (2005) *Sharing Power: Women, parliament, democracy*, Aldershot: Ashgate.

Galtung, J. (1969) *Theory and Methods of Social Research*, Oslo: Universitetsforlaget.

Gamson, W. (1961) 'A theory of coalition formation', *American Sociological Review* 26(3): 373–82.

Ganghof, S. (2010) 'Democratic inclusiveness: a reinterpretation of Lijphart's Patterns of Democracy', *British Journal of Political Science* 40: 679–92.

Garbaye, R. (2000) 'Ethnic minorities, cities, and institutions: a comparison of the modes of management of ethnic diversity of a French and British city' in R. Koopmans and P. Statham (eds) *Challenging Immigration and Ethnic Relations Politics: Comparative European perspectives*, Oxford: Oxford University Press.

Gastil, J. (1997) *Common Problems in Small Group Decision Making*, Madison: University of Wisconsin. Online. Available http://www.fao.org/sd/ppdirect/ppan0009.htm (accessed 13 June 2006).

Geddes, A. (1998) 'Race related political participation and representation in the UK', *Revue européenne des migrations internationales* 14(2): 33–49.

Geisser, V. (1997) *Ethnicité Républicaine: Les élites d'origine maghrébine dans le système politique français*, Paris: Presses de Sciences Politiques.

Gershon, S. (2012) 'When race, gender, and the media intersect: campaign news coverage of minority congresswomen', *Journal of Women, Politics & Policy* 33(2): 105–125.

Girlguiding UK (2009) *Political Outsiders: We care, but will we vote? Active citizenship*, London: Girlguiding UK.

Givel, M. and Glantz, S. (2001) 'Tobacco lobby political influence on US state legislature in the 1990s', *Tobacco Control* 10: 124–34.

Goffman, E. (1976) *Gender Advertisements*, London: Macmillan.

Golder, M. and Stramski, J. (2010) 'Ideological congruence and electoral institutions', *American Journal of Political Science* 54(1): 90–106.

Grafstein, R. (1981) 'The failure of Weber's conception of legitimacy: its causes and implications', *Journal of Politics* 43(2): 456–72.

Gratton, L., Kelan, E., Voigt, A., Walker, L. and Wolfram, H. (2007) *Innovative Potential: Men and women in teams*, London: London Business School. Online. Available http://www.london.edu/assets/documents/Word/Innovative_Potential_NOV_2007.pdf (accessed 3 November 2007).

Gray, T. (2003) 'Electoral gender quotas: lessons from Argentina and Chile', *Bulletin of Latin American Research* 22(1): 52–78.

Green, E. (2005) 'What is an ethnic group? Political economy, constructivism and the common language approach to ethnicity', *LSE Development Studies Institute Working Paper Series*, 05–57.

Grey, S. (2006) 'The 'new world'? The substantive representation of women in New Zealand' in M. Sawer, M. Tremblay and L. Trimble (eds) *Representing Women in Parliament: A comparative study*, Abingdon: Routledge.

Grey, S. and Sawer, M. (2005) 'Australia and New Zealand' in Y. Galligan and M. Tremblay (eds) *Sharing Power: Women, parliament, democracy*, Aldershot: Ashgate.

Griffin, J. and Newman, B. (2005) 'Are voters better represented?', *Journal of Politics* 67(4): 1206–27.

Grofman, B. (1983) 'Measures of bias and proportionality in seats–votes relationships', *Political Methodology* 9: 295–327.

Hall, R. and Wayman, F. (1990) 'Buying time: moneyed interests and the mobilization of bias in congressional committees' in R. Alexander (2006) *The Classics of Interest Group Behavior*, Belmont: Thomson Wadsworth.

Hassim, S. (2009) 'Perverse consequences? The impact of quotas for women on democratization in Africa', in I. Shapiro, S. Stokes, E. Wood and A. Kirshner (eds), *Political Representation*, Cambridge: Cambridge University Press.

Häusermann, S. and Schwander, H. (2010) 'Explaining welfare preferences in dualized societies', paper presented at the 17th Conference for European Studies, Montreal.

Hayward, C. (2009) 'Making interest: on representation and democratic legitimacy', in I. Shapiro *et al. Political Representation*, Cambridge: Cambridge University Press.

Heath, R., Schwindt-Bayer, L. and Taylor-Robinson, M. (2005) 'Women on the sidelines: women's representation on committees in Latin American legislatures', *American Journal of Political Science* 49(2): 420–36.

Heclo, H. (1978) 'Issue networks and the executive establishment' in R. Alexander (2006) *The Classics of Interest Group Behavior*, Belmont: Thomson Wadsworth.

Henig, R. and Henig, S. (2001) *Women and Political Power: Europe since 1945*, London: Routledge.

Herrera, C., Herrera, R. and Smith, E. (1992) 'Public opinion and congressional representation', *Public Opinion Quarterly* 56: 186–205.

Herrera, R. (1999) 'The language of politics: a study of elite and mass understandings of ideological terminology in the United States and the Netherlands' in W. Miller, R. Pierce, J. Thomassen, R. Herrera, S. Holmberg, P. Esaiasson, B. Wessels (eds) *Policy Representation in Western Democracies*, Oxford: Oxford University Press.

Hoddie, M. (2006) *Ethnic Realignments: A comparative study of government influences on identity*, Oxford: Lexington Books.

Hogan, J. (1945) *Elections and Representation*, Cork: Cork University Press.

Högström, J. (2012) 'Women's representation in national politics in the world's democratic countries: a research note', *Journal of Women, Politics & Policy* 33(3): 263–279.

Holmberg, S. (1999) 'Collective policy congruence compared' in W. Miller, R. Pierce, J. Thomassen, R. Herrera, S. Holmberg, P. Esaiasson, B. Wessels (eds) *Policy Representation in Western Democracies*, Oxford: Oxford University Press.

Holmsten, S., Moser, R. and Slosar, M. (2010) 'Do ethnic parties exclude women?', *Comparative Political Studies* 43(10): 1179–1201.

Horowitz, D. (1985) *Ethnic Groups in Conflict*, London: University of California Press.

Htun, M. (2004) 'Is gender like ethnicity? The political representation of identity groups', *Perspectives on Politics* 2(3): 439–58.

Huber, J. and Powell, G. (1994) 'Congruence between citizens and policymakers in two visions of liberal democracy', *World Politics* 46: 291–326.

Hughes, M. (2011) 'Intersectionality, quotas, and minority women's political representation worldwide', *American Political Science Review* 105(3): 604–620.

IDEA (1998) *Women in Parliament: Beyond Numbers*, Stockholm: International IDEA. Online. Available http://archive.idea.int/women/parl/toc.htm (accessed 28 February 2006).

— (2006) *Global Database of Quotas for Women*, Stockholm: International IDEA and Stockholm University. Online. Available http://www.quotaproject.org/ (accessed 20 February 2006).

ILO (2007) *International Labour Migration Database* (computer file), Geneva: International Labour Organization (distributor).

Inglehart, R. (1997) *Modernization and Postmodernization: Cultural, economic, and political change in 43 societies*, Princeton: Princeton University Press.

Inglehart, R. and Norris, P. (2003) *Rising Tide: Gender equality and cultural change around the world*, Cambridge: Cambridge University Press.

Inglehart, R., and Welzel, C. (2010) 'Changing mass priorities: the link between modernization and democracy', *Perspectives on Politics* 8(2): 551–67.

IPU (2009) *Women in National Parliaments*, Geneva: Inter-Parliamentary Union. Online. Available http://www.ipu.org/wmn-e/classif.htm (accessed 10 November 2010).

— (2010) *Promoting inclusive parliaments: the representation of minorities and indigenous peoples in parliament*, Geneva: Inter-Parliamentary Union. Online. Available http://www.ipu.org/dem-e/minorities/overview.htm (accessed 5 January 2010).

Iyengar, S. and Reeves, R. (eds) (1997) *Do the Media Govern? Politicians, voters, and reporters in America*, London: Sage.

Jacobs, L. and Shapiro, R. (2000) *Politicians Don't Pander: Political manipulation and the loss of democratic responsiveness*, Chicago: University of Chicago Press.

Jacobs, R. and Townsley, E. (2011) *The Space of Opinion: Media intellectuals and the public sphere*, Oxford: Oxford University Press.

Jacquette, J. (1997) 'Women in power: from tokenism to critical mass', *Foreign Policy* 108: 23–37.

James, M. (2011) 'The priority of racial constituency over descriptive representation', *Journal of Politics* 73(3): 899–914.

Jenkins, R. (1997) *Rethinking Ethnicity: Arguments and explorations*, London: Sage.

Jenkins, S. (2002) 'Data pooling and type I errors: a comment on Leger and Didrichsons', *Animal Behaviour* 63: F9–11.

Jennings, M. (2007) 'Political socialization' in R. Dalton, H.-D. Klingemann (eds) *The Oxford Handbook of Political Behaviour*, Oxford: Oxford University Press.

Johnson, O. (1998) 'Racial representation and Brazilian politics: black members of the National Congress 1983–1999', *Journal of InterAmerican Studies and World Affairs Winter 1998*.

Johnston, R., Rossiter, D. and Pattie, C. (2006) 'Disproportionality and bias in the results of the 2005 General Election in Great Britain: evaluating the electoral system's impact', *Journal of Elections, Public Opinion, and Parties* 16: 1.

Jones, M. (2005) 'The desirability of gender quotas: considering context and design', *Politics and Gender* 1(4s): 645–52.

Joshua Project (2006) *Unreached Peoples of the World*, Colorado Springs: Joshua Project. Online. Available http://www.joshuaproject.net/ (accessed 18 December 2006).

Jung, C. (2009) 'Critical liberalism', in I. Shapiro, S. Stokes, E. Wood and A. Kirshner (eds) *Political Representation*, Cambridge: Cambridge University Press.

Kang, A. (2009) 'Studying oil, Islam, and women as if political institutions mattered', *Politics & Gender* 5: 560–8.

Kanter, R. (1977) *Men and Women of the Corporation*, New York: Basic Books.

Karp, J. and Banducci, S. (2007) 'When politics is not just a man's game: women's representation and political engagement', paper presented at the *MPSA*.

Katz, R. (1997) *Democracy and Elections*, Oxford: Oxford University Press.

Kellstedt, P. (2000) 'Media framing and the dynamics of racial policy preferences', *American Journal of Political Science* 44(2): 245–60.

Kenworthy, L. and Malami, M. (1999) 'Gender inequality in political representation: a worldwide comparative analysis', *Social Forces* 78(1): 235–68.

Kimmel, M. (2004) *The Gendered Society*, Oxford: Oxford University Press.

King, G., Murray, C., Salomon, J. and Tandon, A. (2004) 'Enhancing the validity and cross-cultural comparability of measurement in survey research', *American Political Science Review* 98(1): 191–207.

Kitschelt, H. and Hellemans, S. (1990) 'The left right semantic and the new politics cleavage', *Comparative Political Studies* 23: 210–38.

Kittilson, M. and Schwindt-Bayer, L. (2010) 'Engaging citizens: the role of power-sharing institutions', *The Journal of Politics* 72(4): 990–1002.

Klingemann, H., Hofferbert, R. and Budge, I. (1994) *Parties, Policies, and Democracy*, Oxford: Westview Press.

Knutsen, O. (1995) 'Value orientations, political conflict and left–right identification', *European Journal of Political Research* 28(1): 63–93.

— (1997) 'The partisan and the value-based component of left–right self-placement: a comparative study', *International Political Science Review* 18(2): 191–225.

Koch, M. and Fulton, S. (2011) 'In the defence of women: gender, office holding, and national security policy in established democracies', *The Journal of Politics* 73(1): 1–16.

Kolinsky, E. (1993) 'Party change and women's representation in unified Germany' in J. Lovenduski and P. Norris (eds) *Gender and Party Politics*, London: Sage.

Kostadinova, T. (2002) 'Do mixed electoral systems matter? A cross-national analysis of their effects in Eastern Europe', *Electoral Studies* 21: 23–34.

—— (2007) 'Ethnic and women's representation under mixed election systems', *Electoral Studies* 26: 418–31.

Krook, M. (2010) *Quotas for Women in Politics: Gender and candidate selection reform worldwide*, New York: Oxford University Press.

Krook, M. and O'Brien, D. (2010) 'The politics of group representation: quotas for women and minorities worldwide', *Comparative Politics* 42: 253–72.

—— (2012) 'All the President's men? The appointment of female cabinet ministers worldwide', *The Journal of Politics* 74(3): 840–55.

Kuklinski, J. (ed.) (2002) *Thinking about Political Psychology*, Cambridge: Cambridge University Press.

Kunovich, S. (2012) 'Unexpected winners: the significance of an open-list system on women's representation in Poland', *Politics & Gender* 8(2): 153–177.

Kunovich, S. and Paxton, P. (2005) 'Pathways to power: the role of political parties in women's national political representation', *American Journal of Sociology* 111(2): 505–52.

Kymlicka, W. (1995) *Multicultural Citizenship: A liberal theory of minority rights*, Oxford: Clarendon Press.

Laakso, M. and Taagepera, R. (1979) 'The effective number of parties: a measure with application to West Europe', *Comparative Political Studies* 12(1): 3–27.

Laponce, J. (1981) *Left and Right: The topography of political perceptions*, Toronto: University of Toronto Press.

Latner, M. and McGann, A. (2005) 'Geographical representation under proportional representation: the cases of Israel and the Netherlands', *Electoral Studies* 24(4): 709–34.

Laver, M. (1997) *Private Desires, Political Actions: An innovation to the politics of rational choice*, London: Sage.

Lawless, J. and Fox, R. (2005) *It Takes a Candidate: Why women don't run for office*, Cambridge: Cambridge University Press.

Leijenaar, M. (1993) 'A battle for power: selecting candidates in the Netherlands' in J. Lovenduski and P. Norris (eds) *Gender and Party Politics*, London: Sage.

Leik, R. (1966) 'A measure of ordinal consensus', *Pacific Sociological Review* 9(2): 85–90.

Lewis, J., Williams, A., Frankin, B., Thomas, J. and Mosdell, N. (2008) *The Quality and Independence of British Journalism*, Cardiff: Cardiff School of Journalism, Media and Cultural Studies. Online. Available http://www.cf.ac.uk/jomec/library/doc_lib/Quality_Independence_ British_ Journalism.pdf (accessed 28 April 2008).

Leyenaar, M. (2004) *Political Empowerment of Women: The Netherlands and other countries*, Leiden: Martinus Nijhoff Publishers.

Lijphart, A. (1977) *Democracy in Plural Societies: A comparative exploration*, London: Yale University Press.

— (1979) 'Religious vs. linguistic vs. class voting: the "crucial experiment" of comparing Belgium, Canada, South Africa, and Switzerland', *American Political Science Review* 73(2): 442–58.

— (1994) *Electoral Systems and Party Systems: A study of twenty-seven democracies 1945–1990*, Oxford: Oxford University Press.

— (1999) *Patterns of Democracy: Government forms and performance in thirty-six countries*, London: Yale University Press.

— (2004) 'Constitutional design for divided societies', *Journal of Democracy* 15(2): 96–109.

Lijphart, A. and Grofman, B. (eds) (1984) *Choosing an Electoral System: Issues and alternatives*, Westport: Praeger.

Lopez-Carlos, A. and Zahidi, S. (2005) *Women's Empowerment: Measuring the global gender gap*, Geneva: World Economic Forum. Online. Available http://www.weforum.org/pdf/Global_Competitiveness_Reports/Reports/gender_gap.pdf (accessed 22 November 2006).

Lovenduski, J. (2005) *Feminizing Politics*, Cambridge: Polity Press.

Lovenduski, J. and Norris, P. (eds) (1993) *Gender and Party Politics*, London: Sage.

Lublin, D. (1997) *The Paradox of Representation*, Princeton University Press.

Luna, J. and Zechmeister, E. (2005) 'Political representation in Latin America: a study of elite–mass congruence in nine countries', *Comparative Political Studies* 38(4): 388–416.

Lutz, G. (2003) *Participation, Cognitive Involvement and Democracy: When do low turnout and low cognitive involvement make a difference, and why?*, Dublin: Trinity College. Online. Available http://www.paltin.ro/biblioteca/Lutz.pdf (accessed 20 October 2005).

McAllister, I. (2006) 'Women's electoral representation in Australia' in M. Sawer, M. Tremblay and L. Trimble (eds) *Representing Women in Parliament: A comparative study*, Abingdon: Routledge.

McAllister, I. and Studlar, D. (2002) 'Electoral systems and women's representation: a long-term perspective', *Representation* 39(1): 3–14.

McDonald, M., Mendes, S. and Budge, I. (2004) 'What are elections for? Conferring the median mandate', *British Journal of Political Science* 34: 1–26.

Mackay, F. (2004) 'Gender and political representation in the UK: the state of the "discipline"', *British Journal of Politics and International Relations* 6: 99–120.

Mackie, T. and Rose, R. (eds) (1991) *The International Almanac of Electoral History*, London: Macmillan.

McLean, I. (1991) 'Forms of representation and systems of voting' in D. Held (ed.) *Political Theory Today*, Cambridge: Polity Press.

McLeay, E. (2006) 'Climbing on: rules, values and women's representation in the New Zealand parliament' in M. Sawer, M. Tremblay, and L. Trimble (eds) *Representing Women in Parliament: A comparative study*, Abingdon: Routledge.

Mainwaring, S. and Scully, T. (eds) (1995) *Building Democratic Institutions: Party systems in Latin America*, Stanford: Stanford University Press.

Manin, B., Przeworski, A. and Stokes, S. (1999) 'Elections and representation' in A. Przeworski, S. Stokes and B. Manin (eds) *Democracy, Accountability, and Representation*, Cambridge: Cambridge University Press.

Mansbridge, J. (1999) 'Should blacks represent blacks and women represent women? A contingent "yes"', *Journal of Politics* 63(1): 628–57.

—   (2003) 'Rethinking representation', *American Political Science Review* 97(4).

—   (2005) 'Quota problems: combating the dangers of essentialism', *Politics and Gender* 1(4):621–38.

—   (2008) 'A "selection model" of political representation' *Faculty Research Working Papers* 10.

—   (2011) 'Clarifying the concept of representation', *American Political Science Review* 105(3): 621–630.

Marsh, M. and Wessels, B. (1997) 'Territorial representation', *European Journal of Political Research* 32: 227–41.

Mateo Diaz, M. (2005) *Representing women? Female legislators in West European parliaments* Colchester, ECPR Press.

Matheson, C. (1987) 'Weber and the classification of forms of legitimacy', *British Journal of Sociology* 38(2): 199–215.

Matland, R. (1993) 'Institutional variables affecting female representation in national legislatures: the case of Norway', *Journal of Politics* 55: 737–55.

—   (1998) 'Women's representation in national legislatures: developed and developing countries', *Legislative Studies Quarterly* 23: 109–25.

—   (2006) 'Electoral quotas: Frequency and effectiveness' in D. Dahlerup (ed.) *Women, Quotas and Politics*, London: Routledge.

Matland, R. and Studlar, D. (1996) 'The contagion of women candidates in single-member district and proportional representation electoral systems: Canada and Norway', *Journal of Politics* 58: 707–33.

Matland, R. and Taylor, M. (1997) 'Electoral system effects on women's representation', *Comparative Political Studies* 30: 186–210.

Messina, A. (1989) *Race and Party Competition in Britain*, Oxford: Clarendon Press.

Miller, D. (1999) *Principles of Social Justice*, London: Harvard University Press.

Miller, W. and Stokes, D. (1963) 'Constituency influence in congress', *American Political Science Review* 57(1): 45–56.

Miller, W., Pierce, R., Thomassen, J., Herrera, R., Holmberg, S., Esaiasson, P., Wessels, B. (1999) *Policy Representation in Western Democracies*, Oxford: Oxford University Press.

Milne, R. (1981) *Politics in Ethnically Bipolar States: Guyana, Malaysia, Fiji*, London: University of British Columbia Press.

Minorities at Risk Project (2008) *Minorities at Risk Organizational Behavior Dataset* (computer file), College Park: Center for International Development and Conflict Management (distributor).

Minta, M. (2011) *Oversight: Representing the interests of Blacks and Latinos in Congress*, Princeton: Princeton University Press.

Moore, G. and Shackman, G. (1996) 'Gender and authority: a cross-national study', *Social Science Quarterly* 77: 272–88.

Moore, R. (2006) 'Religion, race, and gender differences in political ambition', *Politics and Gender* 1: 577–96.

Moser, R. (2004) 'The representation of ethnic minorities in post-communist legislatures: Russia and Lithuania compared', paper presented at the annual meeting of the *American Political Science Association*, Chicago.

Mozaffar, S., Scarritt, J. and Galaich, G. (2003) 'Electoral institutions, ethnopolitical cleavages, and party systems in Africa's emerging democracies', *American Political Science Review* 93(3): 379–90.

Mueller, C. (ed.) (1988) *The Politics of the Gender Gap: The social construction of political influence*, London: Sage.

Murray, R. (2007) 'How parties evaluate compulsory quotas: a study of the implementation of the "parity" law in France', *Parliamentary Affairs* 60(4): 68–84.

—— (2010) 'Second among unequals? A study of whether France's "quota women" are up to the job', *Politics & Gender* 6(1): 93–118.

Mutz, D. (2007) 'Political psychology and choice' in R. Dalton and H. Klingemann (eds) *The Oxford Handbook of Political Behaviour*, Oxford: Oxford University Press.

Nanivadekar, M. (2006) 'Are quotas a good idea? The Indian experience with reserved seats for women', *Politics and Gender* 2(1): 119–28.

Nestle, M. (2002) *Food Politics: How the food industry influences nutrition and health*, London: University of California Press.

Nordlinger, E. (1968) 'Representation, governmental stability, and decisional effectiveness' in J. Pennock and J. Chapman (eds) *Representation*, New York: Atherton Press.

Norris, P. (1985) 'Women's legislative participation in Western Europe', *West European Politics* 8: 90–101.

—— (1987) *Politics and Sexual Equality: The comparative position of women in Western democracies*, Boulder: Rienner.

—— (1993) 'Conclusions: Comparing legislative recruitment' in J. Lovenduski and P. Norris (eds) *Gender and Party Politics*, London: Sage.

—— (1996) 'Do women at Westminster make a difference?', *Parliamentary Affairs* 49(1): 89–102.

—— (2000) *Breaking the Barriers: Positive discrimination policies for women*, Cambridge: Harvard University. Online. Available http://ksghome.harvard.edu/~pnorris/acrobat/QUOTAS.PDF (accessed 9 August 2006).

— (2004) *Electoral Engineering: Voting rules and political behaviour*, Cambridge: Cambridge University Press.

— (2009) 'Why do Arab states lag the world in gender equality?', *HKS Faculty Research Working Paper* 9(20).

Norris, P. and Franklin, M. (1997) 'Social representation', *European Journal of Political Research* 32: 185–210.

Norris, P. and Inglehart, R. (2001) 'Cultural obstacles to equal representation', *Journal of Democracy* 12(3): 126–40.

— (2004) *Sacred and Secular: Religion and politics worldwide*, New York: Cambridge University Press.

— (2010) 'Are high levels of existential security conductive to secularization? A response to our critics', paper presented at the *MPSA 2010*, Chicago.

Norris, P. and Lovenduski, J. (1993) 'If only more candidates came forward: Supply-side explanations of candidate selection in Britain', *British Journal of Political Science* 23: 373–408.

— (1995) *Political Recruitment*, Cambridge: Cambridge University Press.

Norris, P., Curtice, J., Sanders, D., Scammell, M. and Semetko, H. (1999) *On Message: Communicating the campaign*, London: Sage.

Novosel, S. (2005) 'Croatia' in Y. Galligan and M. Tremblay (eds) *Sharing Power: Women, Parliament, Democracy*, Aldershot: Ashgate.

Oakes, A. and Almquist, E. (1993) 'Women in national legislatures: A cross-national test of macrostructural gender theories', *Population Research Policy and Review* 12: 71–81.

O'Brien, D. (2012) 'Gender and select committee elections in the British House of Commons', *Politics & Gender* 8(2): 178–204.

OECD (2006) *Migration Statistics* (computer file), Paris: OECD (distributor): 25th September 2007.

O'Flynn, I. and Russel, D. (eds) (2005) *Power Sharing: New challenges for divided societies*, London: Pluto Press.

Okin, S. (1994) 'Political liberalism, justice, and gender', *Ethics* 105(1): 23–43.

Olson, D. and Crowther, W. (2002) *Committees in Post-Communist Democratic Parliaments: Comparative institutionalization*, Columbus: Ohio State University Press.

Ordeshook, P. and Shvetsava, O. (1994) 'Ethnic heterogeneity, district magnitude, and the number of parties', *American Journal of Political Science* 38: 100–23.

Osborn, T. (2012) *How Women Represent Women: Political parties, gender, and representation in the state legislatures*, Oxford: Oxford University Press.

Overby, M. and Cosgrove, K. (1996) 'Unintended consequences? Racial redistricting and the representation of minority interests', *Journal of Politics* 58(2): 540–50.

Packer, J. (2005) 'Confronting the contemporary challenges of Europe's minorities', *Helsinki Monitor* 16.

Page, E. and Wright, V. (eds) (1999) *Bureaucratic Elites in Western European States: A comparative analysis of top officials*, Oxford: Oxford University Press.

Pantoja, A. and Segura, G. (2003) 'Does ethnicity matter? Descriptive representation in legislatures and political alienation among Latinos', *Social Science Quarterly* 84(2): 441–60.

Paxton, P. (1997) 'Women in national legislatures: a cross-national analysis', *Social Science Research* 26: 442–64.

Paxton, P. (2008) 'Gendering democracy', in G. Goertz and A. Mazur (eds) *Politics, Gender, and Concepts, Theory and Methodology*, Cambridge: Cambridge University Press.

Paxton, P., Hughes, M. and Painter, M. (2010) 'Growth in women's political representation: a longitudinal exploration of democracy, electoral system and gender quotas', *European Journal of Political Research* 49(1):25–52.

Paxton, P., Hughes, M. and Green, J. (2006) 'The international women's movement and women's political representation, 1893–2003', *American Sociological Review* 71: 898–920.

Paxton, P. and Kunovich, S. (2003) 'Women's political representation: the importance of ideology', *Social Forces* 82(1): 87–114.

Paxton, P., Kunovich, S., and Hughes, M. (2007) 'Gender in politics', *Annual Review of Sociology* 33: 263–84.

Peffley, M. and Rohrschneider, R. (2007) 'Elite beliefs and the theory of democratic elitism' in R. Dalton and H.-D. Klingemann (eds) *The Oxford Handbook of Political Behaviour*, Oxford: Oxford University Press.

Pennock, J. (1968) 'Political representation: An overview' in J. Pennock and J. Chapman (eds) *Representation*, New York: Atherton Press.

Peterson, S. (1990) *Political Behaviour: Patterns in everyday life*, London: Sage.

Pettigrew, T. and Tropp, L. (2006) 'A meta-analytic test of intergroup contact theory', *Journal of Personality and Social Psychology* 90(5): 751–83.

Phillips, A. (1993) *Democracy and Difference*, Cambridge: Polity Press.

— (1995) *The Politics of Presence*, Oxford: Oxford University Press.

Pierce, R. (1999) 'Mass–elite issue linkages and the responsible party model of representation' in W. Miller, R. Pierce, J. Thomassen, R. Herrera, S. Holmberg, P. Esaiasson and B. Wessels (eds) *Policy Representation in Western Democracies*, Oxford: Oxford University Press.

Pitkin, H. (1967) *The Concept of Representation*, Los Angeles: University of California Press.

Plotke, D. (1997) 'Representation is democracy', *Constellations* 4(1):19–34.

Powell, G. (2000) *Elections as Instruments of Democracy: Majoritarian and Proportional Visions*, Yale: Yale University Press.

— (2004) 'Political representation in comparative politics', *Annual Review of Political Science* 7: 273–96.

— (2006) 'Election laws and representative governments: beyond votes and seats', *British Journal of Political Science* 36: 291–315.

—   (2007) 'The ideological congruence controversy: the impact of alternative conceptualizations and data on the effects of election rules', paper presented at the annual meeting of the *American Political Science Association*, Chicago.

Pro Quote (2012) *Pro Quote*, Düsseldorf: Initiative Pro Quote. Online. Available http://www.pro-quote.de (accessed 24 February 2012).

Pulzer, P. (1975) *Political Representation and Elections in Britain*, London: George Allen and Unwin.

Rabb, T. and Suleiman, E. (eds) (2003) *The Making and Unmaking of Democracy: Lessons from history and world politics*, London: Routledge.

Rabinowitz, G. (1978) 'On the nature of political issues: insights from a spatial analysis', *American Journal of Political Science* 22(4): 793–817.

Rae, D. (1967) *The Political Consequences of Electoral Laws*, London: Yale University Press.

Ramet, S. (1997) *Whose Democracy? Nationalism, religion, and the doctrine of collective rights in post-1989 Eastern Europe*, Oxford: Rowman and Littlefield.

Randall, V. (1987) *Women and Politics: An international perspective*, Chicago: University of Chicago Press.

Rawls, J. (1999) *A Theory of Social Justice*, Oxford: Oxford University Press.

Raymond, G. (ed.) (2005) *Ethnologue: Languages of the World*, Dallas: SIL International.

Rehfeld, A. (2006) 'Towards a general theory of political representation', *Journal of Politics* 68(1): 1–21.

—   (2009) 'Representation rethought: on trustees, delegates and gyroscopes in the study of political representation and democracy', *American Political Science Review* 103: 214–30.

—   (2011) 'The concepts of representation', *American Political Science Review* 105(3): 631–41.

Reilly, B. (2002) 'Electoral systems for divided societies', *Journal of Democracy* 13(2): 156–70.

Reynolds, A. (1999) 'Women in the legislatures and executives of the world: knocking at the highest glass ceiling', *World Politics* 51(4): 547–72.

—   (2006) *Electoral Systems and the Protection and Participation of Minorities*, London: Minority Rights Group International.

Reynolds, A. and Reilly, B. *et al.* (1997) *The International IDEA Handbook of Electoral System Design*, Stockholm: International Institute for Democratic and Electoral Assistance.

Roemer, J. (2009) 'Why does the Republican Party win half the votes?', in I. Shapiro, S. Stokes, E. Wood and A. Kirshner, A. (eds) *Political Representation*, Cambridge: Cambridge University Press.

Rosenbaum, P. and Rubin, D. (1983) 'The central role of the propensity score in observational studies for causal effects', *Biometrika* 70(1): 41–55.

Ross, J. (1943) *Parliamentary Representation*, London: Eyre and Spottiswoode.

Rothman, S. (2004) 'Political elites: Recruitment and careers' in N. Smelser and P. Baltes (eds) *International Encyclopedia of the Social and Behavioural Sciences*, Amsterdam: Pergamon.

Ruedin, D. (2009) 'The proportion of women in national parliament as a measure of women's status in society', *Sociology Working Papers* 5: 1–7.

Ruiz, R. (2002) *Ethnic Parliamentary Incorporation in Central and Eastern Europe: Finding a Mechanical Explanation*, London: London School of Economics and Political Science. Online. Available http://www.lse.ac.uk/collections/EPIC/documents/C2W2Ruiz.pdf (accessed 9 February 2007).

Rule, W. (1981) 'Why women don't run: the critical contextual factors in women's legislative recruitment', *Western Political Quarterly* 34: 60–77.

— (1987) 'Electoral systems, contextual factors and women's opportunity for election to parliament in twenty-three democracies', *Western Political Quarterly* 40: 477–98.

Rule, W. and Zimmerman, J. (eds) (1994) *Electoral Systems in Comparative Perspective: Their Impact on Women and Minorities*, Westport: Greenwood Press.

Saalfeld, T. (2011) 'Parliamentary questions as instruments of substantive representation: Visible minorities in the UK House of Commons, 2005–10', *The Journal of Legislative Studies* 17(3): 271–289.

Sachs, W. (ed.) (1992) *The Development Dictionary: A guide to knowledge as power*, London: Zed Books.

Saggar, S. (2000) *Race and Representation: Electoral politics and ethnic pluralism in Britain*, Manchester: Manchester University Press.

Saggar, S. and Geddes, A. (2000) 'Negative and positive racialisation: re-examining ethnic minority political representation in the UK', *Journal of Ethnic and Migration Studies* 26(1): 25–44.

Saideman, S., Lanoue, D., Campenni, M. and Stanton, S. (2002) 'Democratization, political institutions, and ethnic conflict: a pooled time-series analysis 1985–1998', *Comparative Political Studies* 35: 103–29.

Sainsbury, D. (1993) 'The politics of increased women's representation: The Swedish case' in J. Lovenduski and P. Norris (eds) *Gender and Party Politics*, London: Sage.

Sanders, D. (1999) 'The impact of left–right ideology' in G. Evans and P. Norris (eds) *Critical Elections: British parties and voters in long-term perspective*, London: Sage.

Sapiro, V. and Shively, P. (2007) *Comparative Study of Electoral Systems (CSES) Module 2: 2001–2006 Full Release* (computer file), Ann Arbor: Centre for Political Studies (distributor).

Sartori, G. (1997) *Comparative Constitutional Engineering: An inquiry into structures, incentives and outcomes*, London: Macmillan.

Saward, M. (2006) 'The representative claim', *Contemporary Political Theory* 5(3): 297–318.

— (2010) *The Representative Claim*, Oxford: Oxford University Press.

Sawer, M., Tremblay, M. and Trimble, L. (eds) (2006) *Representing Women in Parliament: A comparative study*, Abingdon: Routledge.

Scherer, N., and Curry, B. (2010) 'Does descriptive race representation enhance institutional legitimacy? The case of the U.S. courts', *Journal of Politics* 72: 90–104.

Schläpfer, F. and Schmitt, M. (2005) *Choices About Public Goods: The role of information shortcuts*, Zurich: University of Zurich. Online. Available http://www.unizh.ch/uwinst/homepages/Schlaepfer_Schmitt.pdf (accessed 21 October 2005).

Schläpfer, F., Schmitt, M. and Roschewitz, A. (2004) *Information Shortcuts and Stated Preferences for Public Goods: A field experiment*, Zurich: University of Zurich. Online. Available http://www.unizh.ch/uwinst/homepages/Preferences_Information.pdf (accessed 20 October 2005).

Schmitt, H. and Thomassen, J. (eds) (1999) *Political Representation and Legitimacy in the European Union*, Oxford: Oxford University Press.

Schmitt, K. (ed.) (1990) *Wahlen, Parteieliten, politische Einstellungen: Neuere forschungsergebnisse*, Frankfurt am Main: Peter Lang.

Schumpeter, J. (1996/1976) *Capitalism, Socialism and Democracy*, London: Routledge.

Schwartz, N. (1988) *The Blue Guitar*, Chicago: Chicago University Press.

Schwindt-Bayer, L. (2010) *Political Power and Women's Representation in Latin America*, New York: Oxford University Press.

Schwindt-Bayer, L., Malecki, M., and Crisp, B. (2010) 'Candidate gender and electoral success in single transferable vote systems', *British Journal of Political Science* 40(3): 693–709.

Schwindt-Bayer, L. and Mishler, W. (2005) 'An integrated model of women's representation', *Journal of Politics* 67(2): 407–28.

Schwindt-Bayer, L. and Palmer, H. (2007) 'Democratic legitimacy or electoral gain? Why countries adopt gender quotas', paper presented at the *MPSA*.

Semetko, H. (2007) 'Political communication' in R. Dalton and H.-D. Klingemann (eds) *The Oxford Handbook of Political Behaviour*, Oxford: Oxford University Press.

Severs, E. (2010) 'Representation as claims-making: quid responsiveness?', *Representation* 46(4): 411–423.

Shafer, B. and Claggett, W. (1995) *The Two Majorities: The issues of context of modern American politics*, Lawrence: University Press of Kansas.

Shapiro, I., Stokes, S., Wood, E. and Kirshner, A. (eds) (2009) *Political Representation*, Cambridge: Cambridge University Press.

Shapiro, R. and Mahajan, H. (1986) 'Gender differences in policy preferences: a summary of trends from the 1960s to the 1980s', *Public Opinion Quarterly* 50: 42–61.

Sharpe, S. (1976) *'Just Like a Girl': How girls learn to be women*, London: Penguin.

Shella, K. (2011a) 'Choosing between Electing Women or Ethnic Candidates? Ethnic Concentration and Electoral Rules in African States', paper presented at *American Political Science Association Annual Conference*, Seattle, September 2011.

— (2011b) 'Choosing between representing women or representing ethnic groups in Europe? Adding and subtracting plurality, representation, and democracy', paper presented at the *Midwest Political Science Association Annual Conference*, Chicago, April 2011.

Shugart, M. and Wattenberg, M. (eds) (2003) *Mixed-Member Electoral Systems: The best of both worlds?*, Oxford: Oxford University Press.

Simms, M. (1993) 'Two steps forward, one step back: women and the Australian party system' in J. Lovenduski and P. Norris (eds) *Gender and Party Politics*, London: Sage.

Sisk, T. and Reynolds, A. (eds) (1998) *Electoral System and Conflict Management in Africa*, Washington: United States Institute of Peace Press.

Skjeie, H. (1991) 'The rhetoric of difference: on women's inclusion into political elites', *Politics and Society* 19: 233–63.

— (1993) 'Ending the male political hegemony: the Norwegian experience' in J. Lovenduski and P. Norris (eds) *Gender and Party Politics*, London: Sage.

Smith, R. (1995) 'Interest group influence in the U.S. Congress', *Legislative Studies Quarterly* 20(1): 89–139.

Smooth, W. (2011) 'Standing for women? Which women? The substantive representation of women's interests and the research imperative of intersectionality', *Politics & Gender* 7(3): 436–441.

Social Watch (2008) *Gender Equity Index 2008, Montevideo: Social Watch*. Online. Available http://www.socialwatch.org/en/avancesyRetrocesos/IEG_2008/docs/brochure_eng.pdf (accessed 21 March 2008).

Somin, I. (2000) 'Do politicians pander?', *Critical Review: A Journal of Politics and Society* 14(2): 147–55.

Soroka, S. (2003) 'Media, public opinion, and foreign policy', *Harvard International Journal of Press/Politics* 8(1): 27–48.

Spirova, M. (2004) *Electoral Rules and the Political Representation of Ethnic Minorities: Evidence from Bulgaria and Romania*, Budapest: Central European University Centre for Policy Studies. Online. Available http://pdc.ceu.hu/archive/00001920/01/spirova.pdf (accessed 6 March 2007).

Squires, J. (1996) 'Quotas for women: fair representation?' in Lovenduski, J. and Norris, P. (eds) *Women in Politics*, Oxford: Oxford University Press.

Stanley, W. (1995) 'International tutelage and domestic political will: building a new civilian police force in El Salvador', *Studies in Comparative International Development* 30(1): 30–58.

Steenkamp, J., and Baumgartner, H. (1998) 'Assessing measurement invariance in cross-national consumer research', *Journal of Consumer Research* 25(1): 78–90.

Stimson, J. (1999) 'Party government and responsiveness' in A. Przeworski, S. Stokes and B. Manin (eds) *Democracy, Accountability, and Representation*, Cambridge: Cambridge University Press.

— (2007) 'Perspectives on representation: Asking the right questions and getting the right answers' in R. Dalton and H.-D. Klingemann (eds) *The Oxford Handbook of Political Behaviour*, Oxford: Oxford University Press.

Stone, D. (2001) 'Learning lessons, policy transfer and the international diffusion of policy ideas', *Centre for the Study of Globalisation and Regionalisation Working Paper*, 69.

Taagepera, R. (1994) 'Beating the law of minority attrition' in W. Rule and J. Zimmerman (eds) *Electoral Systems in Comparative Perspective: Their impact on women and minorities*, Westport: Greenwood Press.

Taylor, A. (2005) 'Electoral systems and the promotion of "consociationalism" in a multi-ethnic society: the Kosovo assembly elections of November 2001"', *Electoral Studies* 24: 435–63.

Tereskina, A. (2005) T*oward a New Politics of Citizenship: Representations of ethnic and sexual minorities in Lithuanian mass media*, Budapest: Central European University Centre for Policy Studies. Online. Available http://pdc.ceu.hu/archive/00002256/01/media_9_tereskinas.pdf (accessed 6 March 2007).

Thomas, S. (1991) 'The impact of women on state legislative policies', *Journal of Politics* 53(4): 958–76.

— (1994) *How Women Legislate*, Oxford: Oxford University Press.

Thomassen, J. (2012) 'The blind corner of representation', *Representation* 48(1): 13–28.

Thomassen, J. and Schmitt, H. (1997) 'Policy representation', *European Journal of Political Research* 32: 165–185.

Thompson, D. (2001) 'Political representation' in N. Smelser and P. Baltes (eds) *International Encyclopedia of the Social and Behavioural Sciences*, Amsterdam: Pergamon.

Thompson, J. (1995) *The Media and Modernity: A social theory of the media*, Cambridge: Polity Press.

Tinker, I. (2004) 'Quotas for women in elected legislatures: do they really empower women?', *Women's Studies International Forum* 27: 531–46.

Togeby, L. (1994) 'Political implications of increasing numbers of women in the labor force', *Comparative Political Studies* 27: 211–40.

— (2005) 'The electoral system and representation of ethnic minorities', paper presented at the *APSA Annual Meeting*, September 2005.

— (2008) 'The political representation of ethnic minorities: Denmark as a deviant case', *Party Politics* 14(3): 325–43.

Tremblay, M. (1995) 'Gender and support for feminism: a case study of the 1989 Quebec general election' in F. Gingras (ed.) *Gender and Politics in Contemporary Canada*, Oxford: Oxford University Press.

Tripp, A. and Kang, A. (2007) 'The global impact of quotas: on the fast track to increased female legislative representation', *Comparative Political Studies* 41(3): 338–61.

Uhlaner, C. (2002) 'The impact of perceived representation on Latino political participation', *CSD Working Paper*, Center for the Study of Democracy, University of California, Irvine.

UN Statistics Division (2006) *Social Indicators*, New York: UN Statistics Division. Online. Available http://unstats.un.org/unsd/demographic/products/socind/inc-eco.htm (accessed 20 February 2006).

UNDP (2005) *Human Development Report: All tables* (computer file), New York: United Nations Development Programme (distributor): HDR05.

U.S. Department of State (2006) *Country Reports on Human Rights Practices 2006*, Washington: U.S. Department of State. Online. Available http://www.state.gov/g/drl/rls/hrrpt/2006/ (accessed 1 October 2007).

United Nations Office at Vienna (1992) *Women in Politics and Decision-Making in the Later Twentieth Century: A United Nations study*, London: United Nations/Martinus Nijhoff Publishers.

Vallance, E. (1979) *Women in the House: A study of women Members of Parliament*, London: Athlone Press.

Van Cott, D. (2005) *From Movement to Parties in Latin America: The evolution of ethnic politics*, Cambridge: Cambridge University Press.

van Heelsum, A. (2002) 'The relationship between political participation and civic community of migrants in the Netherlands' *Journal of International Migration and Integration* 3(2): 179–200.

Viterna, J. and Fallon, K. (2008) 'Democratization, women's movements, and gender-equitable states: A framework for comparison', *American Sociological Review* 73: 668–89.

Viterna, J., Fallon, K. and Beckfield, J. (2008) 'How development matters: a research note on the relationship between development, democracy and women's political representation' *International Journal of Comparative Sociology* 49(6): 455.

Walby, S. (1997) *Gender Transformations*, London: Routledge.

—— (2009) *Globalization and Inequalities: Complexity and Contested Modernities*, London: Sage.

Walczak, A. and van der Brug, W. (2012) 'The electoral trade-off: how issues and ideology affect party preference formation in Europe', *Journal of Elections, Public Opinion & Parties* 1–24.

Waylen, G. (2008) 'Enhancing the substantive representation of women: Lessons from transitions to democracy', *Parliamentary Affairs* 61(3): 518–34.

Weissberg, R. (1978) 'Collective vs. dyadic representation in Congress', *American Political Science Review* 72: 535–47.

Welch, S. (1990) 'The impact of at-large elections on the representation of Blacks and Hispanics', *Journal of Politics* 52(4): 1050–76.

Weldon, S. (2006) 'The institutional context of tolerance for ethnic minorities: a comparative, multilevel analysis of Western Europe', *American Journal of Political Science* 50(2): 331–349.

Welzel, C. (2007) 'Individual modernity' in R. Dalton and H.-D. Klingemann (eds) *The Oxford Handbook of Political Behaviour*, Oxford: Oxford University Press.

Wessels, B. (1999a) 'System characteristics matter: empirical evidence from ten representation studies' in W. Miller, R. Pierce, J. Thomassen, R. Herrera, S. Holmberg, P. Esaiasson and B. Wessels (eds) *Policy Representation in Western Democracies*, Oxford: Oxford University Press.

— (1999b) 'Whom to represent? Role orientations of legislators in Europe' in H. Schmitt and J. Thomassen (eds) *Political Representation and Legitimacy in the European Union*, Oxford: Oxford University Press.

— (2007) 'Political representation and democracy' in R. Dalton and H.-D. Klingemann (eds) *The Oxford Handbook of Political Behaviour*, Oxford: Oxford University Press.

Wilentz, S. (2003) 'Race, ethnicity, and American democracy: an (unguarded) optimistic view' in T. Rabb and E. Suleiman (eds) *The Making and Unmaking of Democracy: Lessons from history and world politics*, London: Routledge.

Williams, M. (1995) 'Justice towards groups: political not juridical', *Political Theory* 23(1): 67–91.

Wittman, D. (1990) 'Spatial strategies when candidates have policy preferences' in J. Enelow and M. Hinich (eds) *Advances in the Spatial Theory of Voting*, Cambridge: Cambridge University Press.

Wlezien, C. and Soroka, S. (2007) 'The relationship between public opinion and policy' in R. Dalton and H.-D. Klingemann (eds) *The Oxford Handbook of Political Behaviour*, Oxford: Oxford University Press.

Wolbrecht, C. and Campbell, D. (2005) *Do Women Politicians Lead Adolescent Girls to Be More Politically Engaged? A cross-national study of political role models*, Notre Dame: University of Notre Dame. Online. Available http://www.nd.edu/~dcampbe4/xnational.pdf (accessed 2 February 2007).

World Bank (2006) *Gender Stats: Database of Gender Statistics* (computer file), Washington: World Bank (distributor).

World Factbook (2006) *Field Listing – Ethnic groups* (computer file), Washington: Central Intelligence Agency (distributor).

World Values Survey Group (2006) *World Values Survey* (computer file), Ann Arbor: Institute for Social Research (distributor): 20060423.

Wucherpfennig, J., Metternich, N., Cederman, L. and Gleditsch, K. (2012) 'Ethnicity, the state, and the duration of civil war', *World Politics* 64(1): 79–115.

Yach, D. and Bettcher, D. (2000) 'Globalisation of tobacco industry influence and new global responses', *Tobacco Control* 9: 206–16.

Yoon, M. (2004) 'Explaining women's legislative representation in Sub-Saharan Africa', *Legislative Studies Quarterly* 29(3): 447–68.

Young, I. (1990) *Justice and the Politics of Difference*, Princeton: Princeton University Press.

Zetterberg, P. (2008) 'The downside of gender quotas? Institutional constraints on women in Mexican State Legislatures', *Parliamentary Affairs* 61(3): 442–60.

Zimmerman, J. and Rule, W. (1998) 'Women and minorities in parliaments and legislatures' in G. Kurian (ed.) *World Encyclopedia of Parliaments and Legislatures*, Washington: Congressional Quarterly.

index